Videogan

MANCHESTER
1824

Manchester University Press

Videogame, player, text

edited by **Barry Atkins and Tanya Krzywinska**

Manchester University Press
Manchester and New York
distributed exclusively in the USA by Palgrave

Published by Manchester University Press
Oxford Road, Manchester M13 9NR, UK
and Room 400, 175 Fifth Avenue, New York, NY 10010, USA

www.manchesteruniversitypress.co.uk

Distributed exclusively in the USA by
Palgrave, 175 Fifth Avenue, New York,
NY 10010, USA

Distributed exclusively in Canada by
UBC Press, University of British Columbia, 2029 West Mall,
Vancouver, BC, Canada V6T 1Z2

British Library Cataloguing-in-Publication Data
A catalogue record for this book is available from the British Library

Library of Congress Cataloging-in-Publication Data applied for

ISBN 978 0 7190 7400 4 hardback
ISBN 978 0 7190 7401 1 paperback
First published 2007

16 15 14 13 12 11 10 09 08 07   10 9 8 7 6 5 4 3 2 1

Typeset
by Frances Hackeson Freelance Publishing Services, Brinscall, Lancs
Printed in Great Britain
by Antony Rowe Ltd, Chippenham, Wiltshire

Contents

List of contributors   *page* vii

Introduction: videogame, player, text   1
Barry Atkins and Tanya Krzywinska

1   Beyond *Ludus*: narrative, videogames and the split   8
condition of digital textuality
Marie-Laure Ryan

2   All too urban: to live and die in *SimCity*   29
Matteo Bittanti

3   Play, modality and claims of realism in *Full Spectrum*   52
Warrior
Geoff King

4   Why am I in Vietnam? The history of a video game   66
Jon Dovey

5   'It's not easy being green': real-time game performance in   83
Warcraft
Henry Lowood

6   Being a determined agent in (the) *World of Warcraft*: text/   101
play/identity
Tanya Krzywinska

7   Female *Quake* players and the politics of identity   120
Helen W. Kennedy

8   Of eye candy and id: the terrors and pleasures of *Doom 3*   139
Bob Rehak

9   *Second Life*: the game of virtual life   158
Alison McMahan

10 Playing to solve *Savoir-Faire*   175
   Nick Montfort

11 Without a goal: on open and expressive games   191
   Jesper Juul

12 Pleasure, spectacle and reward in Capcom's *Street Fighter*   204
   series
   David Surman

13 The trouble with *Civilization*   222
   Diane Carr

14 Killing time: time past, time present and time future in   237
   Prince of Persia: The Sands of Time
   Barry Atkins

   Index   254

Contributors

Barry Atkins is Senior Lecturer in Computer Games Design at University of Wales, Newport

Matteo Bittanti is a Postdoctoral Researcher at the Institute for the Study of Social Change, University of California, Berkeley

Diane Carr is a Research Fellow at the Institute of Education, University of London

Jon Dovey is Reader in Screen Media, Department of Drama, Film, Theatre and Television, University of Bristol

Bob Rehak is Visiting Assistant Professor in Film and Media Studies at Swarthmore College, Pennsylvania

Jesper Juul is Assistant Professor in Video Game Theory and Design at the Center for Computer Game Research at ITU Copenhagen

Helen Kennedy is Senior Lecturer at the School of Culture Studies, Bristol UWE

Geoff King is Reader in Film and TV Studies at Brunel University

Tanya Krzywinska is Professor of Screen Studies at Brunel University

Henry Lowood is Curator for History of Science & Technology Collections Co-Director, Stanford Humanities Laboratory

Alison McMahan is a documentary filmmaker for Homunculus Productions in New York

Nick Montfort is a Ph.D. candidate in computer and information science at the University of Pennsylvania

Marie-Laure Ryan is an independent scholar in Colorado

David Surman is Senior Lecturer in Computer Games Design at University of Wales, Newport

Introduction: videogame, player, text

Barry Atkins and Tanya Krzywinska

Things move fast in the world of the videogame, and in the world of videogame scholarship. Everything about the industry prioritizes the new and makes grandiose promises about the future potential of the games we have not yet seen. In the context of a highly competitive marketplace, there is an understandable focus on new formats and new platforms, new console generations and new technologies, and this perpetual pushing of (often technological) boundaries drives games forward at a frantic pace. Understandings of videogame history are therefore inevitably progressive in tone, with arguments for how far and how fast things have moved supported by screenshots that show the development from the crude 2D sprites populating the flat landscapes of a couple of decades ago to the complex 3D worlds of the first decade of the twenty-first century. At the opening of a level of the 2006 game *Tomb Raider: Legend* in which the camera pans back to reveal a spectacular image of a huge waterfall falling through an impressively rendered landscape, the game's protagonist remarks that 'If all else fails, I can get into the postcard business', and this is indicative of the promise that many such games hold out: with each new iteration they promise refreshed spectacle of postcards from previously undiscovered lands. The videogame protagonist who is moved by the player through the vast 3D landscapes of today's flagship games (be it *Tomb Raider*'s Lara Croft, or *Metroid*'s Samus Arun, or *Halo*'s Master Chief, or the self-named character of *The Elder Scrolls IV: Oblivion*) is presented as always engaged in the revelation of the new and the previously unseen. There is a continually renewed claim, reinforced by the rhetoric through which games are marketed, reviewed and discussed by their players, that suggests that we ain't seen nothing yet; videogames are regarded by some as an infant media that have not yet grown into their mature form.

Any intersection between the world of the scholar and the world of the videogame, therefore, has to be carefully negotiated. Scholarship is always grounded in careful observation and rigorous examination, and scholars are notoriously reticent about speculating about unseen futures. In reaching any understanding of the object of his or her study the academic has to eschew speculation for evidence, concentrate not on the hyperbolic promise of things that are yet to be realised, but on the games we already see in the stores and on our consoles and personal computers. In engaging in videogame scholarship the individual academic critic has to step back from the maelstrom of imagination of potential, and look with care at what the individual game represents, how it relates to other games (both digital and non-digital) that have come before, how it communicates its meanings, how it functions as played event, and how engagement with it through play generates pleasure. We need to take care, particularly, to focus our attention on the play experience, rather than only on the visual experience that games have to offer. To a degree this collection represents a series of frozen analytic moments, and an opportunity for reflection among a range of critics approaching games from different places and with varied disciplinary backgrounds. There is speculation here, but our request to our contributors was that the majority of their attention be grounded on the specifics of their examples, and particularly on the specifics of the experience of play with specific game artefacts.

There is no real need for any kind of corrective action through a volume such as this to radically undo prior errors in videogame scholarship, however. There was a time when assumptions were made that any academic writing about games would do so from the position of the outsider looking in, rather than from that of a player of games also engaged in professional scrutiny. The writers of these essays need not be shy about claiming the most basic of credentials: these are analytical accounts of play experience undertaken by players. Even if not all the academics gathered here would self-identify as 'gamers', with all the associations that particular label carries with it, their status as players of the games under analysis is made clear through the development of each argument. And these games players are now also situated in a wider context as games academics. Over the course of the past few years academic interest in videogames has grown apace; with several dedicated journals, articles appearing in journals not solely focused on games, and a range of books now published, academia is attempting to catch up with and account for the impact of games on contemporary culture. With games researchers coming from a broad range of disciplinary backgrounds it is inevitable that differences in approach and focus arise. Such diversity is something to be celebrated as collectively these serve well to account for the complex interplay between aesthetics, technological development, and socio-cultural and industrial factors that coalesce in the videogames phenomena. Conversations are taking place, debates entered into, views exchanged and at times contentions turn to battles fought over definitions and territories, orientations and priorities. Many of those who have contributed to this volume have been involved, in different ways, with these ongoing debates and each bring to bear their own particular approach to the core triangulation of videogame, player and text that we as editors regard as central to videogames. The different perspectives that will be found across the range of essays collected in this volume testify to the diversity and differences that characterize contemporary academic studies of videogames.

And yet there is a thesis to this volume that we see as emerging from the combined efforts of all our contributors. Our intention as editors was to bring together essays that show sensitivity to the specificity of videogames as played objects that are only mobilized by the action of the playing subject. It might be extreme to claim, as some have done,[1] that a game without a player is not a game at all, but merely a collection of game components pregnant with the potential to be realised as a game, but there is also something significant about such a position that deserves to be unpacked. Whether we are dealing with physical games or with games working through software, the game in its dormant unplayed state still communicates its status as game, as a glance at a chessboard with its pieces in place or at the screen of an arcade machine in its attract mode would make clear. It does not, however, have much to tell us about the experience of play. The essays collected here each focus on the player's engagement with the games in question, which results in the emergence or construction of what we will term the 'text' of the videogame. While we are anxious to promote and preserve the multi-disciplinary and interdisciplinary diversity of those engaged in the academic treatment of games we have asked our contributors to recognize, and think through, their positions as playing subjects. Academic writing has traditionally pretended to an objectivity which has often been a transparent conceit, and we have asked each writer to work with the recognition of their own action as players. This does not necessitate any dilution of critical authority, however, and a point upon which we both insist is that each videogame text must be treated by the games academic with the same care and rigour afforded to any form of cultural artefact subjected to the scrutiny of an established discipline. That is not to say, however, that there is only one way to analyse the relationships between videogames and their players, and many different approaches to this relationship might happily and advantageously co-exist, as long as the crucial position of the player and the action of play is given due recognition. In centralizing the relationship between the videogame and its player we seek to ensure that there is an object of collective study which does not collapse into incoherence even if it evades any totalizing temptation; in other words the aim of this collection is to represent a truly interdisciplinary area of endeavour circulating about textual production through play.

In itself this is not a demand that such a practice be universally adopted. Videogame studies is not a single thing, but a plural field. There is no orthodoxy of established practice. The games studied in the collection resist closure as single things where any but the most anodyne of statements about all games, let alone videogames, can be made with any certainty. Two scholars can play the same games and come up with wildly different conclusions, and this makes for a healthy and vibrant field of study. One advantage of gathering so many individual scholars together for a volume such as this is the way that it reinforces recognition that any encounter with the work of other games academics exposes each of us to accounts of play that differ from our own and make us think differently about artefacts with which we might be familiar. Seeing familiar things in new ways and, sometimes, new things in old ways is an inevitable consequence of engaging with the varied and diverse range of videogame criticism. It is important therefore to regard videogame studies as a form of heterotopia, with its inherent pluralism acting as a means of creative interaction not just with the games we play but with the play of others. Coming together with different experiences, skills and knowledge makes for strange and fruitful conjunctions, and difference and diversity are positive in and of themselves.

Given that videogames constitute a new arena for academic study, many of the recent publications have tended to address games in a rather generalist manner, often as a means of mapping the field. Rather than providing an overview of videogames, this collection takes a more 'bottom-up' approach, seeking not to survey the entire field, but instead to move closer to the experience of playing particular games. Many of the chapters in this collection draw upon narratological, ludological and remediationist approaches to games, and often these co-exist in individual chapters as an outcome of exploring in detail the particular features that arise from playing an individual game. The specific qualities of any given game, which we might characterize as being both the affordances offered by it as well as its aesthetic components, are designed to locate and shape the player's experience, but they are also shaped to varying degrees, depending on the player and the particular configuration of a game, in accordance with a player's individual physical, cognitive and interpretational engagement. Some games facilitate greater freedom for the player to shape the text through their engagement than others, within which a good range of variation in types of freedoms are available. Other games afford less scope and take a more restrictive approach to player facility (even though they remain open for players to interpret the game content differently). The textual diversity of games becomes obvious when reading the variety of chapters in this study. *Conflict: Desert Storm* or *Prince of Persia: The Sands of Time*, for example, channel the players' actions quite narrowly, providing fairly recent examples of games that take up the 'on-rails' approach often found in earlier games. This contrasts with the more open nature of a multiplayer online game such as *World of Warcraft* that seeks to facilitate different playing styles to maintain broad appeal. Nonetheless in each of these games, and despite their differences in form, affordances are offered in terms of different gameplay features, as well as through the array of resonant and highly 'readable' audio-visual signifiers that comprise the game's stylistic milieu and which are open to different interpretations. In addition these games provide a narrative context, which in the case of *World of Warcraft* can be taken up by players in different ways to inform role-play.

The experience of being-in-the-world of a game is contingent on the particular design, across a range of dimensions, of a given game and that design provides the formal and structural features of a game. These include the game's environment, its particular stylistic, modal and generic characteristics, as well as providing cues and context that aim to make playing that game a meaningful, dramatic and dynamic experience. The types of images, sound effects and music, the balance of play, its learning curve, the capabilities of characters and in-game objects are all features that work textually in concert with the player's particular modes of engagement to create the gameplay experience. Concentrating on the relationship between games and players' use of what is offered to produce text forces the focus on particularities, thereby aiding in the process of avoiding the type of over-generalization that often sidelines subtleties and shades of difference. It is only in the act of playing a game, becoming subject to those formal regimes that act to interpolate the player and shape their experience, that we are able to understand at a deeper level the experience of playing videogames. That is not to say that games are played or interpreted in the same way by each and every player. Cued in part by some types of literary and media studies, a focus on the textual relationship between game and player enables potentially an address of broader issues in play in relation to videogames; issues of politics, ethics, agency, representation, gender and identity for example, or raising questions

about the nature of cognition, as well as addressing why it is that playing in
the skin of a character in a virtual environment has proved so appealing to
many people.

Within the terms of the narratology/ludology debate that so characterized early public discussions about the action of scholarship in relation to
videogames, it might be assumed that any focus on games as texts refers
only to their non-interactive elements. It is certainly the case that games have
a functional dimension that is not present in other media types. However,
functionality also operates 'textually'; the parameters of what a player can
and can't do in a game are scripted into a game – even if we play creatively,
make mods or movies and do things that were not intended or thought of
by games designers. The key performative elements demanded of the player
by a videogame are always located within a set of contexts that give player-
performance its edges, meaning and motivation, and therefore potentially
greater definition and substance. Nonetheless, as with any text, players are
far from passive recipients of the game and its interpolative strategies, a
point underscored by Diane Carr in her essay in this volume on *Civilization
3*. While being subject to a game's parameters including its winning system,
as well as the broader values and social norms that a game carries, a player's
particular investment in a game is also dependent on their own set of predis-
positions. In other words, the text has no life of its own without player
engagement; without the player a game is simply dead code.

Games are often designed in such a way that the player is encouraged to
develop their playing skills over time to become more effective agents in the
gameworld. At the same time games seek to surprise, delight and challenge
the player as a game's textual regimes unfold. Sometimes these factors con-
verge and at other times they might become separated and work in tension.
The challenge for the authors in this collection is to draw out the subtleties
and variability of videogames of such interplay. And, where classical definitions of text and play become strained, it is here that we are likely to see how
videogames differ from other media. The essays collected here each address
a game or group of games in detail and in so doing go some way towards
addressing the very complex and diversely rendered relationship between
videogame text, play and performance. The experience of playing games, in
all its various affective colouring, occurs through the interchange between
technology, aesthetics and the player's own particular investments. An edited collection offers a perfect forum for addressing the diversity that is the
relationship between videogame, text and player. Each article included in the
volume stands alone as a focused analysis, but readers will also be able to
draw their own conclusions by extrapolating particularities, differences and

similarities that emerge across the range of chapters gathered here.

Works cited

Ermi, Laura and Frans Mäyrä (2005) 'Fundamental Components of the Gameplay Experience: Analysing Immersion', in Suzanne de Castell and Jennifer Jenson (eds) *Changing Views: Worlds in Play – Selected Papers of the 2005 Digital Games Research Association's Second International Conference*, Vancouver: Digital Games Research Association and Simon Fraser University, 15–27.

Notes

1 For such an example see Ermi and Mäyrä (2005: 15), where they make the blunt statement that the essence of a game is in its interactive nature, and there is no game without a player.

1

Beyond *Ludus*: narrative, videogames and the split condition of digital textuality

Marie-Laure Ryan

Let me begin by explaining my title: what is the split condition of digital textuality? This new form of art and entertainment reaches both ends of the cultural spectrum. One end is the avant-garde, those regarded as the cool intellectual elite. The other end is the masses of computer game players. But digital texts have yet to reach the middle of the spectrum, namely the educated public who consumes texts for pleasure, not profit, but is also capable of artistic discrimination. In the domain of print literature, this audience reads authors like Günter Grass, Gabriel García Márquez, Toni Morrison, Philip Roth, Umberto Eco or Michel Tournier, all brilliant storytellers, rather than feeding on a lean diet of experimental postmodernism and l*a*n*g*u*a*g*e poetry, nor fattening itself on bestsellers and genre fiction like thrillers, romances and detective stories. To avoid the political connotations of 'right wing' and 'left wing' I will call the experimental end of the spectrum the North Pole, because it is so 'cool,' and also because it takes hardy explorers to venture into this territory, and the other end, the one frequented by the tourists of mass entertainment will be the Tropics, because it is so hot. As for the still sparsely populated area situated halfway between the North Pole and the Tropics, I will call it the Temperate Zone. In digital textuality, the North Pole is represented by hypertext fiction, code poetry, visual poetry, experiments in computerized text generation, browser art, and theoretical fiction, while the Tropics are invaded by the millions of people who spend a large part of their lives playing computer games, especially first-person shooters and MMORPGs. If we look at the major artistic media, namely print literature, drama, and films, as well as music and visual arts, they all cover the North Pole, the Tropics and the Temperate Zone.[1] To me an artistic medium only becomes truly significant when it is able to conquer the centre of the spectrum. This does not mean that I reject experimentalism and popular culture; on the contrary, I believe that the three zones cross-fertilize each other: the North Pole borrows ideas from the Tropics, the Tropics occasionally borrows from the North Pole (but this is much less frequent), and the Temperate Zone is criss-crossed by currents originating at both ends of the spectrum.

In literature, drama, and films, the magic formula for reaching the tourists of the Tropics has been traditional narrative structures, the magic formula for reaching those in love with the North Pole has often been the rejection, or what Alan Liu would call the creative destruction, of these structures, and the magic formula for reaching the population of the Temperate Zone has been the renewal of narrative – a renewal that results from the successful incorporation of ideas from the North into the narrative patterns of the South. For instance, the automatic writing of Surrealism did not produce stories, but it created a fantastic meeting of images that developed narratively into magical realism, perhaps the most important literary development of the second half of the twentieth century. Or to take another example, the New Novel's[2] rejection of most of the immersive features of narrative – interest for what comes next, emotional attachment to the characters – has turned it into a dead-end branch in the tree of literary evolution, yet its self-reflexivity and metaleptic[3] play with boundaries have invaded all levels of culture, from advertisements to movies of the middle ground. Narrative, with its universal human appeal, dominates the Tropical and Temperate zones of print literature, drama, and film. The question I would like to ask here, is whether narrative can cure the split condition of digital textuality and create the audience that this new form of artistic expression currently lacks.

Before proceeding with this investigation, let me propose a definition of narrative that covers (hopefully) all media:

> A narrative is the use of signs, or of a medium, that evokes in the mind of the recipient the image of a concrete world that evolves in time, partly because of random happenings, and partly because of the intentional actions of individuated intelligent agents.

The mental construct constitutive of narrative – let's call it a story, while the material signs are the discourse – can take a variety of shapes, and it can manifest itself in a variety of ways. I call these different ways the modes of narrativity. Here are some examples of modes, some an established part of literary theory and others relatively new to narratologists because they depend on media other than written language:

> *Diegetic mode*: telling somebody that something happened, usually in the past. Novels, oral storytelling.

Mimetic mode: enacting a story in the present by impersonating a character and mimicking action. Drama, film.

Participatory mode: creating a story in real time by playing a role in the storyworld and selecting one's behaviour. Children's games of make-believe, theatre with audience participation.

Simulative mode: creating a story in real time by designing (or using) an engine that will implement a sequence of events on the basis of its internal rules and the input to the system. Story-generating systems (e.g. *Brutus* by Selmer Bringsjord and David Ferucci, 1999).

Some of the modes listed above are mutually exclusive (i.e. diegetic and mimetic),[4] while others can be combined: for instance, a computer game is both simulative and participatory, while children's games of make-believe and improvisational theatre are participatory and mimetic.

Narrative at the North Pole

The aesthetics of the North Pole can be summarized by inverting the traditional slogan of Graphic User Interface: WYSIWYG, what you see is what you get. The only truly distinctive property of the digital medium is the meta-property of algorithmic operation, and for the explorers of the North Pole, a digital literature that truly understands its medium is consequently one that foregrounds the normally hidden layer of the code. This means that literary or artistic value does not reside in what appears on the screen, but in the virtuoso programming performance that underlies the text.

Let me illustrate the anti-WYSIWYG aesthetics with an example from the visual arts. The artist Warren Neidich has produced a number of abstract pictures which look like tangled lines of various colours.[5] If the 'paintings' had been produced by normal means, namely by brush applying colour on canvas, they could have been done by a child of three, and nobody would regard them as significant artworks. But the pictures acquire an entirely new significance when we learn how they were created: lights were attached to the fingers and arms of people conversing in sign language, and the images, titled 'conversation maps', are the visual trace of their gestures (Paul 2003: 51).

The same aesthetic principle applies to computer-generated poetry: the art resides in the productive formula, and in the sophistication of the programming, rather than in the output itself. As Jean-Pierre Balpe writes on the web site of his computer-generated novel *Trajectoires*, 'the code is part of the work'. But since code is invisible, the appreciation of the work requires imagining what lies behind the screen. While the reader responses prompted by standard narrative texts range from 'how moving', 'how dramatic', to 'I can't wait to see how it ends', or 'what a surprise ending', the ambition of authors of the North Pole is to elicit reactions such as 'how cleverly designed' or 'what a cool idea'. These are the reactions typical of conceptual art.

Partly because of aesthetic choice, but also partly because of the aptitudes of the computer, the texts of the North Pole are much more adept at taking narrative apart than at telling coherent stories. Computers are still machines of limited intelligence, and the principal mechanism of automated text production is random combination. The shuffling and free recombining of fragments may work in poetry – think of Raymond Queneau's *Cent Mille Milliards de Poèmes* (1961) – because the meaning of poetry is more spatial than linear, more symbolic than literal, more suggestive than explicit, and overwhelmingly metaphorical. The reader can always imagine semantic connections. But aleatory processes cannot produce narrative meaning, except by letting the legendary 10,000 monkeys hammer long enough on keyboards, because narrative is the exact opposite of chance: the subject matter of stories is human experience, and human experience is a neverending attempt to neutralize the randomness of life through meaningful actions.

The mildest form of narrative deconstruction in digital literature is found in classical hypertext. We cannot really speak here of computerized, nor of randomized creation, because the author writes all the lexia and places all the links, and the linking of lexia should constitute a deliberate process of meaning creation. The ideal hypertext reader is one who constantly asks: why was this lexia linked to this other one? But when the textual network is densely connected, the designer loses control over the order of reading. Since narrativity is based on the fundamentally linear chains of temporal sequence and causal relations, the kaleidoscopic chunking of the text into recombinant fragments constitutes a major obstacle to the construction of narrative meaning. This chunking and shuffling prevents the author from controlling what information the reader possesses when he[6] encounters a given fragment. Even if the reader is capable of mentally rearranging lexia into coherent narrative sequences, the very concept of hypertext prevents the powerful narrative effects of suspense, surprise and sudden turn, because these effects rely on a careful management of the disclosure of information over time. I am not saying that it is impossible to tell stories in hypertext format, but the construction of a stable narrative meaning out of elements presented in a variable order requires a major cognitive investment, and this is the reason why hypertext fiction has not become mainstream.

A much more radical subversion of narrative coherence takes place when foreign elements are randomly inserted in a story. An example of this process is *The News Reader* by Noah Wardrip-Fruin with David Durand, Brion

Moss and Elaine Froehlich (2004). *The Newsreader* is a very clever and often funny program that takes the news stories posted daily on Yahoo! and blends them together, in a process reminiscent of the cut-up technique of William Burroughs. When the reader clicks on a highlighted word, the program generates another text, by replacing part of the text with words randomly borrowed from another story. It does so by preserving the grammaticality of the text, but without concern for semantic coherence. Does this result in meaning? To some extent yes: the absurdity of the resulting texts provides an ironic comment on current politics, the state of the world, and the incessant churning out of news by the media machine. By highlighting the juxtaposition of the trivial and the tragic in the stories posted daily on Yahoo!, *The Newsreader* also forces reflection on what is considered newsworthy in contemporary culture. But if the algorithm produces funny texts – it is an electronic version of the mad-lib party game – these texts appeal through their non-sense, and the meaning of the output resides on the metatextual much more than on the textual level.

The creative destruction of narrative does not necessarily rely on aleatory mechanisms, as my final example, *The Jew's Daughter* (2000) by Judd Morrissey, demonstrates. The text presents itself at first sight as a standard hypertext fiction, but there is only one link per screen. This means that the author retains strict control over the reading sequence. When the user mouses over a link, part of the screen replaces itself, but the new text is inserted without visible mark somewhere in the middle of the screen, leaving the rest of the page unchanged. Only those gifted with perfect recall will be able to tell what is new and what is old. The only clue to the location of the new text is a nervous twitching of the affected area when the substitution takes place. Since it is impossible to return to the previous screen, the reader cannot compare the two fragments. This formula is designed to frustrate memory, and without memory, of course, the reader cannot construct a stable narrative world nor a consistent narrative action. To salvage some intelligibility, readers will interpret the replacement mechanism as an allegorical gesture. For instance, the text could signify the radical instability of meaning, the absence of a definitive story to tell, or it could be interpreted as a simulation of the dynamics of the writing process: the replacement could stand for false starts and for the technique of 'cut-and-paste'. As was the case with *The News Reader*, but for different reasons, the text is only readable on the meta level.

Narrative in the Tropics

The association of stories with computer games is common practice among computer game designers, but has a controversial position in the game studies community. For the Scandinavian school of ludology, and even for some narratologists, games are games and stories are stories and these two types of cultural artefacts cannot hybridize because they present radically distinct essences. For me it is like saying that stories are stories and operas are operas and therefore an opera cannot have a narrative libretto. In my view you can speak of the narrativity of computer games without reducing them to a form of novel or film, because novels, films and games exemplify different narrative modes: the diegetic mode for novels, the mimetic mode for films, and a combination of the simulative and participatory mode for games. But I am not saying that all games, or all computer games, have a narrative basis. There are purely abstract games, such as chess, football, *Go*, and *Tetris* (1985) that do not fulfill the basic conditions of narrativity, namely offering an image of life by creating a concrete world populated by intelligent agents whose actions make this world evolve. But this condition is obviously satisfied by computer games such as *Doom* (1993), *Myst* (1994), *The Sims* (2000), *Morrowind* (1997), *Max Payne* (2001) and *EverQuest* (1999). I would term narrative any game that invites the player to engage in role-playing and make-believe, and to perform, as part of this game of make-believe, actions that lead to practical and inherently desirable goals, like rescuing princesses and saving the earth from evil aliens, as opposed to goals made desirable by conventions, such as kicking a ball in a net or aligning three tokens in a row. The player of a narrative game engages in an act of imagination, while the player of an abstract game like football or tic-tac-toe just follows the rules. For a long time, narrativity was restricted to children's games of make-believe, such as playing house, cops and robbers or 'who is afraid of the big bad wolf', games that were usually not played for the sake of winning. In contrast to games of make-believe, games that were played in a competitive spirit, such as board games and sports games, require some strategic thinking, but no imaginative activity. But the computer changed all that. If there is one significant contribution of digital technology to gaming, it is to have reconciled competition and make-believe, in short, to have introduced a narrative dimension that speaks to the imagination in games of physical skills and strategic thinking.

But the narrative potential of computer games is generally underdeveloped. As Chris Crawford observes (2004: 69), narrative is generally treated by game designers as 'just another tacked-on feature', like animation, sound effects and music, instead of forming the defining aspect of games. This is particularly true of first-person shooters. Games like *Quake* or *Doom* are generally not played for the sake of the story, and the function of the narrative theme is to lure the player into the game, rather than to support gameplay in a strategic way. When hard-core players are engaged in the heat of the action, it does not really matter to them whether they play good guys or bad guys, humans protecting the earth or destroying angels trying to turn the world into apocalyptic chaos. Game designers – with of course some notable exceptions – so far have had little incentive to vary the narrative design of games, because sufficient novelty could be achieved in the domain of technology to sell their new products: better graphics, larger worlds, faster action, more realistic game physics, and the development of built-in cameras that make it possible to record the player's actions. As Andrew Darley has observed, narrative usually takes second seat to the spectacle of technology. But hardware improvement will eventually reach a ceiling, and the game industry will have to pay more attention to what Henry Jenkins (2004) calls 'narrative architecture' because it allows far greater variety than strategic gameplay and the spectacle of technology. 'Narrative architecture' is the design of a fictional world with a diversified geography composed of various locations. Each of these locations offers its own opportunities for experiences, adventures, discoveries, and meaningful action. As the player explores this geography, she meets different characters, receives different missions, forms different goals, and faces different dangers. If by narrative experience one means the pleasure of immersing oneself in a virtual world, of writing through one's actions the life story of fictional characters, and of participating in the collective history of the virtual world, then this experience is fully compatible with the ambition of game designers, which is to create rich worlds that offer players extensive opportunities to exercise their agency. In the future we may see complex characters that arouse emotions, clever dialogue that brings out laughter, situations that create ethical dilemmas, surprising turns in the plot, and we already have games with stunning visual settings that create artistic pleasure. When this happens, narrative will no longer be subordinated to gameplay – the game will be played for the sake of experiencing its narrative design.

Narrative in the Temperate Zone

If we want to extend digital textuality to a new audience, it is imperative to have a clear idea of the likes and dislikes of our targetted users. At the risk of creating these users in my own image, this is how I envision their preferences.

The users of the Temperate Zone do not endorse a philosophy that seems to reign at both the North Pole and the Tropics: 'No pain, no gain'. For the players of the Tropics, this philosophy means having to solve difficult problems, while for the explorers of the North Pole, this means having to struggle with texts that require tremendous mental effort, because they reject the traditional ways of making meaning. At the risk of being called intellectually lazy, the users of the Temperate Zone do not believe that processing difficulty is a guarantee of artistic value, and that what Roland Barthes (1973) called 'jouissance' – the intellectual thrill provided by avant-garde texts – is inherently superior to the pleasure (Barthes' 'plaisir') of narrative. Yet the users of the Temperate Zone do share preferences with the lovers of the North Pole and the Tropics. Like the player of games, they love being immersed in a virtual world, enjoy exploring its geography and inventory, want to play an active role in this world, and appreciate the graphic appeal of the display. They do not like to read on the screen, except for short passages of text on the objects that furnish the virtual world, and they prefer mimetically enacted to diegetically narrated stories. But unlike the game-addict, they do not want to spend over 60 hours with the text, nor to have to do research on the Internet to find out how to progress in the plot. The story, for them, is a focus of attention and not a mere wire frame support for another type of gratification. They care for the characters as human beings, enjoy conversing with them, experience emotions through them, and unlike the game player who regards characters as either helpers or enemies, they appreciate complex personalities. Like the amateur of experimental texts, they are sensitive to the mechanisms that produce the text, and they are able to appreciate what lies below the surface, but they do not endorse radical anti-WYSIWYG aesthetics. The justification for the code lies in the product on the screen, just like the justification for the complex metric and sound patterns of poetry lies in the musicality they impart to language, and not merely in the challenge they pose to the poet. In other words, readers of the Temperate Zone do not regard programming virtuosity as a self-fulfilling activity and as a guarantee of aesthetic merit. They value artistic innovation, but they do not think that innovation requires the dismantling of narrative, because developing narratives that take advantage of the properties of the medium is in itself a major artistic innovation over print literature, drama and movies.

How can the user of the Temperate Zone be wooed? We can approach the issue from two sides: ask how texts of the North Pole can be made more user-friendly, and ask how games of the Tropics can be made more interesting from a narrative point of view. Here I will focus on the second possibility, by looking at some games that have been able to reach beyond the traditional audience of their genre.

The embedded story

My first case is a game structure that Henry Jenkins calls the 'embedded narrative' (2004: 126). This structure covers any attempt by the player to reconstitute events that took place in the past. It connects two narrative levels: the story to be discovered, and the story of their discovery. The prime example of this design is the detective story. The story of the murder follows a fixed internal sequence, while the story of the investigation is 'written' by the actions of the detective, who may discover the facts in a wide variety of different orders, as he wanders across the virtual world in search for clues.

The best-known example of this structure is *Myst*, one of the greatest hits in the history of videogames. In *Myst* there is a hidden story to discover, the saga of the wizard Atrus and his evil sons Sirrus and Achenar, and this story reveals itself progressively, as the player visits the various regions of a richly diversified geography.

But the structure is not free of problems. In a traditional mystery story, the detective performs difficult tasks of problem-solving, but the reader does not *have* to put the story of the murder back together, though he can of course try to guess the solution. Since the actions of the detective are scripted by the author, this makes it possible for the author to control the process of discovery, and to manage effects of suspense, of which the reader is the beneficiary. But in an interactive environment, the user becomes the detective, and it falls to him to reconstruct the embedded story. If the player is granted too much freedom of movement, there is the danger that he may discover cues in a less than optimal order, and suspense will be lost. For instance, he could stumble right away on a tell-tale clue that gives away the solution. Or he may discover bits and pieces of the embedded story in a hopelessly scrambled order, a problem typical of hypertext fiction. To avoid these pitfalls, games can control the order in which the player discovers the embedded story by imposing a more or less rigid linear progression through the space of the game world: you must visit area a, where you will find a certain clue; then you must visit area b, where you will find another clue. In *Myst*, for instance, the gameworld consists of a series of subworlds, and the user must solve often very difficult problems to pass from one subworld to the next and discover more of the story. This design is good for the dedicated game-player who plays for the satisfaction of problem-solving, but it is rather exasperating for our hypothetical user from the Temperate Zone, who plays for the story. The player of *Myst* spends hours in front of closed doors, turning dials, pulling levers, and looking for hidden buttons in the hope of being admitted into the next space. For the player of the Temperate

Zone, who would rather read a novel than solve a crossword puzzle, this is highly aggravating. The game critic Steven Poole eloquently captures this frustration:

> It is as if you were reading a novel and being forced by some jocund imp at the end of each chapter to go and win a game of table tennis before being allowed to get back to the story. (2000: 109)

Chris Crawford has an even better description for this interleaving of puzzle-solving and narrative: he calls it a 'constipated story' (2004: 130) because it consists of a series of bottlenecks. How can we give a laxative to the constipated story? I suggest creating a design that invests in the player's interest in the embedded story, but does not throw 'unnecessary obstacles' in the way of its discovery. Movement in the virtual world should be relatively free, discovery fairly easy, and non-playing characters should spontaneously provide useful information or tell parts of the story. Most importantly, the fictional world should be adaptable, so that when the player returns to a site he has already visited, something will have changed, and different narrative possibilities will open themselves. In other words, he will not encounter the same character who says the same things every time he visits the same spot, as is too often the case in videogames. If progression in the fictional world requires the solving of puzzles, the system should take pity on the player after a number of unsuccessful attempts, and send a helper character who gives hints or takes the player through the roadblock.

This design would no longer be a game in the classical sense of the term, because, if we accept the definition of Bernard Suits (1978), unnecessary obstacles are a constitutive features of games, and it would therefore lose all the hardcore players, but it could offer a rewarding interactive experience that taps into two time-tested sources of narrative pleasure: spatial immersion in a fictional world, and curiosity for its past history.

The emergent story

In contrast to the embedded story, the emergent story (Jenkins 2004: 128) is not preplanned by the designer, but takes shape dynamically as a result of the interaction between the user and the system. The best-known example of an emergent system is *The Sims* (2000), a game which has achieved reasonable success with users of the Temperate Zone because it relies on the quintessentially narrative theme of human relations. In an emergent system such as *The Sims*, the designer populates a world with agents and objects capable of diverse behaviours, also known as affordances, and the user creates stories by activating these behaviours, which affect other agents, alter the total state of the system, and through a feedback loop, open new possibilities of action and reaction. *The Sims* is played by creating a family (or alternatively, by adopting a family with a past history) and by controlling its members. Every significant object and every character in the virtual world is a source of affordances; for instance, with a TV you can watch soaps or work out; with a computer you can play games or look for a job, and with another character you can flirt, argue, or try to have a baby. The possibilities of action evolve during the run of the program, as the members of the family acquire more commodities, as new characters enter the stage – for instance, visiting neighbours – and as affective relations change over time, both in the short run, as a result of the immediate effect of individual actions, and in the long run, as the result of the cumulative effect of behavioural patterns. Affordances are more than isolated actions, they often open the possibility of an entire chain of events. For instance, if a burglar is caught by the police, and if the player, out of curiosity, clicks on the rear door of the police car, the burglar will be freed, and it will be possible for the members of the player's family to start a love affair with him, or even marry him (*Sims2 Game Guide*: 213). The pleasure of the game lies as much in discovering the plot possibilities written into the system as in managing the life of the Sims family members according to the goals set for them by the player.

As is the case with any narrative, the motor that moves the lifestory of the Sims forward is the satisfaction of personal desires. The original version of *The Sims* offered two types of goals to the characters, and consequently to the player who controls them: the implicit long-term or life goal of climbing the social ladder and of acquiring more and more commodities, and the short-term, day-to-day goals of satisfying social and emotional needs, as well as physical needs such as hunger, hygiene, bladder, sleep and comfort. While the long-term goal is an implicit motivation for the player, the short-term goals are explicitly represented on the menu of the character's desires by a bar showing their degree of satisfaction. This bar oscillates with time, since the short-term goals must be fulfilled on a daily basis. *The Sims 2* adds medium-term goals of a more individual and discrete nature, such as writing a novel, seducing a neighbour, or getting a certain job. These goals give the game greater narrative texture than the permanent life goal of acquiring more wealth and the repetitive daily goals, because they are fully and definitely satisfiable. They consequently divide the ongoing lifestory of the characters into distinct episodes. When a medium-range goal is achieved, the system replaces it with another, and since every Sim character has many goals, the player can chose which one to pursue actively. Narrative interest is further enhanced in *The Sims 2* through a more complex inner world than in the original version: characters now have memories, fears, and personalized life goals ('aspirations'), but except for the aspirations, which are selected by the player at character creation time from a fixed menu, these aspects of mental life are all determined by the system. The only thing that the player can do to affect the content of the characters' minds is to take physical actions that lead to certain mental and emotional states. For instance, kissing or arguing have obvious effects on the degree of love of the patient for the agent. The player's control over the evolution of the fictional world is further limited by events randomly thrown in by the system, such as the house catching fire, death taking a character away, or neighbours dropping by unexpectedly, and the player must learn how to respond to these events. This combination of goal-fulfilling actions and random events makes *The Sims* into a believable simulation of life and a powerful story-generating system.

The macro-level goal of climbing the social ladder makes the player's score relatively computable, since it is always possible to compare the relative wealth of different Sims families, but it can be easily subverted into play for its own sake. Players who select their own goals, rather than accepting the 'official' game goal (and ideology) will often select impractical behaviours for their potential to lead to more interesting dramatic situations.[7] Most people play *The Sims* out of genuine narrative interest, whether they are trying to create specific scenarios, or are simply curious to find out how things will turn out for their characters. The game design exploits this narrative interest by offering the option of a 'story mode', through which players create comic strips by taking snapshots of the screen and adding their own text. The stories created in this way are not necessarily the same as the stories created during the game, and most of them require sophisticated thinking and planning from their characters that far exceed the mental abilities of the Sims, but players have been known to manipulate the game, in order to get the snapshots that will fit into the plot they have in mind.

All in all, *The Sims* may be the closest we have to a remedy for what I call the split condition: the failure of digital narrative in the Temperate Zone. But it is far from providing a general and definitive cure. There is a prejudice against videogames in the educated public that will prevent many people from using the system. But even if this prejudice did not exist, there are also internal reasons why texts patterned after *The Sims* will not instantly conquer the Temperate Zone. Here are some of the problems with the current design.

First, *The Sims* and its putative successors are very good at producing comedy, and this is no small achievement, but I do not see how such a system could be used to produce serious drama, because drama requires a control of emotions which can only be achieved through a top-down design. *The Sims 2* repertory of neighbourhoods includes one town, Veronaville, that is divided by the same type of family feuds that underlies the tragic love story of Romeo and Juliet, but the effect is one of parody and comic detachment, not of empathy for the characters. To put it bluntly: most players find it fun to make their Sims suffer and they don't feel empathy for them. We will need other algorithms to cover the full range of human experience.

Second, a large portion of the time spent with *The Sims* consists of performing the chores of daily life, such as taking a shower, eating snacks out of the fridge, or going to the bathroom. This may be fun for a while, but the novelty quickly wears out. Narrative is about the extraordinary, not about routine events. Many novels describe repetitive or trivial gestures, but they only do so to fix the setting and create an atmosphere. When the story starts developing, there is no need to describe these gestures over and over again. In *The Sims*, by contrast, you cannot escape the routine. Imagine that one of your Sims falls in love with the neighbour and invites her to a party the next day. Rather than fast forwarding to the party, as a novel would do, the player will have to make the character live his life minute by tedious minute, eating snacks, taking showers and going to bed. There is admittedly a 'fast' mode, but even this fast mode is painfully slow for the player eager to find out 'how things turned out' in the courting of the neighbour. To increase narrative interest, the game should enable the player to manipulate the clock, in order to jump to the more dramatic moments.

More generally, I think that the user does not have enough control over the plot. She cannot, for instance, put new desires into her Sims: she must wait until the system does it for her. Nor can she construct elaborate plans to fulfill these desires, for instance plans involving lies and deceit, which are one of the main ingredients of well-plotted stories. The reasoning power of the fox of the fable, who satisfies his hunger by flattering a crow and getting her to sing and drop a cheese, is presently far beyond the intelligence of any Sim character.

The most important problem to resolve for emergent systems of the future is to find the right balance between computer-generated and user-controlled events. With too many computer-generated events interactivity is reduced to trivial detail, such as sending your Sims to the bathroom before an accident happens; but with too much user control over the plot, users will be deprived of some of the main sources of narrative pleasure, namely suspense, curiosity and surprise. Some users want to be authors, others prefer to be readers, and the best solution may be to make the balance of control adjustable. The users who want lots of control over the plot would be able to hold the strings of several characters, and to manipulate both their actions and states of mind, for instance by freely selecting their fears and desires, while the users who prefer to watch the plot unfold would manipulate only one character, and this manipulation would be restricted to physical actions, leaving it to the system to compute the physical and mental effects of these actions.

The pre-scripted, but variable story: interactive drama

What would it take for an interactive narrative to produce drama rather than comedy? This is to say, to create an emotional involvement of the user in the fate of the characters, rather than curiosity and ironic detachment. Aristotle associated tragedy with a fixed plot pattern made of an exposition, complication, crisis and denouement, and all the texts that reach a truly dramatic intensity follow this pattern to some extent, because it allows a strict control of the spectator's emotions. Aristotelian dramaturgy has indeed become something of a Bible among Hollywood scriptwriters. This means that digital texts aiming at a dramatic effect will have to rely on a pre-scripted, top-down design. But in order to take advantage of the interactive nature of the medium, they should allow the bottom-up input of the user to introduce variations in the script. This combination of top-down design and bottom-up emergence is the most difficult problem to solve for interactive narrative.

In interactive drama, the user impersonates a member of the fictional world, and she interacts with system-controlled characters through an AI-based dialogue system. To allow the plot to develop according to a relatively pre-defined script, the user should play the role of an active observer, rather than being cast as the main protagonist. Since a top-down design allows only a limited number of variations, interactive drama will be exhausted after a small number of visits. This limited replayability places the genre halfway between the two types of design discussed above. A text relying on an embedded story is not replayable, because the user's motivation is the discovery of a fixed scenario, while an emergent system should be almost infinitely replayable, because stories are created in real time by activating a rich repertory of possible behaviours that allow numerous, but not random combinations.

I will conclude this chapter with a discussion of what could very well be the only working example of interactive drama in existence today, namely *Façade* by Michael Mateas and Andrew Stern. Does *Façade* qualify as game? The project was selected as a finalist at the 2004 Independent Game Festival in San Jose, but it was refused by another conference for *not* being game. These contradictory decisions demonstrate the fuzziness, already noted by Wittgenstein,[8] of the concept of game.

Façade was explicitly designed by its authors to close the digital gap. As Mateas and Stern write, 'We are interested in interactive experiences that appeal to the adult, non-computer-geek, movie-and-theater-going public' (Mateas and Stern 2002:2). Here is how the authors described the text:

> In *Façade*, you, the player, play the character of a long-time friend of Grace and Trip, an attractive and materially successful couple in their early thirties. During an evening get-together at their apartment that quickly turns ugly, you become entangled in the high-conflict dissolution of Grace and Trip's marriage. No one is safe as the accusations fly, sides are taken and irreversible decisions are forced to be made. By the end of this intense one-act play you will have changed the course of Grace and Trip's lives – motivating you to replay the drama to find out how your interaction could make things turn out differently the next time. (Mateas and Stern 2002:2)

While the text permits many variations, it is not a plot with clearly distinct and predefined endings, but rather a compromise between a fixed story and an emergent system. Different runs enact different conversational events in combinations far too numerous to be foreseen by the authors, but all of the runs follow the same basic pattern:

> *Exposition*: Grace and Trip welcome the visitor to their apartment, and engage in small talk with their guest.
>
> *Crisis*: The small talk degenerates into an argument between Grace and Trip that exposes the disastrous state of their marriage.
>
> *Denouement*: The visitor is asked to leave.

Variation takes place less on the level of external events than on the level of the interactor's assessment of the situation: who, between Grace and Trip, is the most responsible for the deterioration of their marriage, and what will happen after the visitor leaves? In some runs Grace and Trip tell the visitor that 'everything will be all right' as they ask her to leave, while in other runs the visitor leaves under the impression that the marriage has been irremediably broken. Each run actualizes 30% of the total material available, and each selection proposes a slightly different portrait of Grace and Trip, depending on what is revealed of their past life, and on who tells the story. For instance, in some runs Grace presents herself as a frustrated artist who was forced by Trip to give up painting for a lucrative career as a magazine designer;

in other runs, Trip describes her as a careerist who poses as an artist but possessed neither the necessary talent nor the dedication to become a painter.

The principal mode of interactivity is typing text, but the user can also move around the apartment, inspect it from various angles and from various distances, pick up or drop some of the objects that decorate the apartment, and perform some physical actions, such as kissing Grace or Trip on the lips. The system uses pre-written dialogue modules which vary depending on the user's input. For each situation, the system maintains a list of discourse acts that constitute appropriate conversational responses: acts such as agree, disagree, thank, criticize, hug, comfort, or judge. The input of the user is parsed by the system and mapped onto one of the currently available discourse acts. For instance if Grace asks the user 'How are you', and the user replies 'I feel terrible' the system understands that the user expressed unhappiness, and it will make Grace respond with commiserating words and a sad expression. When the system cannot parse the text, it ignores the input and selects one of the discourse acts appropriate to the current situation. Users cannot derail the smooth run of the system, but because the AI module that drives the text is rather limited, the system will often respond incoherently to their input.

A major problem for the user is placing a word in the conversation. At the beginning Grace and Trip try to be polite, and ask many questions that give the visitor a chance to express herself. The system pauses until the player responds. But as the story develops, Trip and Grace become more and more focused on each other, and less and less on the visitor. They exchange their barbs in such rapid fire that by the time the visitor has finished typing a line and hit the return key (at which point the input can be processed by the system), Grace and Trip have produced three or four lines of dialogue, and the user's line is no longer relevant. But this incoherence does not lead to a serious loss of credibility, because the problem is minimized by the narrative theme and by the personalities of Grace and Trip. Thematically, *Façade* is about a conversation that degenerates into an argument. In a fight, you feel free to interrupt your opponent, ignore his arguments, make false accusations, or leave questions unanswered. If Grace and Trip fail to respond adequately to the user's input, it is because they are so blinded by their own anger at each other that they become unable to carry a normal conversation. Here we can say that the narrative theme has been masterfully selected to cover up the limitations of the system. This is known among computer programmers as 'graceful degradation'.

One way of giving the visitor more initiative without overburdening the parser would be to extend the possibilities of physical actions, and make the system more responsive to them. Physical actions are much less ambiguous than verbal input because the user can perform them with a mouse click, rather than using a phrase that the parser can understand. For instance, if I you want to leave, it is much more efficient to do so by walking to the door and clicking on the handle (provided a behavior is associated with it) than by saying 'Good bye', 'I want to go', or 'I've had enough', all phrases that may not be in the parser's repertory. In the current version of *Façade*, the possibilities of physical action are still underdeveloped. For instance, kissing Grace or Trip on the lips elicits no more than a pleasantly surprised or offended look, and the ejection of the visitor if the action is repeated. Here the program is missing some interesting opportunities for narrative development: the kiss could for instance introduce a whispering between the user and the other character, the hinting of an affair; or the system could respond differently, depending on whether the kiss involves same-sex or different sex partners.

It would be wrong to say: 'But a system like Façade could not be used to produce the story of *Oedipus Rex* or *Hamlet* or *Little Red Riding Hood*'. The art of interactive narrative consists of thinking with the medium, which means adapting the plot to the features of the system. Mateas and Stern have hit the right plot with their story of a domestic fight that tolerates incoherence and often ignores the player's contributions. But some features are more restrictive than others, and the viability of a system of interactive narrative will consequently depend on the variety of plots that it can accommodate. What remains to be seen is how much diversity the idea of interactive drama tolerates.

I have presented three tentative and partial ways to refocus interest on the story in an interactive environment. Can these three designs be combined for a fuller narrative experience? In a sense no, because each of them presupposes a different type of user involvement. In the embedded story, the user is cast as a member of the virtual world, but he or she has no impact on the story. I call this involvement 'internal-exploratory' (Ryan 2001). In the emergent system, players are not members of the virtual world, but by manipulating the characters they have an enormous influence on the story. Their participation is 'external-ontological'. In the dialogue system of interactive drama, users play a role within the fictional world, and they have limited influence on the story. Their involvement is internal and mildly ontological. It would be a very poor design strategy for a digital text to switch midway from one of these modes of participation to another. Still, some combination of the features of the three types of design is not entirely impossible. For instance, a game can combine the emergent character of *The Sims* with an internal participation. In this type of game, exemplified by the online version of *The Sims*, the user identifies with a single character, rather than holding the strings of an entire family. The idea of the embedded story could be reconciled with a more flexible script. Take the case of *Façade*: there is a fixed embedded story to discover, namely the private life of Grace and Trip before the arrival of the visitor; but this story, rather than being investigated for its own sake, spills into the present and determines the current behaviour of the couple. In contrast to mystery-solving games, different runs of the system reveal different aspects of the embedded story. Or take the idea of a dialogue system controlled by an AI module. It would not be feasible in a God game like *The Sims*, because the player is not a member of the fictional world, but it is very compatible with a design based on an embedded story if the conversation is limited to the characters of the embedding story. And finally, as *Façade* demonstrates, interactive drama can easily integrate the kind of interaction that we find in *The Sims*: clicking on an object to activate its behaviours. The full potential of interactive drama will only be reached when it combines dialogue with simulated physical actions.

There is no simple cure for the split condition. I can write a prescription, but like most doctors I don't know how to manufacture the medicine, and therefore I cannot guarantee that the Temperate Zone will some day be conquered. Here's my prescription:

1　The user should participate and interact out of interest for the story, not for the sake of solving problems or beating opponents. The text should encourage the player who prefers a less efficient action over a more practical way to achieve a goal, when this action leads to more interesting narrative possibilities.

2　Narrative development should not be entirely dependent on non-interactive cut scenes. The user's activities should be part of the story, and move the plot forward, rather than being nothing more than a means to get more of the story.

3　The actions available to the user should be more diverse than the standard repertory of computer games: moving through the fictional world, solving puzzles to get past roadblocks, and fighting enemies.

4　At least some actions should be dependent on the user's construction of the mind of other characters. Decisions should be based in part on such factors as who knows what and who wants what, who likes whom and who does not. Stories are about people, people are scheming social animals, and to attract the population of the Temperate Zone into an interactive digital environment it will take a mode of participation that involves a network of human relations.

Some readers may complain that my proposed remedies for the split condition amount to a basic rejection of the proven pleasures of strategic and competitive play in favour of the utopian dream of an interactive narrativity. In other words, am I suggesting getting rid of what makes a game a game, to attract people who don't like games? The answer depends on whether or not one limits the concept of game to what Roger Caillois called *ludus* and Jesper Juul calls the 'prototypical game situation':[9] rule-based games played for the sake of winning or losing, and requiring 'effort, adroitness, and ingenuity on the part of the players' (Motte 1995: 7). With their tendency to regard shooters as the quintessential games, videogame studies have so far privileged *ludus* at the expense of another type of ludic activity that Caillois called *paidia*, an activity characterized by 'fun, turbulence, free improvisation, and fantasy' (Motte 1995: 7). *Paidia* is represented by toys, games of make-believe, and, among video games, by simulation, dance and construction games.[10] In view of the diversity of activities regarded as play, both in the digital and the traditional sector, my recommendations for the conquest of the Temperate Zone is not an outright dismissal of the game idea in favour of literary models of narrative, but a recognition that computer-based, interactive forms of entertainment cover the whole spectrum from *ludus* to *paidia*, and a recommendation that more attention be devoted to the *paidia* pole.

Works cited

Balpe, J.P. *Trajectoires* (computer-generated novel), http://trajectoires.univ-paris8.fr/.

Barthes, Roland (1973) *Le Plaisir du texte*, Paris: Seuil.

Bringsjord, S. and D. Ferrucci (1999) *Artificial Intelligence and Literary Creativity: Inside the Mind of Brutus, a Storytelling Machine*, Hillsdale, NJ: Lawrence Erlbaum.

Caillois, Roger (1967 [1958]) *Les Jeux et les hommes*, Paris: Gallimard.

Crawford, Chris (2004) *Chris Crawford on Interactive Storytelling*, Berkeley, CA: New Riders Press.

Darley, Andrew (2000) *Visual Digital Culture: Surface Play and Spectacle in New Media Genres*, London: Routledge.

Frasca, Gonzalo (1999) 'Ludology Meets Narratology: Similitude and Difference between (Video)games and Narrative', www.jacaranda.org/frasca/ludology.htm, accessed February 2006.

Jenkins, Henry (2004) 'Game Design as Narrative Architecture', in Noah Wardrip-Fruin and Pat Harrigan (eds) *First Person: New Media as Story, Performance, and Game*, Cambridge, MA: MIT Press.

Juul, Jesper (2004) *Half-Real: Video Games Between Real Rules and Fictional Worlds*, Ph.D. dissertation, IT University, Copenhagen.

Kramer, G. (2004) *The Sims 2: Prima Official Game Guide*, Roseville, CA: Prima Games/Random House.

Liu, A. (2004) *The Laws of Cool: Knowledge Work and the Culture of Information*, Chicago: University of Chicago Press.

Mateas, Michael (2004) 'A Preliminary Poetics for Interactive Drama and Games', in Noah Wardrip-Fruin and Pat Harrigan (eds) *First Person: New Media as Story, Performance, and Game*, Cambridge, MA: MIT Press.

Mateas, Michael and Andrew Stern (2002) '*Façade*: An Experiment in Building a Fully-Realized Interactive Drama', www.quvu.net/interactivestory.net/papers/MateasSternGDC03.pdf, accessed March 2006.

Morrissey, J. (2000) *The Jew's Daughter*, www.thejewsdaughter.com/, accessed March 2006.

Motte, W.F. (1995) *Playtexts: Ludics in Contemporary Literature*, Lincoln, NE: University of Nebraska Press.

Paul, C. (2003) *Digital Art*, London: Thames and Hudson.

Poole, Steven (2000) *Trigger Happy: Videogames and the Entertainment Revolution*, New York: Arcade Publishing.

Ryan, Marie-Laure (2006) *Avatars of Story: Narrative Modes in Old and New Media*, Minneapolis: University of Minnesota Press.

——(2001) 'Beyond Myth and Metaphor: Narrative in Digital Media', *Gamestudies*, www.gamestudies.org/0101/ryan/, accessed March 2006.

Suits, Bernard (1978) *The Grasshopper: Games, Life and Utopia*, Toronto: University of Toronto Press.

Wardrip-Fruin, Noah with D. Durand, B. Moss, and E. Froehlich (2004) *The News Reader*, available for download at http://turbulence.org/Works/twotxt/nr-download.htm, accessed March 2006.

Wittgenstein, L. (1968) *Philosophical Investigations*, trans. G.E.M. Anscombe, New York: Macmillan.

Games

Façade (2005), available for download at: http://interactivestory.net/download.

Myst (2004), Cyan.

The Sims (2000), Maxis.

The Sims 2 (2004), Maxis, Electronic Arts.

Notes

1 The coverage of drama is perhaps the least extensive because the cinema has taken over the Tropics, although in Shakespeare's day it did reach all types of audiences.

2 For instance Alain Robbe-Grillet, *La Jalousie* (1957); Jean Ricardou, *L'Observatoire de Cannes* (1961); Philippe Sollers, *Nombres* (1968), and to a

lesser extent some novels by Michel Butor, Claude Simon and Robert Pinget.
3 Metalepsis is a figure that involves the transgression of ontological boundaries: fictional characters meeting their author, or characters in a work entering the world of an embedded work.
4 Films with voiced-over narration admittedly combine the diegetic and the mimetic mode, but the two modes occupy different channels, and the same signs cannot be said to function both diegetically and mimetically.
5 See reproductions of these paintings in Paul (2000: 52).
6 To avoid clumsy constructions like *him or her*, I alternate randomly between feminine and masculine pronouns.
7 The standard example of a less efficient problem-solving action leading to a more interesting plot is the decision by the wolf, in *Little Red Riding Hood*, to wait until the heroine reaches the house of the grandmother to eat her, rather than doing so during their first meeting in the forest. From the point of view of the wolf this decision makes no sense, because he is taking the risk that Little Red Riding Hood will never find the grandmother's house, or that another wolf will eat her in the meantime, but the plan is certainly motivated from a narrative point of view.
8 See *Philosophical Investigations* (1968), segment 1-32.
9 Juul defines the prototypical game situation through the following conditions: (1) prototypical games are rule-based; (2) they have a variable, quantifiable outcome; (3) values are attached to the outcomes (winning or losing); (4) players invest efforts to influence the outcome; (5) players are attached to the outcome—they want to win and hate to lose; (6) the game may or may not be played with real-life consequences, such as waging money (Juul 2004: 30).
10 The *paidia* dimension of many video games, for instance of *The Sims*, has been pointed out by Gonzalo Frasca in 'Ludology Meets Narratology' (1999).

2

All too urban: to live and die in *SimCity*

Matteo Bittanti

Instructions/diversions/destructions

Videogames allow us to engage in a dialogue with culture. A videogame is not a conventional text. It is an electronic device that builds stories, creates new social dynamics, and generates possible and impossible spaces. A videogame is a set of experiences. A miniature world. A box of possibilities. One can play by the rules or subvert them, finding all the right clues or looking for improbable connections. What follows is a reading of a game, 'an awesome game', where the text is both a point of arrival and departure. This chapter lies at the intersection of videogame/player/(inter)text. There is no cheat mode available. Take it or leave it.

Citizens of the world

There's this awesome game. It's called *SimCity*. You have to be like this city planner. And you have a budget and you get to decide what to buy for the city? And you can make it any time period. So it's like *Castles* or *TeePees*. Or *Forts*. Or regular buildings. And you can build anything you want. You can build airports or houses? And you have to ... Where do you get all this money? From taxes. But the people are always complaining, Fix the roads, Fix the buildings! Build more stuff! It's too crowded! So you raise taxes to pay for the roads and then the people are like, These taxes are too high! We're paying too much! And so you pay more money to pave the roads and you can't raise taxes so pretty soon you have no money left and everybody is complaining! And so you can't take it anymore and so you like take out your bulldozers and like ... *pppfhh! eirr! pfchhhhhh!* It's true. (Maxwell 1999)

In Paul Auster's *Music of Chance* a former Boston fireman, Jim Nashe, is driving across the US in his beamy red Saab. He is missing a clear plan. He would rather squander time aimlessly while drifting from place to place. Near desperation, he meets a bitter young itinerant gambler, Jack Pozzi, also known as Jackpot, a poker player looking for easy money. Pozzi's plan is simple: to rip off two eccentric, secluded millionaires, Flower and Stone, on their Pennsylvania estate. They're millionaires by chance: their fortunes are a gift from the lottery. With their incredible wealth they built a majestic villa outside New York. The eastern wing of this castle-like house, with its black and white chequered floor – one immediately thinks of Charles Forster Kane's Xanadu – hosts the 'Gardens of the Mind', two gigantic rooms where Flower and Stone 'play their games' (Auster 1990: 78). One hosts the 'City of the World', 'a miniature scale-model rendering of a city … a marvelous thing to behold, with its crazy spires and lifelike buildings, its narrow streets and microscopic human figures' (79). It took Stone five years to build the 'City of the World', we are told.[1] The project is both excruciating and exhilarating. 'I like working on it' Stone says, quickly adding: 'It's the way I'd like the world to look. *Everything in it happens at once.*' 'Willie's city is more than just a toy', Flower continues, 'It's an artistic vision of mankind. It's an *autobiography*, but in another way, it's what you might call a *utopia* – a place where the past and future come together, where good finally triumphs over evil' [emphasis added]. Flower's passion is a bit less remarkable than Stone's: collecting. 'Willie makes things; I like to collect them' (82) says Flower. If Stone's model city lies in a large open area, Flower's collection is distributed:

> Into a network of smaller rooms, and if not for the glass dome perched overhead, the atmosphere might have been oppressive. Each of the five rooms was chocked with furniture, overspilling bookcases, rugs, potted plans, and a multitude of knickknacks. (82)

Flower is creating a private exhibition:

> Long rows of glassed-in display cabinets occupied the center of the room, and the walls were fitted with mahogany shelves and cupboards with protective glass doors. Nashe felt as if he had walked into a museum …
> The room was a monument to trivia, packed with articles of such marginal value that Nashe wondered if it were some kind of joke. (82–83)[2]

Question: What does *The Music of Chance* have to do with *SimCity*?
Question: Is there any relationship between Will Wright and Willie Stone?
This essay is an exercise in pataphysics, the science of imaginary solutions, which symbolically attributes the properties of objects, described by

their virtuality, to their lineaments (Baudrillard 2002). In the following pages, I will argue that Paul Auster's novel holds the key to unlocking the mysteries of *SimCity*. *The Music of Chance* can be used as an alternative strategy guide to unveil its inner secrets. It can be read, at times, as a fictionalized version of Wright's urban simulator. Flower and Stone's pastimes are an allegory of Sim games, *SimCity* and *The Sims*. *SimCity*, like Stone's City of the World, is a game of imaginary *construction*. *The Sims*, like Flower's Room of Wonders, is a game of virtual *collecting* (Bittanti and Flanagan 2003). *SimCity* and *The Sims* are the interactive equivalent of the Gardens of the Minds that Auster poignantly describes in his novel. Although the two games differ in many respects, they share affinities as well. They are complimentary, like *yin* and *yang*. *SimCity* inhabits *The Sims*, and vice versa. *Constructing* and *collecting* from what I would call 'the double logic of the Sim games', which is based on four key elements: *miniaturization, display, control* and *self-referentiality*. Additionally, the critical discourse about *SimCity*, that is evident in the ongoing and prolific analysis of Wright's game in academia, can be summarized into six crucial dichotomies: realism vs. fantasy, narrative vs. simulation, single vs. community, pedagogy vs. escapism, immersion vs. detachment and construction vs. destruction (see Figure 1).

The double logic: constructing and collecting

The passion for 'constructing things' might be innate in humans. Like videogames, construction can be both a pastime and a profession, connecting procrastination and occupation, infancy and maturity. If digital games are late modernity's equivalent of traditional games, then *SimCity* is, as Wright likes to say, a 'software toy'. In *Architecture of Intelligence*, Derrick De Kerckhove (2001: 61) defines *SimCity* as a digital application of proto-electronic forms of amusement:

> Building cities on line, whether they be of the 'SimCity' or the Alphaworld variety, is reminiscent of that blissful period when, as children, we used to build cities with the mechanical toys of the times. Dinky toys, Legoland, Tinker Toys, Meccano, Marlin train stations and a host of other tools of the imagination of the industrial era. In Jean Piaget's still revered theory of child development psychology, the imagination of space is supported by precisely such activities, and is one of the key elements of mental growth. The child learns how to control the environment by building cities.

Construction toys that first appeared at the end of the sixteenth century allowed the infant to manage the complexity of the world. 'These magical

Figure 1 The double logic of *Sim* games

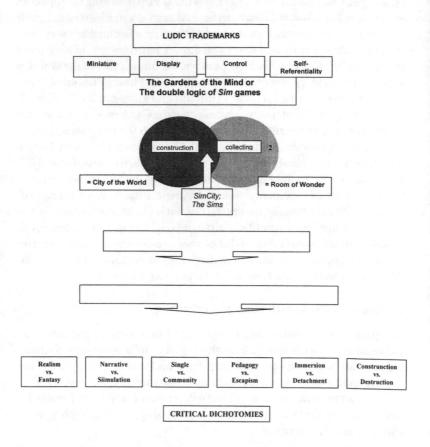

artefacts similarly operated between game and experiment, toy and tech'
(Stafford, Terpak and Poggi 2001: 1). The precursors of *SimCity* are innumerable. One of the most interesting was called *The Pretty Village*, a construction kit that allowed children to build miniature cities, produced since
1897 by New York based McLoughlin Bros. The eighteen models in the box
– which included a hotel, a school, a florist's stand and a church – encouraged children to build 'a city populated by kids'. The print advertisement for
The Pretty Village clearly shows that the game was intended both for boys
and girls, who were supposed to play under the scrutiny of their vigilant
mother. Building a city, or at least, a 'village' was regarded both as an instructive and domestic activity.

SimCity shares *The Pretty Village*'s values, goals and attributes, the difference being that the process of construction here is digital. But production is only one side of the coin. Collecting, too, is an integral part of both *The Pretty Village* and *SimCity*. McLoughlin Bros sold additional sets of the cardboard town, the analogue precursors to videogame add-ons. Similarly, *SimCity* players are actively encouraged to build a City of the World comprising monuments, buildings and objects collected and shared online. The same logic operates in *The Sims*, where constructing a family and a house and collecting a variety of objects are inextricably connected.

While playing a Sim game the computer screen becomes a 'device of wonder', a digital cabinet of curiosities (Stafford, Terpak and Poggi 2001), creating a link between old and new media, that transforms 'the World in a box into Images on a Screen', to paraphrase the title of an exhibition organized by the Getty Research Institute in 2001. As Stafford (1996) writes in her investigation of visual devices from the seventeenth century such as *Wunderkabinett*, *Wunderkabinette* and *Wunderkammern* (cabinet of wonders, tabletop cabinets, and rooms of wonder respectively); early cameras and automatons these 'eye machines' functioned as a filter, a mediation between human beings and the world. They were used to enhance and alter visual perception, but unlike modern museums, their role was to arouse wonderment rather than edification. Their emphasis was on the precious and rare, the novel and the marvellous. They were, moreover, organized according to pre scientific criteria, arranged in some cases to suggest a microcosm, a model of the wider world. They were often compiled by aristocrats and royalty for private rather than public display.

SimCity clearly pays homage to the device of wonders of the past. It is the postmodern equivalent of these archaic visual machines, and it perfectly demonstrates the fluid boundaries between simulation and art, urban planning and literature, technology and entertainment. Thanks to the Internet, a game designed for a solitary, domestic consumption quickly became a portal to a wider world. Sharing and collecting are an integral part of gameplay, if not the essential ones. *SimCity*'s emphasis on collecting items 'found' on the web makes it the modern equivalent of a *Wunderkammern*, although its top-down view renders it more similar to a *Wunderkabinette*. It does not surprise that, in their groundbreaking *Remediation* (1999), Bolter and Grusin consider both the *Wunderkammern* and *SimCity* examples of hypermediation,[3] as they feature 'material links that allow the viewer to retrieve complex personal and cultural references' (Stafford, in Bolter and Gruisin 1999: 62).

SimCity is a gateway to a wider world.

Under the microscope: *SimCity*, or the miniature city

SimCity is a cultural artefact that satisfies a specifically human need: the desire to miniaturize the real, to redefine it in microscopic form, to make the mundane, urban experience intelligible. The diminutive double is readable, manageable, reassuring. Unlike its model, it is proportioned, controllable, balanced. *Ludus*, in this sense, is like a lubricant: it facilitates the cultural acceptance of simulation while redefining the relationship between reality and fantasy. As Susan Stewart (1994: 55) notes: 'There are no miniatures in nature; the miniature is a cultural product, the product of an eye performing certain operations, manipulating, and attending in certain ways to, the physical world' *SimCity*, like other ludic worlds, gives the player the opportunity to experiment, to assess reality through the fantasy. 'The toy world presents a projection of the world of everyday life; this real world is miniaturized or gigantized to test the relationship between materiality and meaning' (57). By miniaturizing the world, we become giants, semi-Gods, contemplating our creation from the top: 'The view from above remains a view from elsewhere, a view in which making the city other must correspondingly employ metaphors of otherness. The view from above could only be a view into a mirror if it were accompanied by a sense of splitting and self-consciousness' (79). The desire to remodel the world is an expression of a solipsistic mind, of an I/eye that considers itself the sole source of reality. Playing God games is a solipsistic activity.

Display: *SimCity* and a virtual landscape

> No Time No Space
> Another Race of Vibrations
> The Sea of the Simulation (Franco Battiato, 'No Time No Space')

As Sandro Bernardi (2002: 20–25) notes, 'The notion of landscape is relatively modern'. In fact, its 'first definition can be probably traced back to Humboldt (1845)'. According to Humboldt, the contemplation of a landscape is an epistemological task. The gaze is actively trying 'to find unity in the diversity of phenomena, to pierce beyond the world of appearances in order to grasp what lies beneath' (21). *SimCity* is not only a game; it is a generator of imaginary landscapes. Thanks to its abstract features, Wright's simulation can reduce the complexity of the real to relatively simple images that appear both 'realistic' and 'fantastic'. *SimCity* leads the players to believing that it is actually possible to locate *kosmos* beyond *chaos* with the aid of a visual interface. If there is a strong tie between the aesthetic experience and the notion of *Weltanschauung*, i.e. a panoramic view of the world, as Humboldt suggests (Bernardi 2002: 22), then *SimCity* is an editor of *Weltanschauung*.

Like all miniatures, *SimCity* 'does not attach itself to lived historical time' (Stewart 1994: 65). The game defines spaces as well as chronologies: the player can alter the flow of time, accelerating it, slowing it down, stopping it at will. By doing so, the player becomes a demiurge, a lesser God. Poole (2000) writes: 'Games like *SimCity* offer two main attractions: the narcissistic instinct in the player: if he or she does well, monuments will be erected and museums will be named in honour of the masterful deity. It's a kind of fame ... Also, the modelling of dynamic processes. Time can be sped up or slowed down at will, and interactions of data over time can be readily visualized' (2000: 48–49).[4]

City of glass: *SimCity* and the imperative of control

> Simulation is about a world that has a measure of autonomy built into its very grammar, but that autonomy is illusory. (Burnett 2004: 199)

City of Glass is the title of one of Paul Auster's most celebrated novels. It is also the most appropriate definition of *SimCity*, a simulation whose logic is founded on the notion of transparent omnivision. With *SimCity* the metropolis of glassy transparency becomes absolute – a vector to pure absence. The simulated, virtual urban environment changes in real time under our watchful eyes. The gaze of the player-as-cyborg (Hayles 1999) is enhanced by filters, menus, pop-up windows. *SimCity* is quintessentially an interactive scopophilic exercise. Wright's simulation is the ludic adaptation of Jeremy Bentham's *panopticon* as it allows the player to see but not to be seen by the simulated citizens, to gaze upon but not to be gazed at, to manipulate without being manipulated. J.C. Herz noted that *SimCity* offers 'a sense of security ... control and containment hard to find in a non-virtual environment' (1997: 218–219). Interestingly, the themes of control and surveillance have become the highest priority in the ongoing debate on urban planning and management, notes Lyon (2002).

Stewart (1994) writes that 'the typical view of the city is though the window – a view within a definite frame and limited perspective, mediated and refracted through the glass of the city's abstraction of experience' (68). *SimCity* allows the players to create and scrutinize virtual cities that exist only on a screen, as if they were protected by glass. Thus, the virtual citizens, also known as Sims, are also virtual prisoners: like fish in a tank, movement is purely illusory. In Jean-Christophe Rufin's *Globalia* (2004), we are presented with a dystopic world in which the cities of the future are protected by transparent bulletproof walls that shield the lucky residents from the poor that live in the 'non-zones'. The need for security leads to many aporia: 'The greatest threat to liberty is liberty itself. How do we defend liberty against itself? By increasing security. Security is liberty. Security is protection. Protection is surveillance. Surveillance is liberty' (Rufin 2004: 56). A similar scenario can be found in George A. Romero's *Land of the Dead* (2004), where the nouveaux riches live in a luxurious cage of glass and steel while the rest of the world is plagued by a contagious disease that turns humans into living dead. But the true cinematic equivalents of *SimCity* are two films of the late 1990s: Alex Proyas's *Dark City* (1998) and Peter Weir's *The Truman Show* (1999). *Dark City* explores the themes of surveillance, control, and simulation with an ingenuity uncommon to contemporary science fiction. Just like Will Wright's *SimCity*, Proyas's fictionalized metropolis modelled after an American city of the 1940s or 1950s is nothing more than an experiment, a simulation gone wrong. The humans trapped in this urban landscape which changes every night are pure automatons that can be reprogrammed at will. The telepathic powers of the rulers of the city, The Strangers, are not unlike the invisible hand of *SimCity* players that can alter significantly the scenario by clicking on the mouse.[5] The film ends with a twist: the 'dark city' is just a lump of matter floating in space. In other words, *Dark City* is a story of a simulation. The film's main preoccupation is memory, or, rather, its absence, its intense fragility: the transformation of the urban space does not really leave any trace in the minds of the citizens. The same applies to *SimCity*. Like Marc Augé's (1995) non-places, the urban structures of *SimCity* are temporary and transient. The Sims are not bothered by the fluidity of the scenario. They have no past, and probably no future either.

Another famous cinematic *experimentum mundi* is Trumania, the simulated city in *The Truman Show*. Trumania, like Wright's game, is an urban simulacrum ruled by a tyrannical, and quasi-omnipotent mayor, Christof.[6] In many ways, Trumania is the antithesis of Dark City. In the latter, all but one citizen (John Murdoch) is unaware that they are living in a simulation. In Trumania, on the contrary, all the virtual citizens but one (Truman) know the truth. Both films are concerned with surveillance and control: they assume that somebody somewhere is controlling everybody, at all times. Unsurprisingly, this obsession for incessant *super*vision is a key element of Stone's City of the World:

> Evil still exists, but the powers who rule over the city have figured out how to transform that evil back into good. Wisdom reigns here, but the

struggle is nevertheless constant, and great vigilance is required of all the citizens – each of whom carries the entire city within himself. (Auster 1990: 80)

This obsession constitutes the very essence of *SimCity*.

SimSimCity: windows, mirrors and Russian dolls

> Simulation is a way of accessing intentionality by entering the world of artifice and living within its confines. (Burnett 2004: 89)

Willie Stone has a dream. Building a second City of the World, 'a smaller one … to fit inside the room within the room', 'a model of the model'. This idea perplexes Nashe. 'But if you did a model of the model – he asks – then theoretically you'd have to do an even smaller model of that model. A model of the model of the model. It could go on forever' (Auster 1990: 81). Stone does not flinch. He is willing to work on his project 'for the rest of his life'. What *SimCity* shares with the City of the World is *openness*, again, both spatial and chronological. They have a definite beginning, but certainly no clear ending. Moreover, they tend to be high in self-referentiality. Willie Stone and Will Wright's projects are fragmentary, a-linear and recursive. The referentiality of *SimCity* reaches its apogee with Steve Alvey's *SliceCity*, a fan-made add-on for *The Sims*. This plug-in allows *The Sims'* players to play a *SimCity*-like game titled *SliceCity* within the game. In other words, with *SliceCity* one can create 'the model of the model of the model'. After designing the mini-cities, the Sims must manage them, satisfying the needs of the mini-Sims, just like a virtual mayor would do (Terdiman 2004). 'The miniature presents us with an analogical mode of thought, a mode that matches world within world' (Stewart 1994: 74).

   This Russian doll-like structure is not peculiar to Will Wright's games, but can be found in many literary texts as well. Consider Andrew Crumey's *Pfitz* (2000), for instance. It tells the story of an eighteenth-century prince who wishes to create the perfect city. He designs a series of imaginary cities, the last of which, Rreinnstadt, he proposes to build in actuality, devoting his entire country to the task. All of Rreinnstadt's elements need to be planned in their tiniest details before the construction can begin. His people are real, as is the work they do on the dream city. The novel has a multi-layered, self-referential structure: one of the characters, a cartographer named Schenck, tries to seduce and conquer the heart of the beautiful biographer Estrella by writing the story of the eponymous Pfitz's travels in Rreinnstadt. Crumey's narrative as a whole is equally recursive and self-referential. With irreverent ingenuity, the author evokes Rreinnstadt in a subsequent novel, *Mr. Mee*, where we encounter a game designer who 'was working at the time on a game program about an eighteenth-century virtual city full of imaginary people' (Crumey 2001: 318). *Medieval Lords*, anyone?

The six dichotomies of *SimCity*

The four aforementioned trademarks are complemented by six dichotomies that inform the discourse about *SimCity*. They are: realism versus fantasy, stories vs. simulation, solitary playing vs. cooperative playing, education vs. escapism, construction vs. destruction and immersion vs. detachment. I will briefly describe each of them.

Realism vs. fantasy

Stone's City of the World is both 'imaginary' and 'realistic'. *SimCity* presents us with the same paradox. Reviewers and critics alike generally emphasize the 'realism' of the game, although here the term is somehow naively associated with the notion of mimetic reproduction of a highly mediated urban iconography. And yet, while it is hard to deny that the graphic depiction of the simcities have become more detailed in the subsequent incarnation of the game, even *SimCity 4* (Maxis 2003) is devoid of the giant logos, billboards and posters that clutter our 'real' cities. In other words, *SimCity* lacks those very elements that define the contemporary urbanscape. The surprising absence of the virtual surrogates of McDonalds, Starbucks, IKEA, Benetton, Pizza Hut and Shell petrol stations makes *SimCity* the ultimate fantasy: a Western-like city where consumerism is present but generic, pervasive yet invisible. Thus, Barry Atkins (2003) is right when he writes that the aesthetics of *SimCity* are somehow cartoonish – not because of iconographic affinities, but because cartoon remains one of the few enclaves of the imaginary relatively free from brand brainwashing and promotional messages embedded in the text.[7]

The evolution of *SimCity* has been characterized by a reduction of abstraction in the graphic depiction of urban and natural elements, to the point that some commentators such as Israels (1999) argued that the game displayed a sense of aesthetic perfection that only true works of art possess.[8] It is interesting to note, however, that while the iconography of *SimCity* has 'improved' significantly, the gameplay, or the inner and outer logic of the game, has remained practically unchanged. The player can only modify the *superficial* aspects of the simulation, for instance the location and aspect of the buildings, but not the *profound* ones, i.e. the models upon which the simulation relies.

> You should be able to experiment with radically different models of urban design (a city of Segways and pedestrians, where cars are forbidden); you should be able to encourage different kinds of businesses in specific neighbourhoods; you should be able to create new forms of urban government … The title is also ripe for historical nuance: the buildings age architecturally as you play the game, but there's no way to build a medieval citadel, or a 19th-century Coketown … Being able to modify the automata rules is exactly what I'd like to be able to do! That would really let you explore different theories about how cities evolve and grow … (Johnson 2003)

As of today, Steven Johnson's requests remain unaccounted for. Yet, one might wonder if *SimCity*'s true reference is not realism, but hyper-realism, both in artistic and philosophic terms. At each inception, *SimCity* is getting closer to a painter's idea of a city. In James Doolin's painting 'Shopping Mall' (1973), a 'faithful' reproduction of Santa Monica's Third Street Promenade, we are looking at the scene as if we were playing *SimCity*. Hyper-realism is both the point of departure and arrival for a simulation whose goal has always been reproducing the 'geography of nowhere' (Kunstler 1994). It is ironic that, in the age of Google Maps, satellite photographs of many locations around the world, the aesthetic of *SimCity* has become, once again, pervasive (Dodson 2005). Like *SimCity*, Google Maps has become a tool for telling stories and constructing narrative:

> Another user Matt Haughey has used the maps in conjunction with photo sharing tool Flickr to give people a potted guide to his childhood in Yorba Linda, near Los Angeles, in California. Haughey, a director at copyright organisation Creative Commons, has used a satellite photo of where he used to live and added annotated notes so that people can follow incidents in his youth at the precise location they happened. The house where he was born, the childhood homes of his friends and past girlfriends, the route of his paper round and where he met his wife for the first time are all shown along with accompanying notes. (BBC News 2005)

Stories vs. simulations

> The toy is the physical embodiment of the fiction: it is a device for fantasy, a point of beginning for narrative. (Stewart 1994: 56)

SimCity is generally considered the paradigm of anti- or post-narrative videogames. According to Espen Aarseth (1997) and Jesper Juul (2002), electronic simulations have nothing that resembles, even tangentially, what is commonly defined as a 'storyline'. However, if the simulation does not rely on a traditional narrative form (linear, sequential), the game stimulates alternative forms of narratives. Its gameplay operates as a 'generator of fiction': it is not a 'story' in itself, rather, it is a narrative machine. Scattered on the Internet are hundreds of 'diaries' of virtual urban planners and mayors that chronicle the origins and growth of "their" imaginary cities. In a sense, this is a paradigmatic example of postmodern, fan-constructed narrative.

SimCity fans love to exchange virtual postcards of their developing metropolis. These iconographic fragments tell us many stories: the story of the virtual urban planner and the story of the fragment that floats in the web in search of a final destination. *SimCity* also represents a paradigmatic example of what Salen and Zimmermann (2003) call 'retelling play', i.e. the players' fictionalization of the ludic experience, stories that cannot only be told in 'first person' as if they were physically immersed in the game.

SimCity's non-identical twin is Italo Calvino's *The Invisible Cities* (1972), a series of imaginary cities expressed through dialogues between Marco Polo and Kublai Khan. If *SimCity* can become a narration of a simulation, Calvino's anti-novel is the simulation of narration. The two are inextricably linked by two elements: *ludus* and *digit*, the Latin terms for play and number, respectively. There is a clear ludic element in *The Invisible Cities*: Marco Polo tells his stories as if he were playing chess, placing the artefacts that he collected in his travels on the black and white majolica floor. The order is not random: he is actively challenging Khan (and the reader-player) to decode the text. *Digit,* the Latin term for 'number' (but also 'finger'), is present because the inner structure of both works, *SimCity* and *The Invisible Cities*, is made of number and alphanumeric strings. In a sense, they're both coded, *programmed. The Invisible Cities* is constructed upon on a very complex but rigid logic of composition which creates an ideal checkerboard made of 64 elements: 55 cities or chapters, in which Marco Polo describes to Kublai Khan, the emperor of China, some city he supposedly visits. These 55 small chapters/cities (i.e. reports) are distributed, on the one hand, in 11 'thematic groups' according to one dominant line or quality of description, and, on the other hand, in 9 big chapters, 5 reports in every chapter, excluding the first and the last chapters, which have 10 reports each. Every chapter is framed with interludes – dialogues between Khan and Marco. If Calvino's cities are invisible, as they exist only in imagination, Wright's cities are virtual, because their visibility does not transcend the borders of the screen.

Alone in *SimCity*

> Hide the geek. That's what it was about. Adulthood was about hiding the
> geek.
> And reclaiming it. I'd been hiding it at Harvard.
> But in our room Tom and I could get back ...
> We got into SimCity and flight simulators.
> The point was to play together. That was the key thing. Together.
> (Bennhaum 1988: 217)

Although *SimCity* was originally designed for a single-player, offline experience, since its inception it has always been a moderately massively online
game. As Will Wright noted:

> Even before we had a website, people were already uploading their cities
> to AOL and trading them. There were big sections with hundreds of cities
> trading. Compuserve was the first place where large collections of cities
> started to appear. (Wright cited in Rouse 2000: 440)

On the Internet, players 'talked strategies, talked urban theory, and actually
swapped cities, posting their files online so other people could download
them' (King and Borland 2003: 84). To encourage players' interaction and
the production of additional content, in the early 1990s, Maxis introduced
an add-on to *SimCity 2000* titled *SimCity Urban Renewal Kit* (*SCURK*).
This tool allowed players to create and customize buildings that could be
used in their virtual cities. Shortly after its introduction, *SCURK* became an
integral part of the game. The players produced an impressive amount of
virtual objects, using the web to both display and swap the outcome of their
work. This form of production is known as 'fanarch', a contraction of 'fans'
and 'architecture'.[9]

It is therefore difficult, if not futile, to map the social space of *SimCity*.
The community that arose around the game is, if possible, more dispersed
and fragmentary than the game itself. Some of the most ingenious architects
in the 'mod' scene, like Wren Weburg, were eventually hired by Maxis. Others, like Lee Sojot became architects *tout court*. Fans production became
even more advanced with the introduction of *Building Architect Tool* (BAT),
Building Architect Plus (BAP) and *Sim City 3000 Unlimited Rendering Kit*
(which became *SC3URK*) for *SimCity 3000*. With the introduction of *SimCity*
4 the landscape evolved even more. The most intriguing feature of the latest
incarnation is *SimCityscape*, which allows the players to 'grab cities from a
region game board, play them, and then upload them to the board for the

next Mayor to develop or evolve. Players work independently from each other on their cities in Mayor Mode, and by participating you will contribute to the collective picture of the region game board' (Maxis website, 2004). Although an in-depth analysis of fans production built by fans transcends the goals of this essay, it seems clear that the fan production oscillates between two poles: *utopia* and *mimesis*. On one hand, the simcities seem to reflect players' idea of the perfect city. On the other, they are modelled after real metropolises, which attests the wish to virtually duplicate 'real' urban spaces.[10] *SimCity* oscillates between interiority and exteriority: the computer screen becomes the mediation between the imagined city and the city that he can see from his apartment window.

SimCity between education and escapism

SimCity is one of the first computer games to be used for pedagogical and educational purposes. According to the Maxis website, in the early 1990s Wright's simulation entered more than 10,000 schools in the United States alone. Since then, however, many commentators have criticized the ideology of the game and the models that underlie the simulation (see, for instance Starr 1994; Bleecker 1995). Others argue that the educational aspects of the game have been highly exaggerated. Martin Lister reminds us that '*Monopoly* and *SimCity* are not accurate models of the complex urban systems. They are – and always been – games' (Lister et al. 2002: 274). The truth lies somewhere in between.

    SimCity is pure escapism masqueraded as edutainment, if such a neologism still bears some meaning in the age of 'serious games'. To play *SimCity* is to immerse oneself in virtual spaces and drown in a flux of images. Here is a confession. I tend to play videogames, and *SimCity* in particular, mostly at night for reasons that oscillate between a genuine lack of time and a sense of guilt induced by Calvinism in condemnation of utilitarian pleasure: indulging in virtual recreation in the hours (allegedly) reserved for compulsive production feels somehow blasphemous. The result is that *SimCity*'s urbanscapes have become my lucid dreams. Interestingly, the conflation between ludic and oneiric is a common theme in cinematic tales of videogame horror (see, for instance, *Brainscan*, 1994). *SimCity* is somehow soporific: its relaxed pace, the muzak in the background, the still images make it the videogame equivalent of a Béla Tarr film. In both cases, distraction from the screen is not only tolerated but even encouraged. *SimCity* is a hypnotizing experience: it creates consensual hallucinations that seem to have come out of a Stanislaw Lem novel. In his underrated *The Futurologist Congress*, a true precursor to *The Matrix*, Lem imagines a dystopian future where human beings use massive doses of hallucinogens that alter sensorial perception, transforming a nightmarish reality into an idyllic fantasy. These pervasive hallucinogens provide a basis for a pseudo-social contract. One of the most common drugs allows the users to create virtual scenarios believed to be real by everybody:

> The older son was an architect with a very promising future, the younger was a poet. The former, unsatisfied with real projects, is now using Constructol and now builds imaginary cities ... If you allow them, dreams have always overcome reality. (Lem 1972: 99)

After all, drugs are both a symptom of capitalist hedonism, and a symbol of the values to which it is dedicated (pleasure). *SimCity* is the new opiate.

Immersion vs. detachment

> Each painter can view the city from only one standpoint at a time, so he will move about the place, and paint it from a hilltop on one side, then a tower on the other, then from a grand intersection in the middle – all on the same canvas. When we look at the canvas, then, we glimpse in a small way how God understands the universe – for he sees it from every point of view at once. By populating the world with so many different minds, each with its own point of view, God gives us a suggestion of what it means to be omniscient. (Stephenson 2003: 265–266)

No matter how hard we seek for *SimCity*'s essence, its real charm ultimately escapes us. Like *The Sims*, *SimCity* can function as a virtual aquarium, where pure observation replaces interaction. You can be playing *SimCity* and yet not be playing it. It is not necessary to keep track of any alteration that happens on the screen, also because many of them are subtle, invisible. This is why J.C. Herz compares *SimCity* to gardening, 'the digital box for those who spend their existence staring at a computer screen and lack the patience to try the "real" gardening' (1997: 214). Gardening is not the most appealing activity for a generation raised on fraggin' and shooting. This explains why many gamers do not hide their deep antipathy for Wright's simulation. Among them, Steven Poole (2000), who considers *SimCity*, and God games in general, a 'tedious pastime'. According to Poole, '[Games like *SimCity*] are not primarily about cities or tribes or any of the putative content ... Perhaps, the fantasy appeal is really about a chance to observe the world over a longer, more sober chronological span than that of a single human life … Such games offer you a position of infinite power in order to whisper the argument that, as an individual in the world, you have none at all' (Poole 2000: 49). Interestingly, Poole, like many other commentators and game scholars, equal freedom of movement with interactivity, implying that the higher the interactivity the better the game. However, the ambiguity of the notion (what is, exactly, interactivity?) makes such a statement almost useless.

The philosopher Pietro Montani (cited in Canova 2004: 52–53) distinguishes between five levels of interactivity: *procedural* (browsing the Internet, using a word processor, etc.); *ludic* (from videogames to hacker activity); *didactil* (multimedia CD-ROM and instructional software); *artistic* (works of art that engage into a dialogue with the user), and interactivity *tout court*, which can 'produce not reversible modifications to the matrix of the program' (53). According to Montani, video game interactivity is nothing more than a simple challenge: 'The player's enjoyment comes from mastering the text. And that's about it' (53). The truth is that many videogames offer a much more sophisticated form of interactivity, since their code can be manipulated to various degrees – one may think of FPS 'total conversion', the radical transformation of *Half-Life* into *Counter-Strike*, and the ever prolific mod scene. *SimCity*'s interactivity is somehow ambiguous. It gives the player the illusion of controlling and customizing the simulated world, but at the same time, it does not allow the player to modify the inner rules (the ideological content). *SimCity*'s charm lies elsewhere. It is not a good example of interactivity, but of interpassivity, as described by Zizek.

> Is, however, the other side of this interactivity not interpassivity? Is the necessary obverse of my interacting with the object instead of just passively following the show, not the situation in which the object itself takes from me, deprives me of, my own passive reaction of satisfaction (or mourning or laughter), so that is the object itself which 'enjoys the show' instead of me, relieving me of the superego duty to enjoy myself … (1997: 111–117)

Interpassivity requires that 'the object itself enjoys the show for me, freeing me from the super ego imperative to enjoy'. According to Zizek, 'in order to be free, I must free myself – and transfer to the other – the inert passivity that contains the density of my substation being' (116). In other words, playing *SimCity* makes the player interpassive. The computer enjoys the game for me, and it keeps playing even when I take a short break from the screen. Interpassivity allows me to correct my students' papers while the computer administers my city. Occasionally, I glance back at the screen to see if 'something is happening'. There is an oscillation between immersion and detachment. The player is always in between stages. Its liminal nature explains why *SimCity* has become so popular with academics even when videogames were not considered worthy of any attention. Playing-and-yet-not-playing *SimCity* perfectly suits a generation of researchers that has had to stand the condescending comments of other faculty members and their rhetorical questions ('You are studying videogames? What is that supposed to mean? Do you actually play them?') *SimCity*'s interpassivity generates several dilemmas: Who is the 'real' player? The human or the machine? Maybe Mel Brooks was correct when he said, half-jokingly that 'Videogames are not for us. They're here to entertain the television.'

SimCity, like Willie Stone's City of the World, stresses detachment over immersion, 'attentive distraction' over 'compulsive involvement'. And yet, this might be a glitch that the game designers have not been able to fix yet. *SimCity* wants to immerse the player in the urban simulated spaces. When Flower shows Jim and Jack the model of his city, the Architect emphasizes that:

> If you look carefully, you'll see that many of the figures actually represent Willie himself. There, in the playground, you see him as a child. Over there, you see him grinding lenses in his shop as a grown man. There, on the corner of that street, you see the two of us buying the lottery ticket ... That's what you might call the private backdrop, the personal material, the inner component. But all these things are put in a larger context. They're merely an example, an illustration of one's man journey through the City of the World. (Auster 1990: 80)

The desire to "enter the simulation" has been expressed by the game designer himself, Will Wright, who once said in an interview:

> I lost my home in the Oakland Hills fire in 1991. So in *SimCity 2000* I made a scenario about the Oakland Hills fire. My house was actually labelled in the scenario so I could put all the fire trucks around my house and save my house. Now that we are working on *The Sims Online*, the boundary is getting blurred. Things are happening to me with real people in the game that are sparking other ideas for the game. We're seeing the in-game and out of game behaviour start to blur. The game is breaking out of the box. (Will Wright, cited in Chambron 2002)

Thus, the evolution of *SimCity* confirms the tension towards total immersion. Clues are everywhere. For instance, the perspective has gradually changed. The top-down view of the original has been replaced by closer views: in *SimCity 4*, it is now possible to zoom in the streets. Moreover, Maxis tried to merge *The Sims* and *SimCity* by allowing the player to move his suburban family to the city. Finally, with the introduction of *Rush Hour* (Maxis, 2004), the player is not required simply to supervise the transportation system, but to directly pilot single vehicles. The player can drive a fire-engine truck that got stuck in the traffic or try to prevent some thieves from escaping on the highway by using the police helicopter. The action is being transferred from the towering observatory to the streets.

The evolution of *SimCity* clearly illustrates that Maxis is progressively abandoning what Michel de Certeau called the 'city-as-concept' to embrace the 'city-as-practice'.[11]

> Michel de Certeau begins his essay 'Walking in the City' (1988: 91–110) with a description of the view of New York City from a skyscraper. From this perspective, thanks to a sanitising distance, the city is reduced to a legible plan, a 'concept city'. In ascending, the subject shakes off the multiplicity of the streets, becoming a reader rather than a participant when his 'elevation transfigures him into a voyeur' (1988: 92). Thus positioned the viewer can savour the 'pleasure of "seeing the whole", of looking down on, of totalising the most immoderate of human texts.' (*ibid*). De Certeau's account of the concept-city is suggestive of the isometric identification invited by *Sim City* – isometric in terms of vantage point, and in the sense that the game generates an identification with its momentum and its system, rather than with any focalised role within the game world. (Carr 2004: 45)

For the 'city-as-practice' to become virtually real it is necessary that the player 'enters' the fantasy. Willie Stone wishes to become part of his creation. Willie is like the statue of baby Jesus that on Christmas Day is placed in the nativity scene to give the representation its full meaning. In *SimCity*, however, this desire is never satisfied. In a sense, the game is truly Buñuellian: pleasure is constantly postponed, delayed and deferred. The outcome is that the simulation creates detachment not immersion. This is true also for *Rush Hour*, whose mission-based structure collides with the open formula of *SimCity*.

Ergo, *SimCity* is a God game *sui generis*. The virtual mayor is the son of a lesser god. He is a stranger in a strange land that administers the world from above. Like Trumania's ruler, Christof, the player cannot live in the world he himself created because he would lose his status as a demiurge. For a city-as-concept to become a city-as-practice a game design revolution is necessary: *SimCity* has to turn into *Vice City* (2003). In Will Wright's simulation, transcendence is not an option, but a prerequisite. As Stewart wrote:

> Today we find the miniature located at a place of origin (the childhood of the self, or even the advertising scheme of a company's earliest product is put on display in a window or a lobby) and at a place of ending (the productions of the hobbyist: knickknacks of the domestic collected by elderly women, or the model trains built by the retired engineer); and both locations are viewed from a transcendent position, a position which is always within the standpoint of present lived reality and which thereby always nostalgically distances its object. (1994: 68)

Construction vs. destruction

> We are like kids left in the game room for too long. After a while, we must destroy our toys, even those we like (Ballard 2003: 77)

> We Americans are always tearing down what we build, destroying the past in order to start over again, rushing headlong into the future. (Auster 1190: 84)

While it is true that construction is the backbone of *SimCity*, it is nonetheless clear that destruction is inherent to the simulation. Clues are everywhere: from the cover of the original *SimCity*, which featured a menacing Godzilla to the infamous 'bulldozer' option that allows players to simply eradicate entire areas of the city (see Kolson 1999), let alone the several natural disasters that the player can turn on at will. If *SimCity* is a virtual sand box, then simcities are sandcastles. No matter how solid and resistant the construction might seem, a tsunami or a hurricane can flatten them in a second. Simcities are fragile and vulnerable: what separates a cluttered screen from an empty wasteland is a mouse click. If Jean Baudrillard (2002) is right in saying that the destruction of the Twin Towers was inscribed in the steel and glass of their structure – an event that fiction had prepared, told and mediated long before the event itself – then total annihilation is embedded in *SimCity*'s source code.

I suspect that, in this era of urban anxiety, paranoia and distress – Paul Virilio's (2005) latest work is aptly titled '*City of Panic*' – the simulation is not simply a duplication of reality, but its memento, souvenir, reminder. The desire of *SimCity* players to virtually reproduce the cities they live in or wish to live can be interpreted as a form of preservation. They are willing to perpetuate the city's existence after their natural or unnatural demise. This scenario has been described by Edward Carey (2003) in *Alva & Irva: The*

Twins Who Saved a City, after the two lonesome twins who create a Plasticine™ model of the city they live in, Entralla. After an earthquake strikes Entralla, their miniature model becomes the only useful tool to rebuild the city.

If death is, according to Martin Heidegger, man's extreme possibility, destruction is not the antithesis of construction in Sim-games. Rather, it is its extreme manifestation. This apparent contradiction is at work also in the cinema of simulation. In Nicholas Roeg's *Track 29* (1988), simulation is present at two levels. A couple live their obsessions: Carolina Linda (Theresa Russell) is still traumatized after being raped as a young girl and she imagines a virtual son, Martin (Gary Oldman), with whom she has an almost incestual relationship. Her husband, Henry (Christopher Lloyd), is a surgeon who displays a maniacal passion for collecting electric trains and spanking his assistant. Henry has transformed his house into a gigantic train set: the miniature locomotives ride from one room to another.[12] The film shows 'things that occupy the same time and the same space even though they do not exist', as a television dialogue strategically placed at the beginning of the film informs us. Simcities do not 'really' exist in time and space, but they do occupy the player's time and space (mental space, at least). Another aspect of Roeg's film that strikes a chord with videogame playing is escapism. Illusion is a form of epistemology that acquires ontological consistency as the game goes on. Both Linda and Henry regress to a childlike stage: the doctor spends more and more time with his beloved electric trains, while Carolina secludes herself in her bedroom, her only company a set of dolls. Even Martin, a byproduct of Carolina's fragile mind, acts like a child. Collapse is inevitable, almost predictable. At the end, the electric train explodes and the evil simulation is finally destroyed. Fascinatingly, death and despair is incumbent in the City of the World, *SimCity*'s non-identical twin:

> For all the warmth and sentimentality depicted in the model, the overriding mood was one of terror, of dark dreams sauntering down the avenues in broad daylight. A threat of punishment seemed to hang in the air – as if this were a city at war with itself, struggling to mend its ways before the prophets came to announce the arrival of a murderous, avenging God. (Auster 1990: 96)

Once again, Luddism seems to be the necessary outcome of ludus. There is no heaven in God games. We build virtual cities just to destroy them. After all, it is just a game, is it not?

Works cited

Aarseth, Espen (1997) *Cybertext: Perspectives on Ergodic Literature*, Baltimore: Johns Hopkins University Press.

Atkins, Barry (2003) *More Than a Game: The Computer Game as Fictional Form*, Manchester: Manchester University Press.

Augé, Marc (1995) *Non-Places: Introduction to an Anthropology of Supermodernity*, London: Verso.

Auster, Paul (1990) *Music of Chance*, New York: Viking.

Ballard, J.G. (2003) *Millennium People*, London: Flamingo.

Baudrillard, Jean (1992) *L'Illusion de la fin: ou La greve des evenements*, Galilee: Paris.

——(2002) *The Spirit of Terrorism: And Requiem for the Twin Towers*, London: Verso.

BBC News (2005) 'Google maps give fresh perspective', http://news.bbc.co.uk/2/hi/technology/4448807.stm, accessed April 2006.

Bennhaum, David (1998) *Extra Life: Coming of Age in Cyberspace*, New York: Basic.

Bernardi, Sandro (2002) *Il paesaggio nel cinema italiano*, Genoa: Marsilio.

Bittanti, Matteo (ed.) (2004) *SimCity. Mappando le citta' virtuali*, Milan: Unicopli.

Bittanti, Matteo and Mary Flanagan (2003) *The Sims: Similitudini, Simboli & Simulacri*, Milan: Unicopli.

Bleecker, Julian (1995) 'Urban Crisis: Past, Present, and Virtual', *Socialist Review* (25), 189–221.

Bolter, Jay David and Richard Grusin (1999) *Remediation: Understanding New Media*, Cambridge, MA: MIT Press.

Burnett, Ron (2004) *How Images Think*, Cambridge: MA: MIT Press.

Calvino, Italo (1972) *Le città invisibili*, Torino: Giulio Einaudi Editore.

Canova, Gianni (2004) 'I cinque livelli possibili di interattività nell'era elettronica. Un dialogo con Pietro Montani', *Duellanti*, February, 52–53.

Carey, Edward (2003) *Alva & Irva: The Twins Who Saved a City*, London: Picador.

Carr, Diane (2004) 'Modelled Cities, Model Citizens', in Matteo Bittanti (ed.) *SimCity: Mappando le citta Virtuali* (Milan: Unicopli), 93–210.

Certeau, Michel de (1984) *The Practice of Everyday Life*, Berkeley: University of California Press.

Chambron, Melanie (2002) 'Interview With the Goddess: The E3 Panel With Yu Suzuki and Will Wright', *GigNews.com*, www.gignews.com/goddess/suzuki_wright.htm, accessed September 2004.

Crumey, Andrew (2000) *Mr. Mee*, London: Daedalus.

——(1995) *Pfitz*, London: Daedalus.

Cubitt, Sean (2000) *Simulation and Social Theory*, London: Sage.

De Kerckhove, Derrick (2001) *The Architecture of Intelligence*, New York: Birkhauser.

Dodson, Sean (2005) 'Get Mapping', *Guardian Online*, 7 April 2005, http://technology.guardian.co.uk/online/story/0,3605,1453293,00.html, accessed April 2005.

Hayles, Katherine (1999) *How We Became Posthuman: Virtual Bodies in Cybernetics, Literature, and Informatics*, Chicago: University of Chicago Press.

Herz, J.C. (1997) *Joystick Nation: How Videogames Ate Our Quarters, Won Our Hearts, and Rewired Our Minds*, Boston, MA: Little, Brown and Company.

Israels, David (1999) 'When Game Imitates Art', *SF Weekly*, 2 November 1999.

Johnson, Steven B. (2003) 'SimCity Redux', stevenberlinjohnson.com, 27 january, www.stevenberlinjohnson.com/movabletype/archives/000037.html, accessed September 2003.

Juul, Jesper (2001) 'Games telling stories?', *Game Studies*, 1:1, www.gamestudies.org/0101/juul-gts/, accessed January 2006.

Kline, Stephen (1995) *Out of the Garden: Toys, Tv, and Children's Culture in the Age of Marketing*, London: Verso.

Kolson, Kenneth (1999) *Big Plans: The Allure and Folly of Urban Design*, Baltimore: Johns Hopkins University Press.

Kunstler, James Howard (1994) *Geography of Nowhere: The Rise and Decline of America's Man-Made Landscape*, New York: Free Press.

Lem, Stanislaw (1974) *The Futurological Congress: From the Memoirs of Ijon Tichy*, New York: Harcourt.

Lister, Martin, Kieran Kelley, Jon Dovey, Seth Giddings and Iain Trant (2002) *New Media: A Critical Introduction*, London: Routledge.

Lyon, David (2002) *Surveillance Society: Monitoring Everyday Life*, New York: Oxford University Press.

Maxwell, Richard (1999) '*House: A Play*', *PAJ: A Journal of Performance and Art*, 21.3, 79–92

Miklaucic, Shawn (2001) 'Virtual real(i)ty: Simcity and the production of urban cyberspace', *Game research: The art, business and science of computer games*, www.game-research.com/art_simcity.asp, accessed December 2006.

Nelson, Victoria (2003) *The Secret Life of Puppets*, Harward: Harvard UP.

Poole, Steven (2000) *Trigger Happy. The Inner Life of Videogames*, London: Fourth Estate.

Rouse Richard (2000) *Game Design: Theory and Practice*, Piano, Texas: Wordware.

Rufin, Jean-Christophe (2004) *Globalia*, New York: Norton.

Salen, Katie & Eric Zimmermann (2003) *The Rules of Play*, Cambridge, MA: MIT Press.

Stafford, Barbara Maria (1996) *Artful Science: Enlightenment Entertainment and the Eclipse of Visual Education*, Cambridge, MA: MIT Press.

Stafford, Barbara Maria, Frances Terpak and Isotta Poggi (2001) *Devices of Wonder: From the World in a Box to Images on a Screen*, Los Angeles: Getty Center.

Starr, Paul (1994) 'Seduction from a Sim', *The American Prospect*, 5:17, 21.

Stewart, Susan (1994) *On Longing: Narratives of the Miniature, the Gigantic, the Souvenir, the Collection*, Durham, NC: Duke University Press.

Terdiman, Daniel (2004) 'The Russian Nesting Doll of Games', *Wired news*, 14 February 2004, www.wired.com/news/games/0,2101,62287,00.html, accessed March 2004.

Virilio, Paul (2005) *City of Panic*, New York: Berg.

Zizek, Slavoy (1997) *The Plague of Fantasies*, London: Verso.

Notes

1 Since the novel was published in 1990 and it is set in contemporary times, one can safely assume that the construction of the City of the World began in 1985. Interestingly, around the same time, Will Wright started to design his urban space simulator.

2 I believe it is necessary, at this point, to mention an inexplicable omission in the cinematic adaptation of Paul Auster's novel, also titled *Music of Chance* (Philip Glass, 1993). In the film we get a view of City of the World, but Flower's Room of Wonders is absent. Auster's cameo at the end is not enough to compensate for the loss. There is, however, one interesting element: Flower and Nashe climb a ladder to contemplate the miniature city. As in *SimCity*, it does not take much to acquire transcendence.

3 For more information about *SimCity* and remediation, see Shawn Miklaucic (1999).

4 See also: J.C. Herz (1997: 219).

5 The analogies between *SimCity* and *Dark City* are also explored by Victoria Nelson (2001).

6 Interestingly, the film was largely shot in Celebration, Disney's 'simulated town' in Florida. For more information, see Cubitt (1999: 104–105).

7 This does not apply to cartoons that were specifically created to promote a correlated toy-line, such as *Pokémon* and *Transformers*. See Kline (1995).

8 See Israels (1999).

9 One of the most interesting examples can be found online at http://freechina taiwan.tripod.com/cosmopolis/cosmopolishome.html.

10 Incidentally, Calvino confessed that the two fundamental themes of *Invisible Cities* are 'memory' and 'desire'. The same themes underline *SimCity*.

11 See Diane Carr's 'Modeled cities, model citizens: overseers and occupants of *Sim City* and *Anarchy Online*', in Matteo Bittanti (ed) *SimCity*.

12 Interestingly, passion for miniature trains tends to border on madness and plain obsession in films and on television. Think, for instance, about the passion Gomez has for miniature trains in *The Addams Family*.

3

Play, modality and claims of realism in *Full Spectrum Warrior*

Geoff King

The aim of this chapter is to examine the balance between notions of play and claims to the status of realism, of various kinds, in the squad-based tactical shooter *Full Spectrum Warrior*. I start here from a definition of play as a distinct *mode* of activity, according to which games are marked off from other aspects of the external world. Some games are designed to blur distinctions between play and the real, however, in making claims to the status of 'realism' or 'authenticity'. *Full Spectrum Warrior* is a useful example of this process, trading on its origins as a training aid designed for the US Army. These include assertions of realism at the level of graphical representation, but more importantly, in this case, claims to the status of a functional variety of realism, in which gameplay is said to be modelled on the embodiment of real-world military tactics. Issues of realism and play are considered in this chapter in relation to the difficulty settings in the game, particularly the difference between the original army version and the standard settings of the commercial release. Some potential clashes are also suggested between different forms of realism, particularly the graphical and functional variants. As a game originally designed specifically to *train* its users in a real-world military context, *Full Spectrum Warrior* is also a good example through which to explore the extent to which games might be understood as functioning to 'position' or 'interpellate' players, in the sense suggested by theories of ideology drawing on the work of Louis Althusser.

First, I want to establish the notion of play as a particular mode of activity or experience, against or alongside which avowedly more 'realistic' dimensions of games have to be considered. This will be covered briefly as it is an issue that has already been quite extensively debated. One way of cutting through a number of definitions of play that have been used in relation to games in recent years is to define play as a distinct mode of behaviour or activity. I am using the term mode here – or modality – in the sense in which it is used by Robert Hodge and David Tripp (1986) in their study of children and television. For Hodge and Tripp, modality suggests a particular attitude towards an activity and how that activity is situated in relation to what is understood to be the real world. All forms of media communication include modality markers that signify their status; distinctive framing routines and formal devices, for example, that establish through convention whether something is meant to be taken as reality or fantasy (one example would be the way television news seeks to situate itself in particular ways as 'serious' and 'important'). Play is usually clearly marked-off in the same way as a distinctive realm. Many definitions of play include the notion that to play a game is to enter into a special experiential area: a demarcated playground as Huizinga (1955) terms it, or the 'magic circle', one of a number of descriptions used by Huizinga and drawn upon by Salen and Zimmerman (2003) to suggest more generally the domain in which gameplay of any kind exists. Even in the animal world, the anthropologist Gregory Bateson (2000) suggests – in another widely cited passage – that the existence of play requires some kind of meta-communication that establishes the frame: a signal that says 'this is play' rather than something to be taken more seriously.

A number of modality markers exist in the case of videogames, starting with the very fact that we call them 'games' (rather than 'simulations') and buy them in games stores or the games sections of other outlets. In some cases dimensions such as cover artwork and interface design clearly establish non-real-world or fantasy frameworks that underline the status of the experience on offer. The actions required by players and player-characters are often limited and arbitrary, an issue to which I will return below in the case of *Full Spectrum Warrior* (*FSW*). Some games, however, send out more confused signals about modality, often claiming a relatively greater degree of congruence with the real-world experiences on which they are based. This can involve a number of different dimensions, several of which are found in *FSW*.

One way of complicating the question of modality is by setting a game in a context that has strong real-world reference: the difference between the location of fantasy or science-fiction related titles and the real-world resonance of many war-related games. *FSW* is given a fictional setting, the imaginary republic of Zekistan, but one that is clearly established as an extrapolation from contemporary military/geopolitical events in the external world. The military action around which the game revolves, urban warfare against forces described as 'ex-Taliban' and displaced 'Iraqi loyalist' fighters, is explicitly situated as an adjunct to its equivalent in the real world. The events leading up to the supposedly NATO-authorized action are described in the game manual as occurring 'After the U.S.-led operations in Afghanistan and Iraq'. Fictional/game material is integrated very smoothly, effortlessly and almost in passing – so much is the process taken for granted – into the stuff of contemporary headline news, a process that raises many questions about the ideological implications of such games, to which I shall return, briefly, later.

Qualities of audio-visual representation are another obvious dimension in which games can seek to make greater or lesser claims to the status of proximity to real-world equivalents. Like many other military-based games, *FSW* trades on levels of realism of this kind, particular in relation to the perceived quality of graphics (generally hailed in reviews as 'highly realistic'), although this issue is always more complex than it might at first seem. The resemblance according to which 'realism' is measured is often towards other representational forms such as film and television as much as to any unmediated notion of 'reality' itself. *FSW* is also marked by claims to the status of functional realism, as suggested above, a dimension to be considered in more detail in this chapter.[1]

Games located in or close to real-world military settings often invest quite considerably in claims to functional realism. Many invest in the notion that weapons function in a manner analogous to the characteristics of the real thing, including the mapping into gameplay of factors such as recoil or the tendency of certain weapons to jam in heavy use. This dimension is largely in the background in *FSW*, however, the principal emphasis of which is on functional realism at the level of tactics. The 'core mechanic' of the game (Salen and Zimmerman), the central, repeated and defining feature of gameplay, is a basic pattern in which two squads of soldiers are manoeuvred through the gamescape. The key lesson taught by the game is the need to move each squad, in an alternating sequence, from one source of cover to another. When enemy forces are engaged, one squad generally has the job of keeping them pinned down with fire while the other moves. Enemies also gain protection from cover, resulting in a gameplay pattern in which it is constantly necessary to find a way to manoeuvre one squad into a flanking position from which existing cover offers no protection. This is the basis of the original Army version of the game, designed as a learning tool for infantry squad leaders. As many reviewers suggested on the release of the commercial version, the basic gameplay routine is extremely repetitive, with few variations, which might be attributable to its origins in a simulation designed to teach a limited number of core tactical skills. This might, inadvertently, constitute another signifier of functional realism for the general market, capturing something of the dull routine involved in real-world military activity (military games in general, unsurprisingly, greatly exaggerate the frequency of instances of actual combat when compared with the reality, something of which *FSW* could also be accused but perhaps to a lesser extent than usual).[2] In some sequences, the player can spend quite lengthy periods carefully negotiating streets, the two squads leapfrogging past each other from one source of cover to another, without encountering any enemy forces. As far as the core mechanic is concerned, there is little difference between its implementation in the Army version and the commercial release, although a number of other distinctions can be made, relating especially to the juncture between 'difficulty' settings and notions of greater or lesser 'authenticity' of gameplay.

The initial commercial release of *FSW* for the Xbox comes in two 'regular' difficulty settings, 'Sergeant' and 'Sergeant Major', distinguished in the conventional manner by factors such as the provision of more ammunition to the player-characters in 'Sergeant' and the greater accuracy of enemy fire in 'Sergeant Major'. A harder 'Authentic' setting is available as a hidden feature, accessible through the input of a 'cheat' code, although this is one of the standard settings available on the subsequent PC version. Also 'hidden' (although this process is something of a confection, a dimension of such games worthy of separate consideration in its own right, as it is not very difficult to unlock) is the original 'US Army' version, which shares some features in common with the 'Authentic' setting such as the absence of 'save' points and the removal of many features from the game-screen's heads-up display (HUD). The 'US Army' version also includes its own difficulty options through which the player can choose different settings for features such as the presence and aggression of 'opfor' (opposition forces) and the 'trained' or 'untrained' status of squad members.

'Difficulty' can be understood as a dimension of gameplay of direct relevance to the questions of realism and modality addressed in this chapter. One of the defining features of 'play' in general is that, where it is modelled on real-world activities, it usually offers a version that is easier than engagement in the real-world activity itself. 'Play' versions of activities are usually less demanding, providing more scope for success than would usually be available to those not highly skilled in the original activity. The separation of play from other activities – a feature of most general definitions of play – includes a separation from much of the difficulty and/or stress of equivalent real-world experiences. This is, arguably, a key source of the pleasure offered by games: the ability to achieve, vicariously, feats unavailable to the player in any other realm (which is not to say that games do not have difficulties and frustrations of their own with which to contend). To play at driving a racing car is much easier (not to mention safer) than doing the real thing. Much the same goes for military games. Player-characters can usually achieve far more – and achieve it far more easily – than would normally be the case in any non-play-world equivalent. It is no accident, then, that the label 'Authentic' has become common parlance for the more difficult settings of games, particularly those with military or other real-world related settings.

Part of the process of turning *FSW* into a commercially viable game, then, is a process of making it easier. Compared with the Army version, the standard 'Sergeant' and 'Sergeant Major' settings provide numerous aids. These include elements such as those cited above: the provision of save points in the commercial release and numerous additional sources of information supplied via the HUD. In the US Army version, whole missions have to be completed successfully or started again from scratch. Extended periods of play have to be repeated if a mission is failed because of the death of squad members, a familiar feature of games in which save points are not included or are very few and far between. It could be argued, in one sense, that this is more 'realistic', a closer analogue of the real-world equivalent experience. In real-world military operations of the kind modelled in *FSW*, there is no option to save progress up to a certain point, to guarantee only having to restart from a mid-way point should a mission subsequently end in failure. Even within the limited confines of a game, more is at stake in every moment of play in situations in which regular saving is not permitted; what exactly is 'at stake' is very different from its real-world counterpart, of course, but the experience might be understood as at least a degree closer to the real than would otherwise be the case. An arbitrary dimension also exists in the Army version, located by the designers of the game as an additional source of 'authenticity' (Berghammer 2004). In the commercial version, the correct following of procedure and the learning of lessons guarantees success. This is not always the case in the Army version, where the player can do the right thing and still fail in some instances; an attempt to factor into the game the capricious nature of real-life military action, a complication of the simpler binary right/wrong structure of the commercial release.

Players of the game in other than Army or Authentic modes are also provided with much more information on the state of play. Helpful icon-shields, appearing over the heads of player-character squad members, indicate whether or not they are in cover, and what state the cover is in should it be a variety that is subject to degradation under fire. Icons above the heads of enemies tell the player when they are 'engaged' (in which case enemies will not shoot at anyone other than the solider engaging them) or 'pinned' (under heavy fire and not able to return fire at all); useful information for the player wanting to know whether or not other player-characters can move safely out of cover. Orientation is also made easier through the provision of an arrow pointing to the direction of the next objective and markers of the compass points. Key aspects of the gamescape are made explicitly legible through extra-diegetic devices, in other words, material that would not be visible to the characters inside the fictional world. Some of these features are also variable within the Army version. The player can choose whether or not opposition forces are identified as such on screen, through the presence of a red shield icon above their heads. Without this assistance, the player is led to look more closely into the game-world, although the presence of enemies is also indicated quite speedily by the automated 'enemy targeted' comments voiced by squad members. In the more difficult modes of play, generally the player has to work much harder to try to establish the status of the various actors or the environment at any time, a process described by the designers as 'much more of an organic experience' (Berghammer 2004), a phrase that implies an experience that grows more 'naturally' from within the simulated activity.

How significant are these differences, though? If we imagine a scale that starts with the real-world equivalent activity, at one end, how might the various versions of the game be located? There are significant differences between the different versions in terms of the balancing of operative modalities: how far different degrees of play or of functional realism are being implemented or foregrounded, whether in the game itself or the game as accompanied by its surrounding marketing, reviews and other discourses. It is useful to tease out these distinctions, as part of a broader process of mapping the various dimensions of gameplay in *FSW* or any other example. But these are all versions of *play*, and the gulf between these and any kind of real-world equivalent is vastly greater than the differences between the alternative versions of the game. This might be an obvious point, but seems particularly in need of emphasis in the case of games such as these in which an overt sense of blurring is sometimes suggested between the realms of, if not *real-world* and play, those of *real-world-training* and play (any games, that is, that have direct associations with actual military training, in a wider context in which there have been significant overlaps between the entertainment- and military-centred developments of game, simulation or virtual world technologies (Der Derian 2000)).

Even in its most 'Authentic' or army-training-developed forms, *FSW* remains clearly identifiable as a game, even if it is a game from which lessons with real-world application might in some cases be drawn. The world of *FSW* is a very limited one. Options for the player and player-characters are tightly restricted. Limitations often seem arbitrary, as is necessarily the case in the demarcated space of any playground. By contemporary game standards, which can include relatively open game-worlds, *FSW* is quite restricted spatially, with player-characters unable to enter buildings or to follow other than what is usually a narrow range of exploratory options. The emphasis on a particular core mechanic is such that little breadth of in-game experience is possible. This might, for some, be a criticism, but my purpose here is to emphasize that arbitrary restrictions of one kind or another are in the essence of games, a central feature of translation into the simplified and abstracting realm of play. In all gameplay, a tension exists between experience of the game-world in diegetic terms (an imaginary experience inside the game, in this case imagining oneself as engaged in particular military activities) and an experience of the game *as a game* (involving awareness of the process of play as an abstracted activity revolving around the performance of core game mechanics). It might be argued that both dimensions are often or usually in play simultaneously or in variable combinations during the process of gameplay. Shifts in the balance of focus might also be associated with different stages of play: the replaying of a sequence, for example, after a mission failure, is likely to be an experience of less 'immersion' in the fictional world of the game. In the example given earlier, in which a stretch of the game-world might be covered very slowly and carefully, without knowledge of the absence of enemy forces, a different mode of play might be expected in subsequent attempts – a faster and more superficial traversal of the gamescape, based on extra-diegetic knowledge gained from the initial experience. Awareness of the game *as game* is never likely to be far from the surface, however, despite all the efforts of designers to create compelling game-worlds, contexts or narrative structures of one kind or another. Explicit markers of arbitrary game-ness, such as the larger number of in-game icons provided in the commercial release of *FSW* on the ordinary settings, might increase this tendency, but only to a relative degree. In the Army version of *FSW*, for example, the attention of the player is unlikely to be devoted primarily to the supposedly 'more organic' experience of a less cluttered game world. That has certainly not been my experience, one example being the process of moving the player-controlled squads around in the game-world.

To move a squad, the player uses the left thumbstick on the Xbox controller. Circular icons appear within the game-world to show the positions the soldiers would take up. At the same time, another icon appears on the surface of the HUD, taking on a different shape to indicate different squad cover formations when cover is available (a straight line to indicate a position where the squad would line up against a wall, an advantageous 'corner' icon for a position looking around a corner and other shapes depending on the nature of the object behind which the squad would be deployed). The positional icons are usually moved around until a suitable spot is chosen. When doing this, the player's attention is pulled by two rival points of focus: the location within the diegetic universe (the actual place in the game-world to which the squad would be relocated) and the cover-formation icon, in the lower right-hand part of the screen (which gives a clear indication of the type of cover that would be provided). A supposedly 'more organic' experience would result from exclusive focus on the former, where what counts would be closer to what could directly be seen of the features of the game world from the current viewpoint of the squad in question. A more effective play strategy, however, requires at least as much attention to the cover-formation icon, if not more, as it is generally an easier and more certain way to establish that a safe cover position will be achieved, especially in anything more than a very short-distance redeployment. There are strong reasons, then, for a 'shallower' point of focus, at the screen-surface of the HUD and at what is clearly a game-specific imposition, rather than a relatively 'deeper' look into the game-world that seeks to establish itself as a 'more organic' diegetic entity.

If *FSW* can be understood as making several different kinds of claim to the status of 'realism', there are certain respects in which these clash, rather than being mutually reinforcing, another factor likely to draw attention to the nature of the game as an arbitrary construct. Graphical representation and functional realism are quite often at odds, for example, a feature common to many games. The figures of squad members might be rendered in detail that provides a reasonable level of (photo)realism, by game standards, along with postures and movements closely modelled on the real-world equivalent, but their positioning on screen often has the effect of undermining the functionally-realist impression sought by the game. Figures standing in a corner position and declared by the game to be safely in cover often appear to be standing quite clearly out in the open: interface icons declare a status contradicted by on-screen appearance (or, in the Army/Authentic versions, the same message is conveyed in less mediated fashion by the fact that that they are not being hit by enemy fire). The same happens in some cases when squad members take cover behind objects such as burned-out cars. In one case, found in an early training session as well as in subsequent missions, a squad of four soldiers is declared to be in cover, and hence safe as far as the game mechanism is concerned, while standing upright along the side of a car situated between them and an enemy shooter. Visuals suggest otherwise: two stand behind the bonnet, clearly exposed in their upper bodies, while the other two could clearly be seen and shot, from an in-game-world perspective, through the car's empty windows.

How important clashes such as these might be is likely to depend, as is much else, on the particular context in which the game is played. Playing the original version of *FSW* unlocked in the commercial release is a very different experience from using the original as part of a training process within the military, a difference that has implications for the modality-nature of the experience that is likely to result. This is a point that can be made more generally in response to claims that certain kinds of games (the focus is usually on first-person shooters, for obvious reasons) can have the effect of 'training' players to perform in-game-type activities in the real world, an issue to which I return below. Context is important. If the original version of *FSW* is played by military personnel, this is not an isolated activity, but part of a broader training context involving other forms of training and rein-forcement and a context of military discipline. If the game offers a rather limited and abstract experience, this might be a positive virtue in the military context. A focus on a small number of key issues is likely to be of greater value, as part of a training procedure, than the more complex, open and multidimensional experience that might be sought by some gamers or game critics.[3] Likewise, a clash between graphical and functional realism might be of little importance: the contradictory impression created by graphical rep-resentation might simply be bracketed-out in a pragmatic context in which the game is designed to perform certain limited training functions, rather than to have any wider aspirations. The same can be said of another prob-lem identified by some reviewers: the fact that enemies located behind cover are *entirely* inviolate, even when they pop their heads or entire bodies into view, whereas in the real world it would be possible to hit them with suffi-ciently accurate fire (as is the case, for example, in *Brothers in Arms: Road to Hill 30*, which mixes the tactical-squad dimension of *FSW* with the direct character control of a third-person shooter). This might also be rational-ized by the game's focus on the pursuit of particular tactics (especially flank-ing manoeuvres) at the expense of attempting a more 'rounded' simulation of military action. If these considerations are particularly germane to the original military training incarnation of *FSW*, however, they might also ap-ply more widely, all games being founded on an essential simplification and reduction in the number of parameters involved in the kinds of activities they model.

Two very different ways of understanding games might be involved in the difference between the experience of *FSW* as a training device used by military personnel or as a game supplied as a commercial entertainment product. Two very different usages are involved, although debates on these issues often blur what I would suggest are some important distinctions. In essence, this comes down to a distinction between notions such as 'training', 'positioning' or 'interpellation' and the notion of 'play'. Functional realism is particularly central to these issues because of its perceived potential to translate into the series of terms that begins with 'training', implying as it does the modelling into gameplay of particular modes of activity or behaviour that might be learned by the player.

The notion that videogames can serve purposes of training, teaching or learning is not only found in the more sensational cases, such as the claims that first-person shooters effectively train people to become potential killers (as is argued most prominently by the military psychologist Dave Grossman; Grossman and DeGaetano 1999). There are also more nuanced understandings of this kind of potential, including the development of games specifically designed to teach children or interventions such as Patrick Crogan's (2003) suggestion that the first-person shooter can be understood as offering a playful variety of a more widely established model of real-time digital information processing. Some of these accounts draw explicitly or implicitly on the concept of 'interpellation', in a sense that extrapolates from Althusser's theory of ideology: the suggestion that games might 'position' players in some way as 'subjects' in society. Videogames can be seen as lending themselves particularly well to the use of this approach, given the active involvement of the player in 'taking up' particular roles during gameplay. Some might suggest that for this reason interpellation might occur in games rather more literally than in other media forms.

There is, however, a key opposition between concepts such as interpellation and how we might understand 'play'. 'Interpellation' suggests a process that has significant and quite powerful real-world resonance; or, more than that, real-world *effect*. It suggests that games can shape players into something, or at least contribute to such effects. Play, on the other hand, suggests 'playing at' rather than 'really doing' or 'really training' for performing any particular activity or kind of activity. What might be the relationship between the two? My argument is that a crucial gap exists between the two, an essential distinction to be maintained between games and any activity modelled in games – however much any individual game, such as *FSW*, might claim or aspire to the status of functional realism – and the kinds of real-world activities that might be simulated. This does not mean that games are entirely separated off from the rest of the world, however. My aim here is to chart a path between two extremes: one that collapses or excessively blurs the distinction between game-world and real-world activity and another that denies any connection at all.[4]

Much of the pleasure of play lies in its clear distinction from the remainder of the real world, as suggested above in the case of difficulty levels. A great deal of play is predicated on the separation between what we play at, or fantasize, and what is available to us in the outside world (see, for example, Jones 2002). To play at an activity is often to acknowledge the fact that such an activity is either unavailable to us or one we cannot perform so well in the non-play world. We also know that gameplay does not have consequences anything like equivalent to the activities it models, which is another reason why we can enjoy it, knowing we are not actually going to die if our character/s gets shot or meet any other untimely end (even if we might be caused some considerable inconvenience by having to replay parts of the game). And if functional realism is often a major factor in the attribution to games of potential effects of interpellation, it is also important to note the extent to which functional realism is usually limited precisely in order to establish the *playful* qualites of videogames – whether this is a gap such as that between one version of *FSW* and another or the much larger gap between the most 'realistic' version and what might be experienced in reality. Functional realism is limited by various pragmatic factors, including finite resources and restrictions imposed by game controllers, but it is also fundamentally limited by the requirement to make games playable and fun. Players might invest in a certain degree of functional realism – marketers and reviewers certainly seem to do so – but this is usually quite limited, because otherwise games would be too difficult and frustrating (even if practical limits to the increase of functional realism were omitted from the equation).

In any contest between the notions of 'play' and 'interpellation', therefore, it is play that should be emphasized. A number of existing accounts that focus on interpellation, explicitly or implicitly, pay insufficient attention to the play dimension of gameplay, including its scope for what Caillois (2001) terms *paidea*, the ability to 'play around' in various ways rather than simply following rule- and goal-bound game activities (for example, see Friedman 1997 and Garite 2003, although not Crogan). This is not to argue, however, for a *total* separation of play and any real-world implications. Play and fantasy can and often do have substantial real-world resonances. Play draws on various sources in the external world. Dimensions such as play, fantasy and the imagination are parts of the broader cultural universe in which they are situated and might be expected to play a part in the wider processes through which particular ways of understanding the world are communicated and reinforced. It is specifically *reinforcement* that I would emphasize here. Videogames do not interpellate us into particular identities (and neither, I would argue, do other media such as film), but the activities structured into play might help to reinforce existing frameworks, as well as providing some more generic skills to do with learning to interact with the digital realm more generally. *FSW* can certainly be read as contributing to certain ideological frameworks as far as its background context is concerned, and in a form of gameplay directed towards the killing of faceless 'alien' others through the mobilization of particular forms of player-character agency.

The concept of interpellation can still be applied to videogames, however, in the more specific way in which it is used by Althusser (1984). Interpellation is understood here as a fundamental mechanism in the maintenance of bourgeois ideology. It refers to a process involved in the constitution or reinforcement of the notion of the individual subject *as* individual subject – through the subject's response to an offer of a position to take-up. The form of interpellation offered by games here would include the role of the player *as* player, a *playful subject* self-consciously aware of the act of playing. This would embrace dimensions such as *paidea*, playing around within the game, and all the other factors that can interrupt any sense of being taken into a specific in-game role; of being interpellated into any *particular kind of* subjectivity. The latter seems much more questionable, because it is based on a rather one-dimensional understanding of the kinds of interactions involved in gameplay. In the broader sense, games can be seen as contributing to powerful ideological effects, but this should be understood as a contribution to something that has a much wider presence; something in which games might be implicated rather than something they can separately be said to cause. *FSW* in its original US Army incarnation might serve as part of a process of interpellation into a particular role, but only as a result of its placement in a broader military training context that is likely to figure much more importantly in the overall process than the game itself.

Works cited

Adair, Bill (2005) 'Did the Army get Out-gamed', *St Petersburg Times* online, 20 Feburary 2005, http://sptimes.com/2005/02/20/Worldandnation/Did_the_Army_get_out_.shtml, accessed April 2005.

Althusser, Louis (1984 [1970]) 'Ideology and Ideological State Apparatuses (Notes towards an Investigation)', in *Essays on Ideology*, London: Verso.

Bateson, Gregory (2000) 'A Theory of Play and Fantasy', in *Steps to an Ecology of*

Mind: Collected Essays in Anthropology, Psychiatry, Evolution, and Epistemology, Chicago: University of Chicago Press.

Berghammer, Billy (2004) 'Full Spectrum Warrior Interview: Pandemic Studios' William Henry Stahl', *Game Informer*, 3 May 2004, gameinformer.com/News/Story/200405/N04.0503.1843.05215.htm, accessed 11 April 2005.

Caillois, Roger (2001 [1958]) *Man, Play and Games*, Urbana, Chicago: University of Illinois Press.

Crogan, Patrick (2003) 'The Experience of Information in Computer Games', *Digital Arts and Culture* conference, Melbourne, http://hypertext.rmit.edu.au/dac/papers/, accessed 12 October 2005.

Der Derian, James (2001) *Virtuous War: Mapping the Military-Industrial-Media-Entertainment Network*, Boulder: Westview Press.

Friedman, Ted (1997) 'Civilization and Its Discontents: Simulation, Subjectivity, and Space', http://www.duke.edu/~tlove/civ.htm, accessed 20 November 2005; subsequently in Greg Smith (ed.) *Discovering Discs: Transforming Space and Genre on CD-ROM*, New York: New York University Press, 1999.

Garite, Matt (2003) 'The Ideology of Interactivity (or, Video Games and the Taylorization of Leisure)', in Marinka Copier and Joost Raessens (eds) *Level Up: Digital Games Research Conference,* Utrecht University, accompanying CD-ROM.

Grossman, Dave and Gloria DeGaetano (1999) *Stop Teaching our Kids to Kill: A Call to Action against TV, Movie and Video Game Violence*, New York: Crown.

Hodge, Robert and David Tripp (1986) *Children and Television: A Semiotic Approach*, Cambridge: Polity Press.

Huizinga, Johan (1955 [1944]) *Homo Ludens: A Study of the Play Element in Culture*, Boston, MA: The Beacon Press.

Jones, Gerard (2002) *Killing Monsters: Why Children Need Fantasy, Super Heroes, and Make-Believe Violence,* New York: Basic Books.

King, Geoff and Tanya Krzywinska (2006) *Tomb Raiders and Space Invaders: Videogame Forms and Contexts*, London/Bloomington: I.B. Tauris/Indiana University Press.

Salen, Katie and Eric Zimmerman (2003) *Rules of Play: Game Design Fundamentals*, Cambridge, MA: MIT Press.

Games

Brothers in Arms: Road to Hill 30 (2005), Gearbox/Ubisoft.
Full Spectrum Warrior (2004), Pandemic Studios/THQ.

Notes

1   For more on the concept of functional realism more generally, see King and Krzywinska 2006.

2   The fact that the game is repetitive, in some cases to the extent of being boring, was noted by 12 out of 50 players in 'community reviews' on the Gamespot website, two of which suggested that this dimension could be taken as adding to the realistic impression created by the game; see www.gamespot.com/xbox/strategy/fullspectrumwarrior/readers.html, accessed August 2005.

3   A contrary suggestion is made in claims, including those of some involved in real-world infantry training, that the realistic dimension of the original version suffered as a direct result of design features intended to serve the commercial/entertainment prospects of the subsequent release (see Adair 2005). Reviews of the game that I have read tend to go along, however, with the view that 'fun' is in some respects sacrificed in favour of increased functional realism.

4   The balance between the two may be somewhat different in massively multiplayer online role-playing games, where the social-relationship dimension of collective gameplay can take on a substantial reality of its own.

4

Why am I in Vietnam?
The history of a videogame

Jon Dovey

Rain falls vertically down the screen, we're in some kind of bunker with a slit window looking out on a green and blue jungle. Three men, un-shaven and sweaty, sit smoking and drinking. Hanoi Hannah squawks from a transistor radio, 'It must be very confusing for you, why you have to live and die far from home, go home GI Joe'. One of the men turns the radio off, 'What you do that for?' 'I had enough of that shit, bad enough we have to be here when everyone else is chasing poontang and kicking back'. The argument is curtailed by a barked command 'stand to,' the base is under attack. A caption tells me it is January 31st 1968, The Tet Offensive. (Author's Gameplay Diary 10.12.04 from a cutscene in *Conflict: Vietnam*)

This is the story of a computer game called *Conflict: Vietnam*. How did it come to be in the world? What pressures determined that it would be as it is? What kind of passions sustained the stupendous creative effort that goes into the production of any computer game? As critics and academics we spend most of our time thinking about how texts are interpreted – how do readers/users make sense of them? What kinds of experiences do they produce? What are the structural mechanics of textuality? We have developed great expertise in understanding readers', users' and players' responses to mediation – we claim privileged insight into the kind of interpretive responses available to us. However, we seldom consider how the wide range of these experiences are already prescribed by the choices made by media producers. The great global enterprises of media production are often left untroubled by our concentration on audience–text relations. Of course there is a small academic industry that attempts to understand the social function of media institutions by interpreting their products, through further practices of hermeneutic surgery on the ideological body. However there is still very little work that subjects the process of production to critical analysis. Ethnographies of audiences far outnumber studies of producers. So, why do we get the games we get? How is my play structured by the business, the technologies and the cultures of design studios?

This chapter is based on a production case study undertaken in Pivotal Games' studios in Autumn 2003. The study was based on several days of workplace observations plus ten one-hour interviews with a cross section of the production team from game testers to the Managing Director. Comments from game designers are also intercut with my own gameplay diary as I played the game through the winter of 2003/04. I am attempting therefore to reconstruct the history of the game in three modes; the voices of designers, the experiences of a player and through critical writing. By triangulating the designers' perspective with the direct experience of a player I aim to exemplify a way of writing about new media that is rooted in situated material practices rather than technophiliac abstraction.

Conflict: Vietnam is a tactical squad based shooter. The player commands a squad of four soldiers on a series of missions set in the period of the Tet offensive in the Vietnam war of 1968. The game can be multiplayer or single player. The gameplay follows the usual navigate, accumulate, annihilate formula of the action game; finding your way round the level map, discovering the always mysteriously abandoned caches of arms and ammunition that litter the landscape and killing all enemies until you complete your mission and find your exit, in this case often a helicopter or boat that transports the squad to its next mission. Managing your squad requires a constant level of tactical awareness to make sure they are all in the right place and possessed of the right mix of weaponry and medikits.

> It's Friday night and TV is dismal as usual. I'm still stuck on Hill 933. As soon as it opens we get a new objective, put down smoke. But by the time I find the guy with the yellow smoke the VC are all over us, every time – time to get organized. Finally after several restarts I work out who's got the smoke and where it has to go. I'm not sure what I'm doing. My ten year old daughter has told me the smoke is amazing, it kills all your enemies and looks fantastic when you mix the yellow with the pink. (Author's Gameplay Diary 16.12.04)

> 9 times out of 10 we will have lots of effects but we're limited, we can only have so much of this and so much of that … for instance we have a limit on the amount of particles that can be in the world at one time and when the limit gets hit it has to take one out. So you might have some

smoke columns going up and you fire a rocket which kicks out a ton of smoke and stuff but then those other smoke columns are going, shooting down, they're all getting deleted because this rocket's kicking off loads of new ones. You want to push to have more of this, more of that, that's definitely the first and foremost, then new technology comes along and you can see what you can do with that. (*Conflict Vietnam* Lead Artist, Pivotal Games, 2003)

OK! She was right, that smoke does look fantastic. But, as I'm hanging round enjoying it, bam! Game over. The whole squad's creamed by the air strike called in by the yellow smoke, now I understand why she thought it killed all your enemies. (Author's Gameplay Diary 18.12.04)

Margins of choice

Most producers, most of the time, in most cultural industries have very little margin of choice about what they make. The determinations of the market, financing your product and bringing it to consumers, exercise a powerful logic that takes its own particular shape in each studio. The Pivotal Games Technical Director eloquently describes the console games market context at the time of *Conflict: Vietnam*'s production,

> Even if you have got a million pounds in the bank and that is very rare, most developers won't, you quite simply can't function. So team sizes have got huge, they have gone up and they are continuing to rise at a frightening rate. We used to create games with just sort of seven or ten people and now it genuinely is thirty to forty people and I don't think we are particularly big. But the cost of the games hasn't gone up by anything like the same amount, arguably it has gone down. Playstation 1 games used to cost thirty, forty pounds and that is what they cost today, ten years on. So the retailers are pretty much making the same margins as they used to, they get those games in at twenty, twenty three pounds and they sell them at forty. The publishers have got greater overheads, everyone's salaries have gone up, the world has got bigger, the market place has got bigger, it is more international, you have to distribute and sub-contract, so their costs have gone up. So I really see it as being the developer that is being squeezed. Costs have gone up, number of people have gone up, cost to the consumer hasn't gone up, something has got to give and that is why there has been an awful lot of consolidation in industries, a lot of companies and industries going under. (Technical Director, Pivotal Games, 2003)

Competition within the mainstream console games market has increased faster than its overall expansion; in 2001 there were 270 games available for the three main consoles, this figure jumped to 750 in 2002 (Edge 2003: 8). As production costs have increased studios have found themselves having to ship more and more units just to stay viable in the face of a more or less static price point; most developers would aim to ship between 500,000 to 1,000,000 units to now break even. It has been estimated that while development costs have doubled sales have only increased by 50% (Edge 2003: 9). In the mainstream console market it has been increasingly true that developers now look to publishers to bear the risk of production investment and publishers find themselves minimizing risk by opting for titles with a proven track record, thus reducing the space for innovation.

> There are four air strike targets to hit, but by the time you've got round them all Junior is riddled. Since he seems to be the only squad member with the flares I have to keep him alive. I could always go back and make sure more of us have them – but, go back and repeat just to re-equip? So I take him into a bunker to patch him up, but every time the tank comes, finds me and blows us up as I'm doing the medikit. How does it find me every time? Twenty restarts so far and still I can't get past the tank. I went to a walkthrough, didn't help. I hadn't realized the tank is triggered by anyone crossing the road – but how the hell do you plant the flares without doing that? (Author's Gameplay Diary 19.12.04)

Tastes and technicities

While market conditions determine the margin within which choices can be exercised they do not necessarily determine the choice itself. Knowing that a studio has to ship one million units and keep a staff of 70 on the payroll does not explain how it comes to produce a squad based military shooter set in Vietnam, as opposed to a racing game or a fantasy role play . There is then still an originary space for an auteur's input, for the generation of ideas that will fit the market but which are driven by designers' pleasures and passions. At Pivotal these tastes, pleasures and passions have originated with the Managing Director, the visionary and driving force who has pushed the studio forward from its earliest days. His own cultural biography drives the Pivotal brand:

> I always played toy soldiers, still do, and role playing games, make believe. I actually read a lot of history. I think for me it was a classic time growing up, you had Robin Hood on TV, Richard the Lion Heart, Lancelot, you

know. I remember them as being great but they are probably rubbish if I saw them again today. . . I was an avid history reader, I went on to do an Economics and Social History degree as well. After that I was a Role Playing Games Designer and Board Game Designer for major product lines, Dungeons and Dragons, Games Workshop's *Warhammer*, and various other companies. (Pivotal Managing Director, 2003)

Kline et al. argue that a dominant 'semiotic nexus' around 'war, conquest and combat' 'focuses gaming culture on the subject-positions and discourses of what we term "militarized masculinities"' (2003: 254). The biographical description above seems at first to confirm this kind of hegemony at work within the Pivotal studios. But what does the 'miltiarized masculine' subject look like? How might we know him? Survivalist fatigues and a pick-up truck? At Pivotal the MD's interest in military history is seen as a positive creative generator; a producer at the studio underlines this appreciation:

The MD is very, very war orientated, to make a game about something you need to know about that subject. It is easy to make something about fantasy because you can create your fantasy world. He has a very, very good background knowledge on military war through the ages, so therefore lets use that knowledge, that is certainly one of the elements which have pushed for it to be a semi-realistic environment. (Pivotal Producer, Pivotal Games, 2003)

Kline et al. reduce this sensibility to its alleged technological origins, 'This situation . . . tracks back to the military origins of interactive play. The game industry conjured into being by technologically adept and culturally militarized men, made games reflecting the interests of is creators' (2003: 257). Our evidence suggests that if there is 'cultural militarization' at work its evolution is more subtle and more interesting than Kline et al.'s account suggests.

In our work on computer games Helen Kennedy and I have developed the concept of *technicity* to think about the dominance of certain kinds of taste (and people) in game culture. This term has a particular history within cyberculture studies. David Tomas (2000) draws on the work of cultural anthropologist Lee Drummond in order to account for the new kinds of social and cultural relationships being formed through the use of technology. The significant aspect of our appropriation of the term technicity is to encapsulate within it the connections between an identity based on certain types of attitude, practices and tastes *and* the deployment of technology in the construction of that identity. To be subjects within the privileged twenty-first century first world is to be increasingly caught up in a network of technically and mechanically mediated relationships with others who share the same attitudes/tastes, pleasures and preferences. Technicity therefore becomes the expression of particular tastes and affiliations through technological engagement. The Pivotal interviews were able to furnish us with a good deal of evidence of particular biographies of technicity (see Dovey and Kennedy 2006).

The senior designers in our study did not become 'technologically adept or culturally militarized' through the 'military origins of interactive play'. Four of the ten respondents – significantly all senior figures within the company both in age and authority – expressed strong childhood and adolescent attachment to paper gaming, to the mathematically systematized pastime of role play gaming, fantasy and *Dungeons and Dragons* (D&D). A Pivotal lead designer is typical of this group:

> I was about nine when I started playing *Dungeons and Dragons*. I mean I had been into fantasy stuff for quite a while which I think stemmed from the fact that both my parents were quite into *Lord of the Rings* and I used to get read *The Hobbit* as a bedtime story by my mum .... so I'd always been really interested in that whole fantasy thing, and had you know, fantasy toys and soldiers and that ... I was really quite hooked on that sort of thing and absolutely loved it. Then I discovered the *Warhammer* stuff a bit later, probably when I was about twelve or thirteen and again got really into that. Some of my earliest ever attempts to write serious rule systems was for *Warhammer 40,000*, which I sent into Games Workshop and they liked enough to send back release forms to say well we might use this, so sign the copyright over to us ... I read a lot of the Dungeons and Dragons sort of novels, a lot of the fantasy stuff. I used to read enormous amounts of comics, whatever I could get my hands on, *Batman, Daredevil*, the Marvel comic called *The Punisher* and again any sort of films related to that, the Star Wars films, the usual. I was very into *Battlestar Galactica* and all that kind of pop culture sci-fi. But I was also, and I think it stems from my dad being in the army, I was very into sort of military stuff as well, very interested in military history, so I read an awful lot of that kind of thing as well. (Lead Designer, Pivotal Games, 2003)

These common cultural histories have three main consequences. The first is that generations of designers learnt the maths of game mechanics in table-top gameplay that could be easily transposed to computer algorithms when the technology became widely available. Just as television remediated the parlour game as quiz show, so the computer remediated the table-top role play game.

The fundamental mechanic is all down to numbers and probabilities, percentage chances of hitting and missing; all our vehicles are just a bunch of numbers, there is a 3D model there and there are 3D surfaces set, as a number value, hit point value and then something that says what happens when you penetrate and destroy that, is it catastrophic damage? That is stuff I played with for years, just on table-tops or role playing and ditto with characters, movement speeds, hit points, actions you can do and it is all number based. (Managing Director, Pivotal Games, 2003)

In the case of *Conflict: Vietnam*, and indeed the whole 'Conflict' brand, there is a more direct design consequence of this common cultural history; the MD also loved social play:

For me with the role playing table-top background, I always wanted to do things on computer that you couldn't do. I mean a lot of people just took board games and put them on computer and that to me, that is just loneliness. That is I haven't got anybody to play with and it misses the social interactivity that really table-tops and role playing is all about, it is what people come up with playing together. (Managing Director, Pivotal Games, 2003)

Hence the Conflict brand is up to four player (and now online multiplayer); in multiplayer mode the game is very busy, with a lot of affordance for verbal exchange between players commenting, explaining and suggesting gameplay tactics.

Finally, and here we approach Kline et al.'s ground, the table-top role play heritage is of course based around agonistic scenarios of conflict, combat and mastery. However it is clear from the cultural biographies referred to above that these subjects are very far from a simplistic definition of 'militarized masculinity' that might be 'read off' from game content. The boys who stayed at home reading fantasy literature and playing D&D weren't the same guys who were on the football team, or who were out jacking cars, pulling birds or doing any other supposedly 'normal' alpha male behaviours. In my experience of table-top gaming trying to play with the alpha males was always a nightmare, their physical energy always won out over their powers of concentration and the table-top would finish up on the floor or else the game would spin off into some real world pursuit. No, these games and the sensibilities they articulate might be better understood within a paradigm of competing masculinities in which we observe the virtual revenge of the nerds on the jocks. This is a place where bright boys with imagination and technical prowess get to design worlds where they don't get sand kicked in their faces any more, a world in which they can be in control and can kick ass for once (see for example, Pargman 2003 for discussion of 'controllable worlds').

> I realize that to crack the level I'm going to need a buddy. I ask my son but for weeks he just responds with a kind of Beavis and Butthead snigger, 'Dad's stuck in a game and he needs my help – cool, ngngng'. Eventually he agrees and on the third start we get every fox hole accounted for and – as the tank comes over the ridge, catching me by surprise – I swing the rocket launcher up and in one glorious moment fire one off right down the tank's throat blowing it to bits before it can even get a shot off. Yess! (Author's Gameplay Diary 10.01.05)

Branding

To find out why this particular Vietnam game emerged from this particular cultural and and economic matrix we have to understand a little of the history of Pivotal Games, since this game is in effect the product not only of the enthusiasms described above but also of a successful technology and a successful brand. Pivotal was formed from the ashes of a previous studio which had produced *War Zone 2100*, a real time war strategy sim for Eidos. Although *War Zone 2100* sold 350,000 copies Eidos, flush with the extraordinary *Tomb Raider* sales, turned down the next iteration. The core creative team from *War Zone 2100* then set up a new studio and sat down to decide what to do next. Given the personnel and the game engine technology already developed, a war game of some kind was a given. In fact Pivotal had to rebuild their game engine from scratch because the *War Zone 2100* engine was contracted by Eidos. What was to become the Conflict series was originally conceived of as a World War II game, however Pivotal then became aware that numbers of other studios were also working in the same genre and decided to change tack. The decision was taken in 2000 to set the new game in the first Gulf War of 1990:

> We want to be doing something a bit different and I said 'Let's do something modern, let's do something we don't have to explain' because in *War Zone* I had to explain the world, lots of exposition, lots of background. So it is taking a real world event, everybody knows what SAS forces are, it is all very obvious. It was a ready-made setting which at that time, as far as I'm concerned was history, and had I been able to predict it would have all blown up the way it has, I don't know whether it would have changed my mind. (Managing Director, Pivotal Games, 2003)

Conflict: Desert Storm was released in 2002 and has sold more than one million copies. The Publisher SCI immediately commissioned a *Conflict: Desert Storm 2*. A 'Conflict' brand has been established in the marketplace which has, for the time being, force and staying power. The first three 'Conflict' titles all hit the number one slot in the all formats game chart with the more recent *Conflict: Global Storm* getting to number four. The brand is characterized by multiplayer possibility, they are all four-person squad based and each member of the squad is individualized as far as their skills go; one can fire better on the run, another soldier is heavier and can take more bullets. They also all have different weapons skills which improve with experience (Experience Points). The optimal deployment of your group therefore becomes a matter of strategy as well as action. The player is constantly checking the level of each squad member's supplies making sure that enough appropriate weaponry, ammo and medipaks are distributed throughout the squad. The Pivotal engine developed for the 'Conflict' brand also allows for a good deal of group ordering making strategic decisions about who does what – for example, does the squad all move together or does one soldier move ahead alone for stealth action? The *Desert Storm* games are set in the 'behind-enemy-lines' thriller scenario familiar to audiences from books and television series made from the memoirs of ex-SAS personnel (such as McNab 1993). As Pivotal's MD indicates above, they were making a decision to work within what audiences felt was a 'familiar enough' world. Interestingly, the *Desert Storm* games do not in any way actually echo the oft repeated cliché that the Gulf War was the first videogame war – in fact they simply use the real historical events as a background for a pure *Boy's Own* adventure. There is little sense in the *Desert Storm* games of war by remote control, instead more of close-up engagements and a narrative of escape.

> I mean realism is a funny word in the sense that we know it is a made up world and it is not a realistic portrayal of how that war was fought for most of the soldiers, because it predominantly was fought through air strikes, through bringing air cover, you know, it wasn't a particularly good war in terms of gameplay because they didn't do a lot. You look at the footage that has come out now of the Gulf War, generally you would drive forward, you would come under fire, you would call in an Air Strike and there would be a bit of mopping up. Then these very exciting stories of Special Forces actions came out, basically we take that as a basis and then add on loads of other stuff to make it more exciting. But it is kind of a hyper real version of reality if you like and if you want a war with modern weapons, modern equipment, that people recognise, then I think that is why that setting has been picked. (Lead Designer, Pivotal Games, 2003)

So, in deciding what game to produce in late 2002 after the success of *Conflict: Desert Storm* and the hoped for success of *Conflict: Desert Storm 2* , the company had a successful brand and a preference for 'semi realistic' game worlds, to which I will return in more detail below.

> Why don't the choppers ever take me out of here? I'm still not sure what we're supposed to be doing, I just want the transport to drop me off somewhere for some R&R instead of which they always leave us in some VC infested rat hole. And the boat! How boring was that – OK lots of big guns to fire but the auto aim was frustrating and it sent me crazy that we couldn't control the speed of the boat. No run like hell option. Took me ages to figure that every time the boat stopped I was supposed to be blowing things up. Eventually got through after taking the auto aim off. This is becoming a walkthrough isn't it? (Author's Gameplay Diary 3.04.05)

The engine

Apart from the brand Pivotal also by now had a game engine that would do certain things and not others; this is a compelling determination in the choices open to any studio which has not been fully understood outside the immediate gaming production community. A proprietary game engine represents a massive financial and creative investment that cannot easily be replaced. The Pivotal MD likens their engine to a virtual studio:

> So we have now got a great game engine…my usual analogy is the movie business, we spent years struggling how to make cameras stay on tripods and look the right way, save the information and edit it, we have now got that in our engine. We can do any third or first person based game now, it doesn't have to be four characters, all that physics, processing, all the stuff that lets you do that, is there. So I sort of look at it as my movie set now, and we need to now be moving that forward in interesting ways. (Managing Director, Pivotal Games, 2003)

In deciding what game to make after the first two *Conflict* titles the engine is an inescapable determinant,

> The obvious thing is looking at what our engine does … So one of the things that the designers would have been looking for is, is how do we take the engine that we have got and use it really well? So it would have been silly to have gone and written a football game for instance because our technology would really have to be re-written from the ground up to do a football sim. Whereas doing another war sim means that we can

basically build on our experience and build on the things that we have learnt to improve them. So it was kind of inevitable that it was going to be some kind of squad based shooter – as a result you are looking for a scenario that the audience would be familiar with. (Level Programmer, Pivotal Games, 2003)

To date the game engine has been at the core of production decisions. It remains to be seen how the spread of middleware and the adaptation of commercially available engines such *Half-Life* and *Unreal* will affect future game technologies. However it is possible to speculate that the capital investment needed to develop a game engine might become more flexibly available as engine licensing becomes more widespread.

Woke up this morning running round the jungle, that's what happens when you play last thing at night. Found a whole new part of the map, no idea how I got here. But just as I thought I must be getting to the end of the level after an hour, I ran into a huge firefight, running low on ammo and medikits, got into a horrible muddle and got creamed. Must work out how to get there quicker. In this Vietnam a rocket doesn't have the slightest impact on a bamboo fence? I just want to blow the thing up to get through – but no, nothing so simple allowed. (Author's Gameplay Diary 19.03.05)

Vietnam: history as storyworld

This is where you are kind of aware of your market in the sense that, you know ... I would love to do a game set in the Spanish Civil War, but not many people know anything about the Spanish Civil War. So, there is no saying that a game set in the Spanish Civil War couldn't be a hit, but you have got a lot more people to persuade. (Level Designer, Pivotal Games, 2003)

Given the preferences and constraints of the production context described above, then Vietnam almost inevitably emerges as a site for the next game in the *Conflict* series.

So there are an inordinate number of wars that have happened in the world, but picking a war that the American market is going to be aware of then becomes the question. And I think really there are three wars that they, the majority, the industry considers they are aware of, World War II which is done a lot, the Vietnam event, which I think is a slightly more trickier setting for a game, and then the Gulf War, the two of them, because they happened most recently. (Level Designer, Pivotal Games, 2003)

But there are an 'inordinate number of wars in the world'. The studio in this case, given its preference for a kind of historical realism, is looking for a kind of paint-by-numbers familiarity where the player does the colouring-in based on their intertextual knowledge of the genre background.

> To be honest we are cheating. We are seeking what has gone before to have done some of the work for us. It is Vietnam, people immediately go, 'I know what Vietnam was about, I have seen *Apocalypse Now*,' they know what that is, they have set the scene, twenty pages of the book have already been read for us, and that is great. So we are in familiar territory already. (Technical Director, Pivotal Games, 2003)

This position is of course only another version of the kind of genre choices that all kinds of media producers make. However, just as 'character' in computer games often becomes 'skill' (see, for example, Newman 2004; Dovey and Kennedy 2006), so 'setting' becomes 'map' – a function of gameplay navigation rather than a meaningful dramatic *mis-en-scène*. Here genre is clichéd intertextual reference to previous Vietnam films. The cut scene at the start of the 'Charlie's Point' level begins with the squad finding a gunboat on the river to help them in their journey, 'The Chief', the gunboat captain is a refugee from *Apocalypse Now*; he explains tersely, 'Bin dropping off Green Berets up river, saw some strange shit up there.' The desperate nihilism of grunts trapped in a chaotic and meaningless war is reiterated by the repetition of 'It don't mean a thing, not a fucking thing' as part of the script in several cut scenes. The game licenses iconic songs from the late 1960s, Jefferson Airplane's 'White Rabbit' and the Rolling Stones' 'Paint it Black', to add 'period' flavour.

We might extend this intertextuality to intermediality. By intermediality I mean the contemporary market driven form of intertextuality in which texts and activities may refer to the same fictional 'world' despite presenting themselves on different media platforms (Lehtonen 2000). Other commentators have also drawn attention to the imperatives of political economy driving intermediality. Henry Jenkins, for instance, identifies intermediality as one of the key characteristics of emerging new media landscapes; there are, he argues, powerful 'economic trends encouraging the flow of images, ideas, and narratives across multiple media channels and demanding more active modes of spectatorship' (2003). Jenkins suggests that these trends are altering 'the way media consumers relate to each other, to media texts, and to media producers' (2003). In these conditions storyworlds can become franchises –

quoting the total revenue attributed to *Star Wars* products, the British-based newspaper, *The Observer*, claimed 'If *Star Wars* was a country, its $20bn would place it 70th in the World Bank's rankings of countries according to Gross Domestic product' (Smith 2005). At the time of writing the *Game Spy* web site lists 21 PC games set in Vietnam, with three each for the PS2 (apart from *Conflict, ShellShock: Nam '67* and *Vietnam: The Tet Offensive*) and three on the Xbox consoles: *Conflict, Men of Valor* and *ShellShock* again). Here, then, Vietnam becomes neither historical event nor media franchise but an intermedial setting for actions amenable to gameplay adaptation:

> I can kill, but boy I just can't navigate. Put me on a real mountain and I do fine, even a forest; but these endless circular maps! Bad Moon is done I'm sure – but I've been running round the jungle for half an hour, enemies all dead, objectives completed, every bit of booty hoovered up and still I can't find the exit. I've been here so long even the NPC corpses have disappeared. Then a booby trap that I swear I'd already cleared mercifully ends my play session. Damn – no save. (Author's Gameplay Diary 16.03.05)

The trouble with authenticity

It is clear enough, then, how an innovation-averse market, individual technicities, and technological constraint produce the game *Conflict: Vietnam*. However this matrix is too neat, and raises further, more interesting questions which take us into the designer–player relationship. As we have seen, the *Conflict* designers see their games as 'semi-realistic'. An analysis of this discourse suggests that actually this means certain elements of the game design will be authentic in terms of character design, weapons and vehicles.

> Part of the appeal of the *Conflict* games is there is a degree of realism in it, you know they are not using laser guns, they are using M16's, and I think because for us as developers it is important to get some of that right, there is obviously a degree within our audience that appreciate the effort that has gone to make that slightly more realistic. (Level Designer, Pivotal Games, 2003)

The background interest in military history also manifests itself in character artists' concerns for authenticity of uniforms, hats and insignia. As the comment above suggests, there is a clear assumption that certain consumers appreciate this kind of historical authenticity.

Certainly with current affairs, there is a certain thing about having a realistic game that attracts people to it. I find people prefer realistic racing games rather than fantasy racing games. Fantasy, to some people it's just just a load of goblins and fairies, [they] don't care, not interested. Because there is no realism to it. (Producer, Pivotal Games, 2003)

In this reading the contemporary setting, the authenticity of particular details is seen as creating a viable fantasy world for a certain kind of male player.

I think because the industry is still very male dominated there is a huge element of it is still toy soldiers and people love the fact that it is soldiers. Everyone rather fancies the idea that you know, if push came to shove they could get in there and take out the enemies with their gun. Reality is completely different of course but people like doing that and it is role play, escapism and role play. People like contemporary settings because it is not too far away. It is conceivably close and they can kind of rather fancy themselves in that setting, whereas space setting, fantasy setting, the leap to imagine yourself there is not practical. (Technical Director, Pivotal Games, 2003)

However, both the problem *and* the advantage of this order of realism as a ground for imaginative engagement is that reality might just return to trouble the fantasy. 9/11 occurred during the production process of *Conflict: Desert Storm 1* – the implications for the production team were not immediately obvious as the American response in Afghanistan was followed by the long build-up to the second Gulf War. However, this period was clearly troubling for some members of the team such as the studio's Head of Audio discussing here why the shift was made from Iraq to Vietnam:

I think a setting other than the desert and other than Iraq especially with you know September 11th, because we were halfway through developing *Desert Storm 1* [based on the first Gulf War] which was ten years ago so we thought we were pretty safe, we thought it would be a good thing, you know get all the special forces with all the radio mics and all the new gear what a great environment to set a game around. Then the fact that September 11th went off and then the war on terror and George Bush etc etc is unfortunate and I wasn't sure about *Desert Storm 2* really. It's a bit near the knuckle in places, you know with the oil fields burning and this that and the other, some stuff in there which was too close I feel to present day stuff and reality. And I don't think that was a particularly good move. (Head of Audio, Pivotal Games, 2003)

Pivotal's 'semi-realistic' brand has once again been troubled by the reality of history in the run-up to the launch of its latest title. *Conflict: Global Terror* (2005) is 'Set within the modern day context of counter-terrorism. A new force in global terrorism, "March 33", is emerging. Tasked with defeating March 33 is a rapid response counter-terrorist unit: Bradley, Jones, Connors and Foley – the heroes from the original *Conflict: Desert Storm* games are back.' (www.pivotalgames.com, 13 July 2005) Less than a week before writing this in July 2005 London became the latest place to experience the terror of the suicide bomber.

What is it about 'authenticity' represented by particular in-game details that appeals to certain kinds of player? What does this order of 'realism' signify? Do such games simply reflect and reinforce the pleasures of 'militarized masculinity'? The designers' comments above seem to me to challenge this assumption by making it more complex. There are 'an inordinate number of wars in the world', however the post-babyboomer generation of men in the West are probably one of the first generations of men *ever* for whom the threat of war has not been immediate. Nevertheless, 'Everyone rather fancies the idea that you know, if push came to shove they could get in there and take out the enemies with their gun.' These games are 'escapism', 'role play'. One way to understand this relationship between authenticity and fantasy might be through recourse to the psychology of D.W. Winnicott as it developed out of his accounts of childhood development published in *Playing and Reality* (1971). Winnicott offers a great deal to our understanding of the ways in which play is *both* identity production and culture making.

> ... on the basis of playing is built the whole of man's experiential existence ... We experience life in the area of *transitional phenomena*, in the exciting interweave of subjectivity and objective observation, and in an area that is intermediate between the inner reality of the individual and the shared reality of the world that is external to individuals. (Winnicott 1997: 64, my italics)

In Cultural and Media Studies researchers such as Matt Hills (2002) and Roger Silverstone (1999) have used Winnicott to resolve text/reader problematics by arguing for the productive 'interweave' between text and user in fan communities. Silverstone describes media consumption as a form of play and makes some broad claims for the importance of play as a site of cultural production as well as identity formation:

> Play enables the exploration of that tissue boundary between fantasy and reality, between the real and imagined, between the self and the other. In play we have license to explore, both our selves and our society. In play we

investigate culture, but we also create it. (Silverstone 1999: 64)

In this reading the desires of designers and players alike to construct military worlds or to enjoy playing as an anti-terror operative can be seen as positively healthy. A constant recapitulation of the realities and threats of the world that we do all actually share. A world of 'an inordinate number of wars' and the viral threat of terrorist action.

> How pissed off am I? Two dozen mission starts tonight alone and two dozen fails. And why? 'D'Hione' the tribal villager has to lead us to the Sacred Statue so we can supposedly exchange it for a radio that will allow us to call in rescue. But every time, she gets shot; she hangs around at the back or else races off and gets killed, mission over. So I'm totally subject to the NPC AI, can't go ahead and clear the way, can't hang back 'cos no matter what I do she always gets shot. Annoyingly she advises stealth in her dialogue but I've resorted to frustration blasting. I want to know why I can't just go back to the village and torture them till they give up the radio. How am I ever going to get out of here? (Author's Gameplay Diary 5.04.05)

Works cited

Dovey, Jon and Helen Kennedy (2006) *Game Cultures*, Maidenhead: Open University/McGraw Hill.

Edge (2003) August 2003, p. 8.

Hills, Matthew (2002) *Fan Cultures*, London: Routledge.

Jenkins, Henry (2003) 'Interactive Audiences: The Collective Intelligence of Media Fans', http://web.mit.edu/cms/People/henry3/collective%20intelligence.html, accessed April 2006.

Kline, Stephen, Nick Dyer-Witherford and N. Greig de Peuter (2003) *Digital Play: The Interaction of Technology Culture and Marketing*, Montreal: McGill Quarry University Press.

Lehtonen, Mikko (2000) *The Cultural Analysis of Texts*, London: Sage.

McNab, Andy (1993) *Bravo Two Zero*, London: Corgi.

Newman, James (2004) *Videogames*, London: Routledge.

Pargman, Daniel (2003) 'Word and Code, Code as World', Melbourne DAC http://hypertext.rmit.edu.au/dac/papers/Pargman.pdf, accessed April 2006.

Pivotal Games (2003) Staff interviews with the author, December 2003.

Silverstone, Roger (1999) *Why Study the Media?*, London: Sage.

Smith, David (2005) 'Star Wars Empire Strikes Gold', *Observer*, 15 May 2005, 3.

Tomas, David (2000) 'The Technophilic Body: On Technicity in William Gibson's Cyborg Culture', in David Bell and Barbara Kennedy (eds) *The Cybercultures*

Reader, London and New York: Routledge.

Winnicott, D. W. (1971) *Playing and Reality*, London: Tavistock

Games

Conflict: Desert Storm (2001), Pivotal Games, SCI.

Conflict: Desert Storm 2 (2002), Pivotal Games, SCI.

Conflict: Global Storm (2005), Pivotal Games, SCI.

Conflict: Men of Valor (2004), Vivendi.

Conflict: Vietnam (2004), Pivotal Games, SCI 2004.

War Zone 2100 (1999), Pumpkin, Eidos.

ShellShock: Nam '67 (2004), Eidos.

Vietnam: The Tet Offensive (2004), Oxygen Interactive.

Acknowledgement

The author wishes to thank Pete Johnson and the staff of Pivotal Games for their cooperation in this research which was undertaken with support from the Arts and Humanities Research Council.

5

'It's not easy being green': real-time game performance in *Warcraft*

Henry Lowood

Warcraft III begins with two short missions, 'Chasing Visions' and 'Departure'. They introduce the game as prologue, tutorial in the rudiments of *Warcraft* game mechanics, and first moments of play set in the narrative arc of the game. This mini-campaign, called the 'Exodus of the Horde', is introduced by two pre-rendered trailers, the second a troubling dream from which the great Orc Warchief and shaman Thrall awakens. This is a land scarred by 'remnants of the past; the dreams reveal a new enemy', a 'burning shadow', that threatens all mortal races. At the end of this vision, the prophet points directly to the dreamer and through the screen to the player, '*You* must rally the horde and lead your people to their destiny!' In the next scene, rendered by the game engine, Thrall gathers himself and rides out. The prophet promises to reveal his future, and Thrall agrees to 'play along'. So he does; at this moment the player takes control, guiding Thrall's actions and learning how to play along. The Orc Warchief has become the liminal 'you', the player on the threshold of spectator and character who has a mission to perform.

    Warcraft played a significant role in defining the game form, or genre, known as real-time strategy (RTS). The historical transition from turn-based, table-top play (boardgames, miniatures) to multiplayer, real-time computer games was an important moment for digital games. Yet, with the exception of Sid Meier's *Civilization*, strategy and RTS games received relatively scant attention in game studies. The RTS game is particularly interesting, because it was a transmutation of historical simulations and wargames that required computer technology. This history of *Warcraft* and its antecedents will argue that competitive RTS games redefined strategy gaming by adding performance of interface mastery skills to contemplative problem-solving and decision-making. *Warcraft* as a competitive game shared play dynamics and the mission structure of the single-player campaign, but created a different narrative potential grounded in performance rather than linear storytelling.

Warcraft in the history of real-time strategy

Blizzard Entertainment, founded as Silicon & Synapse in 1990, was primarily a third-party developer during its first few years. It produced games for several platforms, the best known being *The Lost Vikings* (Interplay, 1992). *Blackthorne* and *Warcraft: Orcs and Humans*, both released in 1994, were the first PC games released under the Blizzard label. *Warcraft: Orcs and Humans*, Westwood Studios' *Dune II* (1992) and *Command & Conquer* (1995), are recognized today as the founding trio of the RTS genre. *Warcraft*'s sequels were *Warcraft II: Tides of Darkness* (1995) and *Warcraft III: Reign of Chaos* (2002). The series spawned expansions, patches and derivative games. *Beyond the Dark Portal* (1996) and *The Frozen Throne* (2003) added new content (maps, campaigns, new units, etc.) to *Warcraft II* and *Warcraft III*, respectively. *Warcraft II: Battle.net edition* (1999) updated *Warcraft II* for compatibility with Blizzard's proprietary network for competitive play. Blizzard also published 'battle chests', anthologies, collector's editions, and gift sets (1996, 1999, 2000, 2002, 2003) with games, expansions, and extras such as strategy guides, art books or soundtrack CDs. Tewi Verlag's *Levels and Add-ons for Warcraft II* in 1995, Sunstone Interactive's *W!Zone* (1996) and Aztech New Media's *Aztech's Armory: Campaigns for Warcraft II* (1997) contributed independently developed content, and Electronic Arts published *Warcraft II: The Dark Saga* (1997), a version of *Warcraft II* for the Sony Playstation and Sega Saturn consoles, while players added countless 'puds' (maps), 'custom games' and software such as replay tools.

　　Warcraft's story world and characters literally played a role in the success of the series. The positive response of players to the story-based campaign in Blizzard's *Starcraft* (1998) emboldened *Warcraft*'s developers to intensify their focus on character and story development in the sequel to *Warcraft II*, called *Warcraft Adventures: Lord of the Clans*. The initial design was more a 2D adventure than an RTS game. When *Lord of the Clans* was cancelled during development in May 1998, Blizzard reassured the player community that it would not abandon 'the Warcraft world, because there are still chapters to be told' (Ocampo 1998). The promise of these added chapters and hints of a revised 3D game system at first dubbed 'real-time roleplay' nonetheless fuelled expectations that emphasized the narrative space, rather than competitive qualities for the next game. Indeed, *Warcraft III* and its expansions, supplemented by novels and a table-top role-playing game, delivered a story world popular enough to push past other intellectual properties such as *Star* Wars, *The Lord of the Rings*, or *The Matrix* as the basis for a game set in a persistent virtual world. The appropriately named *World of Warcraft* launched at the end of 2004 by early 2005 had easily attracted more subscribing players than any other massively multiplayer game based on an externally developed IP.

Ten years before *World of Warcraft*, *Warcraft* emerged from a tradition of strategy games associated more with historical than fantasy worlds. Like most fantasy gaming from miniatures to *Dungeons and Dragons*, the antecedents of *Warcraft* were wargames. By the end of the nineteenth century, Von Reisswitz's *Kriegsspiel* and its variants established a war college tradition of wargaming strategic and operational levels of battle as a means for training staff officers or rehearsing campaigns. Fred Jane's *Naval War Game* (1912) and H.G. Wells' *Little Wars* (1913) established tactical and skirmish (individual combat) wargames as a form of civilian entertainment, often with toy soldiers, miniatures or models. After World War II, Charles S. Roberts' *Tactics* (1952), *Tactics II* (1958) and Avalon Hill Game Company (1958) connected commercial and strategic military boardgame design. By the early 1970s, a second generation of commercial game companies led by Jim Dunnigan's Simulations Publications Inc. (SPI) was publishing a 'flood of games' for hobbyists (Patrick 1983: 21). Dunnigan firmly shifted game design from abstract strategy to gritty 'simulation' by emphasizing data and systems that could be modelled and read as historically realistic (Lowood and Lenoir 2003: 433–437).

Historical simulations greatly influenced computer game designers in the late 1970s and 1980s, perhaps more than any other existing games including *Dungeons and Dragons*. Even after the popularity of SPI-style boardgames peaked, microcomputer games such as Chris Crawford's *Tanktics* (1977) and *Eastern Front – 1941* (1981); Joel Billings's *Computer Bismarck* (1980); Tactical Design Group's *The Battle of the Bulge: Tigers in the* Snow; and Gary Grigsby's *Guadalcanal Campaign* (1982) borrowed visual representations, rules or data from boardgames and miniatures systems. Billings's Strategic Simulations Inc. (SSI) published a catalogue full of these wargames through the 1980s. Like SPI, SSI's games used hexagonal map-grids and units could be 'stacked' on the displayed map like cardboard counters. They played the same, too, as players usually moved one unit at a time in turn-based sequences of play. Loftus and Loftus (1983: ix–x) observed that 'video games are fundamentally different from all other games in history because of the computer technology that underlies them', but most computer wargames published during the 1980s hardly seemed 'fundamentally different'. A moment's reflection on the history of printing technology or other media innovations reminds us, however, that the impact of a technology does not have to be immediate to be fundamental. For a decade or more, most computer wargames replicated earlier games in many respects, and some still do.

The distinctive application of computer technology in David Hille's *Combat Leader* (1983) and *Battalion Commander* (1985) was the introduction of real-time computing to wargames. Both were published by SSI, the *Hochburg* of turn-based games such as Gary Grigsby's *Kampfgruppe* (1985). They simulated armoured warfare since World War II, based primarily on the US Army's field manual for mechanized infantry tactics. The metaphor governing play was the officer pointing to a spot on the map and ordering a platoon to move or fight there. On the Commodore 64 home computer, the player did this by moving the joystick cursor to a position on the displayed map, pressing the joystick button to select that location, then pressing the letter A on the keyboard to select A platoon, and finally G to give the order to move out to the location indicated by the cursor. All this happened while on-map units moved about. *Combat Leader*'s instructions reassured players unfamiliar with 'point-and-click' interfaces, who probably felt like Charlie Chaplin falling behind on an assembly line, that 'you are in the role of a Lieutenant. If you were too knowledgeable, you would not be convincing as a Lieutenant.' But this was a computer, the 'tool for modern times' announced by IBM's advertising featuring Charlie Chaplin, the 'Little Tramp' only two years earlier. Conscious of the novelty of his approach, Hille affirmed the 'great promise' of point-and-click wargames as 'more enjoyable and more realistic', citing possibilities such as 'robot' subordinate commanders and the use of 'arcade speed and graphics' (Hille 1983). In the *Combat Leader* designer notes, he noted that 'time management' would be crucial for both players and programmers, because 'quite a bit goes on all at once' when one hundred or more units are in a battle In catalogues of the mid-1980s, SSI marketed *Combat Leader* as a 'real-time wargame' that 'you'll call a strategy arcade game' and the 'ideal first-born' of a 'new hybrid of strategy and arcade wargames'.

Hille anticipated a relationship between player and computer that inverted the usual meaning of 'real-time' in the literature on real-time industrial systems of the mid-1980s. Real-time systems depend 'not only on the logical result of computation, but also on the time at which the results are produced' (Stankovic 1988: 10). Applications such as flight control, military command and control, or highway and rail control software set up a *controlling system* that monitors the environment of a *controlled* system in order to regulate it. The controller must keep up with 'real time' interactions in the environment. Hille's inversion had the player pointing and clicking to keep up with the simulation time of the game, more accurately described as *uninterrupted* time. Turns no longer froze the passage of time while a contemplative player plotted the perfect move. As Clausewitz himself noted, the 'slower the progress and the more frequent the interruptions of military action, the easier it is to retrieve a mistake' (1976: 85). In the strategy arcade, there was no such luxury.

Hille's games suffered in one major comparison to turn-based games. Home computers of the 1980s strained to keep a real-time game moving and at the same time provide a challenging AI-controlled player; there were only so many processing cycles available. Dani Bunten Berry's *Modem Wars* (Electronic Arts, 1988), *Command HQ* (Microprose, 1990) and *Global Conquest* (1992) sidestepped this problem as head-to-head multiplayer games. *Modem Wars* (originally *War*) was modelled on the backyard play of boys, without 'any of the complicated rules and relationships' of wargames. Berry explicitly designed it to reward hand–eye coordination and interface mastery as well as strategic thinking, so that 'each person had their own specialized style of play'. The technical design of the game made it possible to store data from which replays, or 'game film' as Berry called it, could be produced, and these movies allowed players to rerun and study their performance. Berry was amazed at 'how people used this opportunity the game films offered to rationalize their loss and to create stories out of the intense and ephemeral experience of the battle'. Berry recognized that player communities would thrive on the ability to make 'legends out of their best performances' and 'game film' was included in both *Command HQ* and *Global Conquest*. (Berry n.d.) *Global Conquest* was also one of the first games to offer network-based competition. Berry's games thus brought competitive player performance and spectatorship to real-time strategic gameplay.

Released in 1992, Westwood Studio's *Dune II* put together the elements that would characterize RTS as a genre: resource-gathering, base-building, map exploration, construction and selection of units and tactical combat, all set in the fantasy world of Frank Herbert's *Dune* novels. When reviewers or players posting to bulletin boards began to react to *Warcraft* in 1994, they greeted it with remarks like '[*Warcraft* is] kind of like *Dune II* meets *D&D*' (Cirulis 1995: 38). In fact, games based on the *Advanced Dungeons and Dragons* (AD&D) system directly inspired *Dune II*. Beginning with *Pool of Radiance* (1988), SSI published licensed computer games based on *AD&D* and its story worlds, just as it had brought wargames from paper to the computer. Westwood developed *Eye of the Beholder* (1991) and *Eye of the Beholder II* (1991) for SSI, introducing first-person perspective, a point-and-click interface, cinematic cutscenes and, especially significant, real-time play to *D&D*-style role-playing. During development of *Eye of the Beholder*, Bretty Sperry wondered if real-time play would also work in a game with 'resource management and a dynamic, flat interface' (quoted in Geryk 2001). This concept was realized by *Dune II*.[1] It differed markedly from the global perspective of Berry's titles – still looking down at a map, but displaying individual buildings and combatants. Perhaps *Dune II* put gameplay nearer to the ground as a legacy of the skirmish-orientation of Westwood's role-playing games. What mattered was that *Dune II* thus introduced the distinctive convention and contradiction in RTS games of showing tactical action and strategic resource management at the same scale of time and place.

Warcraft and *Dune II*'s successor, the *Command & Conquer* series, refined RTS play during the 1990s; players struggled at first with the similarity and newness of these games. The *Warcraft FAQ and Strategy Guide* called *Warcraft* a 'real-time fantasy strategy game', a 'point-and-click strategy game' and a 'fantasy-strategy game' (Kang and Asher 1995). Players wondered about similarities among these games. A reviewer of *Warcraft* remarked that by switching out a few unit graphics, resources and buildings, 'you have Westwood Studio's *Dune II*'. He catalogued similarities in gameplay, quipping that 'it's a good thing for Blizzard that there's no precedent for "look and feel" lawsuits in computer entertainment' (Lombardi 1995: 229). A player agreed that 'If ever there was a case for duplication of "look and feel" it would be between these two games' and concluded that '*Warcraft* is a direct "sequel" to *Dune II*. Or maybe something in between that and a remake' (Kang 1994). Another said, 'It is almost the EXACT same engine as what *Dune 2* used' (Wehmann 1994). Judging from comments posted to the Usenet discussion list devoted to computer-based strategy games, players speculated that these games had been made by 'the same company' or that Blizzard had licensed Westwood's game engine. 'Blizzard denies this of course, but us *Dune II* addicts know better … :-)' (Choo and Green 1994). Westwood's Louis Castle thought Blizzard were 'knockoff kings' when he first saw *Warcraft*; most designers of RTS games acknowledged *Dune 2* as the 'blueprint for the modern RTS' (Chris Taylor, quoted in Walker 1999). Bill Roper, who joined Blizzard as *Warcraft II* was being completed, credited *Dune II* as having 'started it all' for real-time strategy, but noted that it was more important to Blizzard that for two years after its publication, there had been no imitators (Walker 1999; Asher 2000). *Warcraft* was a response to that gap, and Westwood soon followed with *Warcraft*'s primary rival in the RTS arena,

Command & Conquer (1995). But while *Warcraft* and certainly *Command & Conquer* were 'born out of *Dune II*', the crucial difference was that Blizzard identified multiplayer competition as the essential form of real-time strategy play (Castle and Morhaime, quoted in Keighley 2000).

Point-and-click

What is Warcraft? The first player-authored FAQ and strategy guide for the first game in the *Warcraft* series responded that,

> *Warcraft: Orcs and Humans* is a point-and-click strategy game of 24 levels.
>
> The objective is to build a town that can create an army strong enough to beat your opponent. (Kang and Asher 1995)

The first notion, although referring to strategy, encompassed the *interface* and *structure* of gameplay. The second stated the *strategic problem* of the game. In *Warcraft*, the craft of war is not chess-like problem solving or decision making at the strategic scale. Preparation for battle put the strategy in real-time strategy, exemplifying Clausewitz's dictum that 'in strategy there is no such thing as victory', but only 'timely preparation for a tactical victory; the greater the strategic success, the greater the likelihood of a victorious engagement' (Clausewitz 1976: 363). In *Warcraft*, the actual battles were small scale missions, hardly more than skirmishes in the grand scheme of war. Yet, *Warcraft* squeezed planning, preparation *and* battle tactics within this constricted framework of time and place. RTS players learned to multi-task, switching non-stop between these modes of activity. Point-and-click, *do* or die, '*perform* or else' (McKenzie 2001).

War and battles are typically divided realities outside RTS play. The *Total War* series, for example, separates modes and maps of its turn-based strategy game, with resource collection, technology trees, and army-building, from a tactical game for fighting battles. *Warcraft*'s strategy and tactics had to be presented abstractly for the sake of real-time and visual continuity. Resources are mined, barracks built, and troops trained within a matter of minutes, while a 'warlord' leads at most a few dozen soldiers. More than that, and players would be overwhelmed by the task of pointing and clicking to give commands without the interruptions and pauses of turn-based play. They must *construct* a base by commanding workers to make buildings and technology according to a pre-determined 'technology tree' or gather resources for construction (gold, lumber and also oil in *Warcraft II*). Sending units out to explore the map plays a part by locating resources and the opponent's forces. These are *strategic* aspects of play. They *manage* resources and train units appropriate for a particular 'strat' (harass, rush attack, tower siege, 'creep and counter', etc.), often adjusting the force 'build' in response to an opponent's actions. These are *transitions* from strategic planning to battle. Finally, players *control* units during combat versus the opposing player or team, relying on computer control of some units ('artificial intelligence') and direct control of others, such as moving damaged units out of harm's way or casting spells ('micro-management'). These are *battle tactics*. Wargamers of every ilk understand strategy and tactics as the core of their games; simultaneity and the common scale of these activities set *Warcraft* apart as a distinctly computer-based version of wargame.

Like id Software during the making of *DOOM, the Warcraft* developers team became its first player community. During coding and playtesting, they learned that multiplayer, networked play transformed strategy gaming:

> The feeling of sitting alone in front of a computer, looking at your screen and realizing that off in cyberspace somewhere there is another sentient being building, exploring, and plotting your destruction was exhilarating. It was a totally different feeling from the hundreds of strategy games I had played against computer AIs, or even multiplayer games where your enemy sat beside you and shared a monitor. It was really creepy. Definitely a defining gaming moment for me. (Adham, quoted in Blevins 2001)

The multiplayer version of *Orcs and Humans* could be played via modem, serial link or local area networks. The boxed game included more than 20 custom maps to determine, as Blizzard marketing urged, 'who among you is the supreme warlord' (Blizzard 1998). It was a competitive game calibrated in Blizzard parlance for 'sentient vs. sentient' play ('Human' is designated as a race in the game). In response to negative comments about its computer-controlled players, Blizzard insisted that *Warcraft* be judged as a multiplayer game, because 'strategy gaming really depends upon two (or more) learning sentients, and until technology has made some pretty large advancements, personal computer AI's at least are not going to ever replace playing against another human being'. (Loving 1995). Moreover, Blizzard's developers were convinced that linear storytelling 'very seldom' motivates players to replay a game (Roper 2005). They believed that *Warcraft* featured the 'single greatest improvement to the [RTS] game genre to date, multiplayer support' (Pardo, quoted in Walker 1999; Roper 2000: 56).

Warcraft emphasized elements of competitive play that were fundamentally different as a result of computer technology. By the mid-1990s, competition in computer games meant networked play, first via peer-to-peer Local Area Network (LAN) connections, then client-server technology and the Internet. In 1994, perhaps ten computer games featured networked versions; one year later, support for networked, competitive games was snowballing, so that 'with all the talk of the survival of the wargame, making the experience more singular and isolated is probably a bad idea' (Cirulis 1995). So it was with *Warcraft II and III*. Network support made it possible to play with others and to watch others play. As Berry's vision of turning strategy gaming into a space for social performance had predicted, networked players made movies for other players to document their prowess (Lowood 2006; 2005). Demo movies, spectator modes, machinima and other game-based performances by 'worthy gamers' ready to participate in 'the next stage in online gaming' (id Software 1996) were first associated with first-person action games such as *DOOM* (1993) and *Quake* (1996). The publication of *Warcraft II* and *Command & Conquer* within months of each other (and between *DOOM* and *Quake*) fuelled similar impulses among multiplayer RTS players. New technology served their needs. Matching services such as Kali spoofed LAN connections over the Internet to match players and connect them; Blizzard licensed *Warcraft* to commercial networks, such as TEN (Totel Entertainment Network), Mpath and Engage Games Online for this purpose. The player community grew rapidly as a result.

As *Quake* was about to bring client-server networking to FPS players, Blizzard hired Mike O'Brian in 1995 to work on *Warcraft*'s support for online play and matchmaking. O'Brian had been 'just blown away' by *Warcraft* as a player; he contacted Blizzard and soon was applying his knowledge of real-time programming in rail traffic control to the architecture of multiplayer gaming (O'Brian 2000). The move from player to game programmer (he led the programming team for *Warcraft III*) led to Blizzard's Battle.net. Launched in early 1997 for Blizzard's action role-playing game *Diablo*, Battle.net hosted millions of *Diablo* games in the first year alone (Sams 1997). It matched players and provided a game server for massive numbers of *Diablo* and *Starcraft* players, especially in the United States and Korea. The Battle.net edition brought *Warcraft II* into the fold in 1999. Having decided that Battle.net would be integrated into all Blizzard games, beginning with *Starcraft*, Blizzard organized tournaments and a laddered ranking system, matched players for pick-up games, and provided social communication tools such as chat and buddy lists at no cost to players. Player-created software tools such as War2BNE captured replays of Battle.net games. *Warcraft III* players naturally expected multiplayer competition to be the primary mode of play; Blizzard agreed, attributing much of their games' popularity to 'play over Battle.net' (Roper 2000: 56). *Warcraft III* changed much about the game, from its 3D environment and more in-game races (night elves, undead) to camera control, and a 'real-time roleplaying' element, but the editor of a FAQ devoted to *Warcraft III* stated the obvious for most players: 'Of course the most famous and most played part will be the multiplayer function' (Tam: 2003). In *Warcraft III*, built-in spectator modes and replay capture, websites for distributing replays from Video on Demand and shoutcast commentaries of games fostered a player–spectator relationship around competitive game performance. Player, replay, game news and replay sites proliferated, building a huge community database of multiplayer tips, star players, advice on micro and strats, fee-based play training and reports of league or championship competitions. Berry predicted that game replay movies would make legends out of performances; the *Warcraft III* FAQ documented the practice: 'You can transfer your replay files, so you can trade them with other players. This can also be useful in distributing champion or particularly skilled player's games, or to catch cheaters as well' (Tam 2003).

As a competitive game with an enthusiastic player community, *Warcraft* followed *Starcraft* into the realm of high-level, even professional e-sports, especially in Korea and Europe. In 2003, *Warcraft III* joined six other titles in the annual World Cyber Games (WCG), founded three years earlier as the international 'Cyber Game Festival'. A total of 74 players from 44 countries participated in the first WCG *Warcraft* tournament, with $20,000 in prize money for the championship. In October 2004, San Francisco hosted the 4th annual WCG. The crucial match from that tournament, the second of three to decide the *Warcraft III* champion, documents how game dynamics, competitive player skills, and spectatorship shaped high-performance competitive play (Lowood 2004; WCG 2004). After three days of competition, this game matched two of the best *Warcraft* players in the world. The favoured player, WelcomeTo (aka Zacard; realname: Hwang Tae-Min), was from Korea, the world hotbed of RTS competition with professional leagues, star players and television coverage. His opponent, [4k]Grubby (realname: Manuel Schenkhuizen) of the 4 Kings clan came from the Netherlands. Played before a live crowd, the virtual *Warcraft* community viewed a webcast with shoutcast commentary, or downloaded replays later from the WCG website. During the match, spectators in the Civic Auditorium also gazed at a neutral observer view of the game map, identical to the webcast and piped to a large overhead screen. Although they could watch the players or marvel at the mastery of their hands furiously clicking away at keyboard and mouse, even those present at the match mostly kept their eyes glued on the avatars in combat on the giant video display.

The set of three matches, which Grubby would win 2–1, revolved around a few pivotal seconds in the second match. As usual for both players, they each commanded Orc armies. About six and a half minutes into the game, spectators observed the following: the armies were skirmishing around Grubby's main base. After some back-and-forth, WelcomeTo's army fell back. His main hero, a 'Farseer' was badly wounded, so WelcomeTo used a town portal scroll to teleport his army back to their home base. This they did, and a few seconds after landing, the farseer toppled over, dead. WelcomeTo was unable to recover from this loss, and a few minutes later, he conceded the game. Despite loud cheers from the audience when the Farseer died, only a few expert players and referees immediately grasped all that had just happened. By looking carefully at replays, we can translate these events, which transpired in perhaps 10 seconds, into player actions. Grubby's own Farseer hero had earlier in the game taken a 'wand of lightning' from a gnoll assassin while 'creeping', and it sat in his inventory. When WelcomeTo's activated the portal scroll, his Farseer was invincible, but Grubby instantly clicked on his wand (or hit a key selecting it), moused his cursor over WelcomeTo's *second* hero, a Firelord, then clicked the mouse to cast a lightning shield on him. This shield would now do damage over time to any unit standing *next* to the Firelord. As Grubby knew instinctively, WelcomeTo's heroes would land together in their base; instead of finding safety, the wounded Farseer died from standing next to his charged brother greenskin.

A spectator cannot discern Grubby's mastery of the syntax and tactics of *Warcraft* from staring at a screen. A replay movie cannot tell anyone what Grubby was thinking as he worked out his strategy; if he clicked on the wrong unit or randomly cast the spell, everything would look the same. In the Civic Auditorium or listening to the shoutcast, we might fill in a few blanks from the commentator noting 'the farseer has fallen' and 'good work by Grubby', from the sudden applause and singing by the European fans in the audience or from the pained expression on Zacard's face. A knowledge-able player, tapped into *Warcraft* discussion forums and replay sites, knows right away. Grubby had performed. He grasped an instant opportunity, made a preposterously rapid decision in the real-time heat of battle, and applied masterful knowledge of game syntax and 'micro' (the term used by players for micro-management of individual on-screen units) to carry out this game-winning performance. His interface mastery, tactics and strategy translated into a 'story' about this match that cannot be isolated at any of these levels. It is hardly true that such competitive gameplay lacks narrative potential, or that we can only describe this game's meaning – paraphrasing Beethoven regarding one of his musical performances – by simply replaying the game. *Warcraft* websites and forums offered chronicles of Grubby's victory. These accounts fit the events of the match into stories such as the amazing comeback, the startling defeat of the suddenly demoralized Korean favorite, payback for the arrogance and hubris of WelcomeTo's choice of the inferior Firelord as second hero, or even a morality tale on the superiority of quick tactical thinking over high 'actions-per-minute' counts. Such stories arranged details of gameplay to fit into discernible narrative structures; they distilled the rapid, perhaps even bewildering syntax and actions of high-performance RTS play through 'narrative tactics' akin to what Hayden has called 'explanation by emplotment' in his seminal work on the structures of historical writing (White 1975: *passim*, but especially 7–11).

While the pace of *Warcraft: Orcs and Humans* was deliberate, it began the shift from calculated decision making as the hallmark of turn-based games to the quick reactions, keyboard skills, and micro-management of units that increasingly dominated play in later versions of the game. The editor of *Computer Gaming World* described the 'panicked pace', 'split-second decisions', and 'mad-dash juggling of resources and demands' already in the original game, concluding that 'if you can't manage the carpal calisthenics to right and left mouse click in rapid succession, you can forget about *Warcraft*' (Lombardi 1995: 229). *Warcraft* retained much of the core gameplay from turn-based wargames focused on the strategy and tactics of battle, but added *syntax* of play requiring mastery of the computer interface.[2] Networked, competition created the conditions for a culture of spectatorship and performance. Surprisingly, the computer-specific dimension of interface mastery emphasized physicality (reflexes, fast hand movements) absent in 'physical', paper-based boardgames. Computer-mediated dimensions of RTS play transformed the strategy game into a form of competitive e-sports. The criticism levelled at RTS games of reducing strategy play to mindless mouse-clicking misunderstands the denigrated 'clickfest' or 'button-mashing' by missing the connections between mastery of syntax and strategy, both invisible on the screen. *Warcraft*'s visual representation is a charming, if comical abstraction of warfare at the strategic level, but one that perfectly incorporates new skills in the tactics of digital competition as well as computer interfaces. In gamer's terms, the essence of competitive play *à la Warcraft* is the combination of successful 'strats' *and* point-and-click 'micro'. The moral of Grubby's victory is that real-time strategy is powerless without real-time interface mastery; it really isn't easy being an Orc.

Reading player performance?

Warcraft added a new aspect to strategy play as performance of game interface and syntax. Together with game dynamics depicting the mixed realities
of tactics and strategy as unified and continuous and networked, multiplayer
competition, *Warcraft* thus created conditions for player performances that
were intimately connected to computer technology. As compelling as all this
might be when talking about the success *of Warcraft* or the transformative
power of digital play with respect to strategic games, the *Warcraft* series also
evolved in a rather different direction. Blizzard's success, both North (*Diablo*)
and South (*Warcraft, Starcraft*), has also been read as demonstrating the
importance of narrative threads and touches in games. *Warcraft* became
more ambitious with each new version by this measure, whether in the
continuity of the world history, the quality of cinematic cut-scenes or the
charming 'pissed sounds' emitted when a player clicked repeatedly on unit
avatars (Orc Grunt: 'It not easy being green'). The developers explicitly shifted
their focus on the game as a fictional story form with *Warcraft Adventures*,
the original successor to *Warcraft II*, considering 'real-time roleplaying' and
the adventure game during the early stages of work on this project to be a
suitable replacement for the RTS mode of play and storytelling. Their eager-
ness to put the narrative cart before the RTS horse perhaps provides some
evidence to support the observation that 'the idea that games have something to do with stories has such a hold on designers' and gamers' imagination that it probably can't be expunged ...' (Costikyan 2000).

   Warcraft, in other words, exhibits a tension between the developer's notion of game story-lines, authored and continuous, and player-generated
stories based on game performance and experience. However, RTS games
were not the first to put narrative precision and player possibility in the
same package. As Dunnigan pointed out, 'The object of any wargame (historical or otherwise) is to enable the player to recreate a specific event and,
more importantly, to be able to explore what might have been if the player
decides to do things differently' (Dunnigan 1980: 11). The older conception
of how wargames do this might be thought of as counterfactual play in a
historical world. The famous boxcover art for Avalon-Hill's *Afrika Korps*
(1964) provided a quaint, but surprisingly rich account of this view of game-
based narrative play. It presented the historical right on the box with text
and pictures – 'Early in 1941, a general named Rommel ...' and so on. The
story took the player to a moment, the beginning of the game. Then, the
game took over as historical fiction, previewing Thrall's vision by turning
you into the subject: 'Now YOU command in this realistic Desert Campaign

game ...' It was the player's role to venture into a ludic possibility space of counterfactual moves and *change* history. For Dunnigan and SPI, however, historical simulation modeled a reality underlying *wie es eigentlich gewesen ist*. The advantage of the 'simulation game' allowed, 'within well-defined limits, a great deal of variety in an otherwise strictly pre-determined historical event'. He realized that many boardgame wargamers actually never explored the possibilities offered by agonistic play. Dunnigan pointed out that the historical simulations could be read quite literally as authored accounts: 'Many gamers "collect" games. They buy them, but never play them. This does not mean they are not used. Quite often, the hobbyist will spend several hours with the game.' He unfolded maps, looked at counters, read rules, or maybe set up an opening move for solitaire play to discern orders of battle, the lay of the land and the historical commander's options. For every player who departed from the 'linear rendering' offered by historical monographs by exploring the dynamic potential in these games, which was 'meant to be exercised', another played boardgames in single-player mode, exercising this potential 'in his head with the aid of the game components' (Dunnigan 1980: 109–117).

In a linear medium, the author controls the pace of plot development, knowing exactly that when a particular plot device is applied, the reader or viewer will be positioned at a certain point in the story. Warcraft's single-player campaigns surrender some aspects of this control, but pull it back by cleverly matching 'story nodes' with the mission structure of these campaigns. Blizzard's designers aligned the story line in synchronization with a player's progress through the game by reaching these nodes through gameplay appropriate for the introduction of significant story elements, such as letting the player know in Starcraft 'what characters were going to die, where betrayals were going to happen, etc.' (Roper 2005; Pardo 2000 142). These nodes were introduced primarily in two ways. First, and exceptionally, they would occasionally pause progress through the game for a 'major story point'. Second, as a 'reward' for achieving goals within the game structure, it was 'perfectly fine to have a scripted cut-scene at the end of a level', when the player could mark progress and relax by watching a dramatic narrative leap forward (Pardo 2000: 141). *Warcraft's* single-player campaign structure positioned 'story' as the reward for accomplished missions and as the thread connecting these missions.

Multiplayer performances also demonstrated a narrative potential, but as we have seen, as chronicles or emplotments of competitive play. Like SPI's boardgames, *Warcraft* can be experienced in different ways that reverse the agency of authored narrative and player performance. In the single-player game, the developer is in charge; the player is 'there', but he must contextualize his experiences in terms of the story world and character motivations provided by the game's back story, story nodes, and mission assignments. In multiplayer competition, like Grubby's turnaround victory, performances of syntax, tactics, and strategy of play are displayed, interpreted and supplemented by subsequent retelling.

The crucial roles played by spectatorship, multiplayer competition and player communities in extending real-time strategy offer persuasive arguments that *Warcraft* can be understood (even if metaphorically) as a performance space rather than as a text. We should pay more attention to the modes of performance available to the player in competitive games and the ways in which these play performances are viewed, interpreted, and narrated within a virtual community of players. Maybe if green is all you want to be, that's not such a problem.

Works cited

Asher, M. (2001) 'The Spellcaster', *Computer Games*, 122, January 2001.

——(2000) 'Almost 10 Years Strong: A Brief History of *Warcraft* and Blizzard', *Computer Games*, www.cdmag.com/articles/031/005/warcraft_feature.html, accessed March 2005.

Berry, D. B. (n.d). 'Game Design Memoir', reproduction of website on Dani Bunten Berry memorial site, www.anticlockwise.com/dani/personal/biz/memoir.htm, accessed March 2005.

Blevins, T. (2001) 'A Decade of Blizzard', http://pc.ign.com/articles/090/090953p1. html, accessed March 2005.

Blizzard (1998) Warcraft website, www.blizzard.com/war1, available from Internet Archive, http://web.archive.org/web/19981202194850/http://blizzard.com/war1/, accessed December 2004.

——(1996) Blizzard Entertainment website, www.blizzard.com, available from Internet Archive, http://web.archive.org/web/19961019175340/blizzard.com/info.htm, accessed December 2004.

Choo, E. A. and Green, A. J. (1994) 'Re: Dune 3 and Warcraft', Comp.sys.ibm.pc. games.misc, accessed February 2005, http://groups-beta.google.com/group/comp.sys.ibm.pc.games.misc/browse_thread/thread/f861ad4f1ba4f740/a02cc74b94c465f7?q=warcraft+dune+conquer.

Cirulis, M. E. (1995) 'Take Ten Steps, Turn, and Dial', *Computer Gaming World* 127, 38–47, available from Expanded Academic ASAP Plus, accessed February 2005.

Clausewitz, C. (1976) *On War* [*Vom Kriege*] trans. M. Howard and P. Paret, Princeton, NJ: Princeton University Press.

Costkiyan, G. (2000) 'Where Stories End and Games Begin', *Game Developer*, 8 (6), 44–53, available from: http://www.costik.com/gamnstry.html, accessed March 2005.

Davies, J. (2001) 'Blizzard's Moment of WOW', *Computer Games*, 132, November 2001.

Dunnigan, J. F. (1980) *The Complete Wargames Handbook: How to Play, Design and Find Them*, New York: William Morrow.

Geryk, B. (2001) 'A History of Real-time Strategy Games: Part 1: 1989–1998', *Gamespot*, www.gamespot.com/gamespot/features/all/real_time/, accessed September 2004.

Golden, C. (2001), *Warcraft: The Lord of the Clans*, New York: Pocket Books.

Hille, D. (1983) 'Designer's Notes', in *Combat Leader* manual, Mountain View, CA: Strategic Simulations, Inc.

Id Software (1996) Corporate Website, via Internet Archive, available from http://web.archive.org/web/19961220085757/www.idsoftware.com/clans/index.html, accessed June 2003.

Jane, F. T. (1912) *How to Play the 'Naval War Game'. With a Complete Set of the Latest Rules, Full Instructions and Some Examples of 'Wars' that have Actually been Played*, London: S. Low, Marston & Co.

Kang, W. (1994) Re: *Warcraft* vs. *Dune II*, Comp.sys.ibm.pc.games.strategic, accessed February 2005 from http://groups-beta.google.com/group/comp.sys.ibm.pc.games.strategic/browse_thread/thread/7a1a3d70d91a0b92/a5d05582c2981596?q=warcraft+dune.

Kang, J. and Asher, C. (1995) *Warcraft: Orcs and Humans*, Frequently asked questions (FAQ) and strategy guide, Version 1.00, retrieved March 2005 from http://members.tripod.com/~stanislavs/games/warcraft.faq.

Keighley, G. (2000) 'Eye of the Storm: Behind Closed Doors at Blizzard', *Gamespot*, 14 November 2000, available from www.gamespot.com/gamespot/features/pc/blizzard/, accessed November 2004.

Loftus, G.R. and Loftus, E.F. (1983) *Mind at Play: The Psychology of Video Games*, NY: Basic Books.

Lombardi, C. (1995) 'War Crime in Real Time', *Computer Gaming World*, 126, 228–230, available from Expanded Academic ASAP Plus, accessed February 2005.

Loving, T. (1999) 'Re: Hey, PC Game writers why do you do this ?!', comp.sys.ibm.pc.games.strategic, available from http://groups-beta.google.com/group/comp.sys.ibm.pc.games.strategic/browse_thread/thread/118299733ace82b9/076fd3b17a2de3bf?q=author:blizzrdent@aol.com, accessed March 2005.

Lowood, H., (2006) 'High-performance Play: The Making of Machinima', *Journal of Media Practice*, 7:1, 25–42.

——(2005) 'Real-time Performance: Machinima and Game Studies', *The International Digital Media and Arts Association Journal*, 1:3, 10–17.

——(2004) Personal Notes, Conversations, as Head Referee, *Warcraft III* tournament, WCG 2004.

Lowood, H. and Lenoir, T. (2003) 'Kriegstheater: Der Militär-Unterhaltungs-Komplex', in J. Lazardzig, H. Schramm and L. Schwarted (eds) *Kunstkammer, Laboratorium, Bühne—Schauplätze des Wissens im 17. Jahrhundert*, Berlin: Walter de Gruyter.

McKenzie, J. (2001) *Perform or Else: From Discipline to Performance*, London: Routledge.

O'Brian, M. (2000) Mike O'Brian interview, *Infoceptor*, www.infoceptor.com/interview/arenanet.shtml, accessed March 2005.

Ocampo, J. (1998) 'Company Asks Gamers to Trust its Judgment on Game's Cancellation', *Computer Games: Strategy Plus*, www.cdmag.com/articles/013/181/blizzard_on_wacraft_petition.html, accessed February 2005.

Patrick, S. B. (1983) 'The History of Wargaming', in Staff of *Strategy & Tactics* Magazine (eds) *Wargame design*, New York: Hippocrene Books, 1–29.

Perla, P. P. *The Art of Wargaming: A Guide for Professionals and Hobbyists*, Annapolis: Naval Institute Press.

Roper, B. (2005) Lecture and personal conversation, Stanford University, 1 March 2005.

——(2000) 'Bill Roper, Blizzard Entertainment', in Marc Saltzmann (ed.) *Game Design: Secrets of the Sages*, 2nd edn, Indianapolis: Brady Games, 54–57.

Sams, P. (1997) 'Battle.net Defines its Success: An Interview with Paul Sams of Blizzard', *Gamasutra*, www.gamasutra.com/features/19971128/battlenet_01.htm, accessed February 2005.

Stankovic, J. (1988) 'Misconceptions about Real-time Computing: A Serious Problem for Next Generation Systems', *IEEE Computer*, 21:10, 10–19.

Tam, K. (2003) *Warcraft 3 Reigns* [sic] *of Chaos*, FAQ and Walkthrough for Warcraft III on PC, Version 1.81, http://db.gamefaqs.com/computer/doswin/file/warcraft_iii.txt, accessed March 2005.

Walker, M. H. (1999) 'The Wind of Change: A History of Real-time Strategy', *Electric Playground* website, via Internet Archive, http://web.archive.org/web/20001024115152/http://www.elecplay.com/features/rts/rtshistory.html, accessed October 2000.

——(1996) *Warcraft II: Beyond the Dark Portal: Official Secrets & Solutions*, Rocklin, CA: Prima.

WCG (2004) World Cyber Games 2004 website available via Internet Archive from http://web.archive.org/web/20041012082117/http://www.worldcybergames.com/ accessed March 2005.

Wehmann, B. H. (1994) 'Re: *Dune III = Warcraft*', at Comp.sys.ibm.pc.games.strategic, available from http://groups-beta.google.com/group/comp.sys.ibm.pc.games.strategic/browse_thread/thread/7a1a3d70d91a0b92/a5d05582c2981596?q=warcraft+dune, accessed February 2005.

Wells, H. G. (1913) *Little wars: A Game for Boys from Twelve Years of Age to One Hundred and Fifty, and for that More Intelligent Sort of Girl Who Likes Boys' Games and Books*, London: F. Palmer.

White, H. V. (1975) *Metahistory: The Historical Imagination in Nineteenth-century Europe*, Baltimore: Johns Hopkins University Press.

Games

Battalion Commander (1985), Strategic Simulations Inc.

The Battle of the Bulge: Tigers in the Snow (DOS version) (1982), Tactical Design Group/Strategic Simulations Inc.

Blackthorne (1994), Blizzard.

Combat Leader (1983), Strategic Simulations Inc.

Command & Conquer (1995), Westwood.

Command HQ (1990), Ozark Softscape/Mindplay.

Computer Bismarck (1980), Strategic Simulations Inc.

Dune II (1992), Westwood.

Eye of the Beholder (1991), Strategic Simulations, Inc.

Eye of the Beholder II (1991), Strategic Simulations, Inc.

Global Conquest (1992), Ozark Softscape/Microplay.

Guadalcanal Campaign (1982), Strategic Simulations, Inc.

Kampfgruppe (1985), Strategic Simulations, Inc.

Sid Meier's Civilization (1991), MicroProse.

Modem Wars (1988), Ozark Softscape/Electronic Arts.

Pool of Radiance (1988), Strategic Simulations, Inc.

The Lost Vikings (1992), Blizzard/Interplay.

Tanktics (1977), Chris Crawford.

Tanktics (1981), Avalon Hill Game Company.

Warcraft: Orcs and Humans (1994), Blizzard.

Warcraft II: Tides of Darkness (1995), Blizzard.

Warcraft II: Beyond the Dark Portal (1996), Blizzard.

Warcraft II: The Dark Saga (1997), Electronic Arts.

Warcraft II: Battle.net edition (1999), Blizzard.

Warcraft III: Reign of Chaos (2002), Blizzard.

Warcraft III: The Frozen Throne (2003), Blizzard.

World of Warcraft (2004), Blizzard.

Notes

1 *Dune II* was not the sequel to *Dune,* an adventure game by Cryo. They were developed independently for Virgin Interactive, who held the license for games based on the novels.

2 I am indebted to Rene Patnode for this notion of game syntax.

6

Being a determined agent in (the) *World of Warcraft*: text/play/identity

Tanya Krzywinska

As an extension of the well-established *Warcraft* series, *World of Warcraft* is a subscription-based massively multiplayer role-playing game that came online in late 2004.[1] Alongside an analysis of the game's specific stylistic and textural milieu, it is the way that this particular multiplayer game facilitates a balance between player agency and restriction and the relationship between interpellation and identity that provide the main focus of this chapter. I am interested here in the way that *World of Warcraft* configures and draws on the dynamics of agency and determination at aesthetic, semantic, experiential and psychological levels within a modal context of a high fantasy role-playing game. The game offers players an extensive, graphically detailed and socially-oriented environment within which a range of play styles and 'make-believe' are possible. In many respects the game follows the model set by *EverQuest*. As is typical of role-playing games, experience points are gained by completing quests and 'killing' various non-playing characters (NPCs), which can be looted for items that can be used, traded for money or passed on to other players. Such tasks can be undertaken solo or in a group of two to five players. In addition, 'raids' on opposing factions that include many more players may be undertaken, which give honour and rank. There are a number of overarching parameters based on the particularities of the game's programming infrastructure and its online delivery that determine many of the conditions of play. In combination with the social aspect of playing with others, it is the availability of a range of set tasks and scope for less predetermined activities that help to keep players engaged with the game over potentially longer periods than single-player games. This is financially important for the game providers who seek to sustain continued payments of the monthly subscription fee.

The relative balance between player agency and restriction has a bearing on the manner in which the game's textual features shape the player's experience. This is not, however, a one-way process as the player's identity, engagement and experience realises and activates the game's text. The interplay between the game as a predetermined textual construct and as an emergent user construct works with intertextual, contextual and interpretational factors; the meanings derived from *World of Warcraft* depend on the particular knowledges and predilections a player brings to the game-world and the experience of playing within this context. In addition, a variety of issues around player identity arise because of the social context afforded by the game and it is a core contention of this essay that it is the complex interactions between text and player/s that breathe vitality and drama into this world.

Context/intertext/gameplay

Any game can be said to comprise of a set of 'textual' features and devices that provide its environmental, stylistic, generic, intertextual, structural and semiotic characteristics. Such formal and formative components combine with the player's inter-actions to make a coherent game 'world'. These elements include the balance of play and the capabilities of in-game objects and characters which construct for the player a defined aesthetic and ludic experience. Some of these features operate at surface level, while others work behind the scenes to constitute the game's fictional 'diegetic' world. The surface features make the player's interaction with the game's complex computational infrastructure meaningful in contextual and game-play terms while deeper structures determine the conditions of play. In order to preserve the integrity of the high fantasy modality that characterizes *World of Warcraft*, its computational infrastructure is hidden, at least ostensibly, from view (although it is visible in mediated form in the game's quite complex user interface and graphical properties, such as mountain ranges and seas that disguise the spatial limits of the game world). As Eddo Stern has said, 'most fantasy game designers would regard visible signs of any technological underpinnings as unwanted anachronisms that would threaten the constitution of the immersive fantasy they are attempting to construct' (2002: 263). Nonetheless, the game's programming infrastructure plays a core role in shaping a player's experience and it is integral to the game's textual effects. As such, and in order to accommodate the specific attributes of digital games, I define text here neither as the written word nor just in terms of the dimension of representation but more generally. I regard the game-text as a holistic entity. Surface features work with the parameters set at the level of programming to shape, through certain designer-determined limitations, the potential for 'being' and 'doing' things in the game-world; in conjunction these produce a ludic and aesthetic experience. Text is also used in a semiotic sense as something that can be activated by a player's cognitive engagement to produce meaning through intertextual referents and connotation (game determinants can be 'read' for meaning in just the same way that audio-visual representations can be 'read'). The concerted action of a game's overt and covert textual strategies facilitate, at least in part, the generation of emotional, interpretative, physical and cognitive engagement, orchestrating the player's experience of game-play and the game's world. To understand the fiction-making and affective qualities of a game's design, the way it seeks to shape the player's experience while giving scope for choice, and to evaluate the values of a game, it is important to address its particular textual configuration. It is only by addressing the way that *World of Warcraft* operates as text, which shapes through a dynamic relationship between agency and determination the experience of playing the game, that it is possible to understand how the game works as a 'prop' for a collective, play-centred, fantasy and the types of possible pleasures on offer.

World of Warcraft presents itself to players as an expansive, persistent and carefully structured 'world' with a well-developed back-story. As a multiplayer game, its social dimension is largely composed of interactions between players who are represented in the game-world by a predefined game character. A sense of the game as a fantasy 'world' is diversely comprised, ranging from the inclusion of mythic material, presented as history, through to the coherent audio-visual design of the game, the logic of which dictates the types of landscape, character-types, objects and quests. Underpinning the coherency and stylistic character of the game's design is the use of well-established high fantasy rhetoric, which can be characterized as neo-medievalist.[2] A great deal of *World of Warcraft* refers to other texts of that type, of which J.R.R. Tolkein's *The Lord of The Rings* is a primary source. Following this model, and as a means of constructing 'world-ness', the game assembles different 'cultures', each supported by a range of audio-visual and ficto-historical features. The presence of a host of generic conventions derived from high fantasy, along with the game's role-playing tag, means that the game-world is presented not just as a virtual space but also as a *fantasy* space, acting as an open invitation to be playful and where players adopt heroic personas fighting, ostensibly at least, for a preordained just cause, no matter which character-type they play. While the game requires real-world activities (from paying for subscriptions through to growing more skilful in the use of the game's multifaceted user interface), the player's willingness to engage in *make-believe* is also an important factor in making gameplay multi-dimensional, vivid and evocative; in other words bringing the game-world to life. This is cued by the marked presence of high fantasy rhetoric, as well as the fact that players engage with others while inhabiting the skin of a fantasy-based character (as I will show later, the embodiment of the player in the game world as a predefined character calls to attention the sticky relationship between identity and interpellation and which underlies the term 'player-character').

A chief component of the way the game predetermines player experience, and on which much of the gameplay is based, is that player-character sets are split into two discrete factions: the Alliance and the Horde. This division establishes an important regime of difference in the game, including the way that space is organised on territorial lines; there are, for example, areas that players of opposing factions cannot easily occupy. It is possible, however, for players to band together to raid areas populated by the opposing faction, although it is not possible to colonize such areas for any length of time. Each faction and race has a pre-given history outlined briefly in the character creation screen and expanded on in voice-over as a new player-character first enters the world. The Horde races (Orc, Troll, Undead and Tauren) are outcasts who in the past have been enslaved, 'corrupted' or subject to aggression, which in part contextualises the Horde's hostility to the Alliance. The Alliance races (Human, Dwarf, Gnome and Night Elf) are united in their loathing of what the game guide calls 'things demonic'. The imparting of such historically-framed information is important in creating 'world-ness'. As well as interpellating the player into the game's extensive diegetic milieu, the availability of such information provides cues that can be taken up by the player for the ways that they might choose to act, perform and play in the game-world. There is, however, no straight Manichaean split into good and evil in this game-world, as is the case with *The Lord of the Rings*; each race and faction has a sense of injustice and of wrongs done to them. In effect, whatever faction the player-character belongs to, the core task-set – tasks that are intrinsic to progression and which make *World of Warcraft* a goal-based game and not just a prettily furnished chat-room – remain much the same.

How much the contextualizing back-story might come into play for players is variable, however. It rather depends on the goals players set themselves, the level of their commitment to role-playing and other broader investments in the back-story and the situation, social or otherwise, in which they find themselves. Players can choose to play on a dedicated role-playing server, where the back-story is likely to come into the foreground as a cue for player's to adopt identities in the game that are in keeping with the game-world (of which more later). Nonetheless, whatever server is chosen and no matter what the player-character type, the fundamental internal mechanics of the game impel the player-character to fight for their side, a feature that is important to the player vs. player dimension of the game.

Such rigidity of allegiance operates as an effect of game-play balance but is also one of the ways that the game can be said to interpellate players into predetermined roles which govern to an extent the way players regard one another. *World of Warcraft* refers back to earlier *Warcraft* games as a means of building its fictional history; the coming together of the two factions in *Warcraft 3* to defeat the Burning Legion, is in *World of Warcraft* a memory that functions as back-story (making coherency and capital from player-history in the case of those who played the earlier games); since that victory the two factions are now once again on the brink of war, providing a rationale not just for player-character identity and the organisation of space but also for the game's organisation of its player vs. player dimension and its concomitant honour and ranking system. The historical narratives generated from a range of perspectives not only function as a form of predetermination and lend a sense of contingency but also penetrate into the organization and character of game-play and player-character identity; in addition, they also play an important role in constructing the game as a modally-determined prop for make-believe.

It is into an agitated, brink-of-war state that the newly made player-character enters the game. The player begins by selecting a character from the available range of different races as well as selecting their functional type (warrior, druid, rogue, priest, hunter, etc.). Choices about trade-skills, specialisms and in some cases alignment are made at other stages in the game. The particular combination of these determines the abilities that the player potentially will be able to develop when playing their character and therefore determines certain aspects of play and player-character identity. Players enter the game at an initial stage with the aim of becoming competent with the user interface and a number of factors are built into the game to aid that process, with tasks becoming progressively more complex (this provides another example of the way the textual features of the game operate to structure the experience of players). On first entering the game the player is in a 'home' area; quests are easy and readily available, each functioning to acquaint players with the basic interface functions and the task types that persist throughout much of the game. Some of these provide information on the class and race of their character. Quest instructions are delivered in scribed (written) format and kept in the quest log, where they can be consulted at any time. Quests are automatically deleted once completed as the log can only show twenty-five quests at any one time. This 'rule' demands that players make choices about their actions forced by the game's infrastructure; it is an arbitrary rule, but operates, along with many other features, to foreground choice and management as an articulation of player agency. As well as imparting fragments of information about the gameworld's fictional history, instructions on how to undertake a quest must often be read carefully as they contain sometimes less than obvious clues. Close reading also encourages players to engage more closely with the contextualising mosaic of back-story which in total has led up to the state of affairs of the world in its present condition.

Cues as to the state of affairs are also inscribed in the landscape and nonplaying characters and creatures. In the case of the Night Elf homeland of Teldrassil, for example, the woods and shores are littered with the ruins of once splendid temples and the various creatures that roam these lands have become 'corrupt' – made aggressive by a supernatural force released by the unwise and decadent use of dangerous magics (a theme often found in high fantasy). The present condition of the Night Elf homelands stands in testimony to the history of the race, as is also the case with the homelands of the other races. Night Elves are characterized along Tolkeinean lines: they are an ancient race with a strong affinity to nature and regard themselves as superior to others, even though their sophisticated civilisation has been reduced by war and home-grown degeneration. As Walter Benjamin (2003) says of the cultural use of ruins, they cast an aura of mystery and nostalgia. Vestiges of once splendid temples and cities act within the game (as in real life) as *in memoriam* signifiers of past glory, representing in romanticized terms a lost object of desire (in this case the loss of a balanced and nature-friendly use of knowledge). These ruins work with the 'lost object' conditions that govern desire investments in, and thematic concerns of, the fantasy genre (a factor that also underpins many real-world historical narratives). The presence of such ruins is one of the ways that the '*mise-en-scène*' of *World of Warcraft* is used to invoke resonances that have a charge derived from the real world; in this case, and important perhaps for some players predisposed to such things, an imaginary investment promoted by the 'magical revivalism' promoted in part by so-called new age culture's promotion of knowledges and beliefs that fall outside rationalism and Christianity/monotheism. Things of importance lost through war, greed, corruption or degeneration also play a defining role in the histories of other races, as well as underpinning the thematic logic of gameplay. In allowing players a range of races to choose from, the game seeks to accommodate different playing styles and personal predilections, at least to some extent, but while the cultures of the available races are diverse and have different real-world resonances, the activities undertaken by all player-characters are, in fact, much the same as each are determined at base by the same computational determinants.

The presence of signifiers and narratives of a diegetic historical past is one of the primary ways that the game creates the illusion of a coherent and persistent world in cultural, spatial and temporal terms, and, in addition, provides a rationale for the way that the player-character is assigned a particular, predetermined, morally and emotionally loaded history and identity. As with the real world, the player-character is born into this symbolic order and its concomitant 'subject' positions (although players bring their histories to the game text). In addition, the provision of history and culture with its apparent breadth and depth helps to efface what is in fact a technologically generated domain. The evocative use of *mise-en-scène* and narrative hides arbitrary rules and parameters that are necessary to construct a game and a virtual-physical world which variably, and conditionally, is orchestrated to sustain the suspension of disbelief. These forms of meaning generation have a significant impact on the types of play encouraged by the game. A variety of game scholars have argued that digital games should be regarded as spatial narratives. This is not just inherent to the media-specific nature of the majority of games, but also in a wider sense to the nature of the fantasy genre. As George R.R. Martin notes,

> J.R.R. Tolkein was the first to create a full realized secondary universe, an entire world with its own geography and histories and legends, wholly unconnected to our own, yet somehow just as real. 'Frodo lives,' the buttons might have said back in the sixties, but it was not a picture of Frodo that Tolkein's readers taped to the walls of their dorm rooms, it was a map. A map of a place that never was. (Martin 2001: 3)

The nature of *World of Warcraft*'s quest system forces players to be nomadic, travelling the world to undertake the tasks required to progress. There is, therefore, a strong sense of a journey structure in the game, working on the lines of the blueprint hero quest found in Homer's *The Odyssey* (c. 750 BC). The various maps available aid travel and effective play. They are part of the game's functional realism,[3] used in much the way one would use a map in the real world, yet they also promote a sense for the player that they are free to travel the realm, either to see the sights and/or undertake tasks, and contribute to the sense of the game as world by locating the player spatially, but as becomes clear quite quickly, not all places are hospitable because they are populated by guards from the opposing faction. The maps available are geographical and do not clearly show the effect of history on territory (names of areas might be read so, however), which determines where a player can and cannot roam.

Alpine and agrarian regions, desert, savannah, forests, towns and cities, caves and mines, rivers, lakes, seas and marshes are all compressed into two fairly small continents. These differently cast areas contribute to making the world culturally meaningful within the terms of the game and aesthetically interesting; they are often designed to look spectacular on first entry. Sometimes this works with the spectacle of scale (the towering statues that stand guard at the entrance to Ironforge and the glowing molten material that falls from a great height at its core for example), sometimes through the visually arresting detail of forest flora and in other cases because of perspective enhancing vistas, islands reaching skyward out of the sea, for example. (The graphical qualities of the world might be experienced variably by players as the game enables players to reduce the quality and depth of the visual field to enable frame-rates to be increased – again this helps to facilitate different playing styles – more generally this user determined facility also accommodates variability in the resources of home computers and internet connection speeds.) The range of different culturally-defined landscapes is also pleasing visually through their relative diversity, as are the creatures that differ according to the putative ecological specificity of a particular environment. In addition, different sound schemas characterize aurally each space: the sound of footfalls crunching through frosted snow, the heroic music played on entry into Stormwind, the shimmering sounds of Ashenvale forest, to which are added the particular sounds emitted by creatures that inhabit a given area, which often alert players to their proximity. While all these components are used to signify a fantasy world, the sights and sounds that players encounter through their travels are often integral to game-play. As a form of determinism, they often signal where to find something, in conjunction with quest information, or they may alert the player to potential dangers to avoid or to engage in combat, or encourage exploration; in this sense the aesthetic and the ludic come together to form the game's 'readable' text. In total, the carefully structured text of *World of Warcraft* offers the player a fantasy world that seeks to seduce through stylistic and ludic craft and an attuned balance between agency and determination.

Social-play

One of the pleasures – and sometimes frustrations – of being in the *World of Warcraft* is the presence of other players. Castulus Kolo and Timo Baur's empirical data on *Ultima Online* found that '[the] dominant motive for playing is the social experience of the distributed virtual environment' (2004: 21), which as they point out supports the conclusions made by Mikeal Jakobsson and T.L. Taylor (2003) in their earlier study of *EverQuest*, that 'the production of social networks and the circulation of social capital proves to be one of the most important aspects' (cited in Kolo and Baur 2004: 22). The active promotion of social interaction in online role-playing games has a significant impact on game-text, play and player experience. Social interaction is facilitated and encouraged by the game in numerous ways. The social nature of *World of Warcraft* is also important to the types of game-play and more general playfulness offered within the world. In terms of game-play, getting in and playing in a group is often required if certain preset goals are to be achieved. For the new, inexperienced player it can prove somewhat intimidating to join with others; play, including mistakes or lack of knowledge, is subject to public scrutiny. For this reason, the game makes earlier levels easier to play 'solo' and this is always an option for players of any level. There is an advantage to playing in a group, beyond the opportunity to interact with other players in a task-based context, however. As the game manual states, quests available within a given level range are of a different level of difficulty. If the quest title is listed in the log in orange or red type, then it should be undertaken in a group or failure/death is the likely outcome. Such quests offer the greatest rewards in terms of experience and loot, thereby encouraging grouped activity.

The game provides a number of ways for the player to find a group. In the chat window there are different channels dedicated to certain types of player 'speech' (which is typed), one of which is the Looking For Group channel. This can be used to advertise one's services (a player will state which quest they are looking to embark upon) and groups looking for members might also advertise here. Many players with greater experience are often more likely to group with people with whom they have played regularly; reliability and skill being issues of contention at times. Another window can be accessed in the user interface which allows the player to see which 'friends' are online. Most players will add people to the player-generated friends list when they have grouped with another player with whom they feel some form of affinity (often based on being roughly the same level and competency). Most groups quickly disband after completing a task, but not always and longevity may depend on how a group gels socially and/or in terms of success. Some quests and tasks take little time, while others involve a longer time commitment, as is the case when a group undertakes to do an 'instanced dungeon', described by the game manual in these terms: 'once you step through the instance portal, you are taken to a unique version of the dungeon that appears only for you and your adventuring group … this enables groups to play *World of Warcraft* through the most rewarding sections of a dungeon without the intrusion of other players' (*World of Warcraft* 2004: 123–124). It is considered bad etiquette to embark on an instanced dungeon and then leave before the group have completed it (unless explained or pre-warned). As with any social environment, conventions of etiquette are in play; in this case behaviour and speech are policed by Blizzard and by player censure. While the social rules set by Blizzard seek to be unequivocal, player sensibilities inevitably differ, but both are likely to determine in some ways play and inter-player interaction. On the whole, being helpful and polite is likely to make a player more popular with others and therefore help in the acquisition of aid, experience and loot ('grief play' and rudeness are rarely tolerated, likely to push other players into assigning 'ignore' status to such players).

There are also a number of parameters that determine the composition of groups. The maximum number is five (a seemingly arbitrary number but based on balance of play equations) and for optimum results a range of player-character types of a comparable level are required. A healer and a 'tank' (a player-character type with maximised hit-points) are essential if a fairly tough and therefore rewarding task or quest is undertaken. The other group slots can be occupied by a wider range of player-character types; but preferably drawn from casters and hybrids such as paladins or druids (the latter can heal, tank or cast). A group of casters, for example, are less likely to prosper than a well-balanced group in terms of class type. Group play can be extremely rewarding, but when things go awry acrimony can ensue; patience with inexperience and inattention sometimes wears rather thin, especially when the stakes are high. The way such situations are handled differs from one context to another, depending on how well players know one another, what their history is and on personality-based factors. Generally greater tolerance and more deft ways of demonstrating frustration are exhibited in groups where players are more closely bonded.

As well as interactions with others such as trading, 'buffing' (casting beneficial spells on other players), general chat, flirting and banter, the social dimension of the game is given shape by the facility for players to create guilds. The guild system potentially counteracts the more transient nature of passing inter-player interaction and grouped activities and can help to bond players. Guilds have a dedicated chat channel, seen by all members. Some guilds advertise for players to join, particularly in the early stages, often describing their main aims and what they require: guilds with more ambitious aims state the minimum playing time per week for example, while others describe themselves as focused on fun and friendliness. Membership of a guild has the advantage of potentially providing a more stable social experience; often players get to know each other well, even if they have player-characters of widely-spread levels. Members are likely to help each other out, either in tasks, or by donating or passing on objects and providing advice. My own experience of being a member of a guild has been very positive, making game-play more vivid, providing a forum for discussing game tactics and more general friendly chatter, as well as a pool of trusted people with whom to group and raid. Most players are likely to belong to a guild for such reasons. Being a guild member ties the player into a social contract, another dimension within which a balance between agency and determination operates.

One of the significant differences between *EverQuest* and *World of Warcraft* is that in the latter only players of the same faction can belong to a guild, a group or be designated as a friend. It is also the case that speech forms of interaction between opposite factions are limited (each faction speaks a different language, a Night Elf cannot understand the 'say' speech of an Orc for instance, nor can they speak to one another in 'tells'). This makes for some rather creative if somewhat aggressive interactions – 'mooing' at the anthropomorphised bovine Tauren, for example, or using a predefined 'emote' to trigger a non-verbal animated gesture. Such predetermined limitations on inter-faction communication tie into the historical tensions between factions and also encourage players to engage in making honour kills by fighting with players and NPCs of the other faction. Honour points assign staged prefixes to names that operate hierarchically (private, sergeant, knight etc). Players consent to Player vs. Player (PvP) fighting by manual command or by taking an aggressive action. Most NPCs are PvP activated, and guards are favoured targets. However, 'civilian' kills (killing merchants or same faction guards for example) lead to the player accumulating dishonour points. This heightens a sense of contingency and consequence for the player and the deterministic qualities of PvP are obvious, even if we are free to choose not to do it.

PvP can be undertaken in the context of a raid, where groups band together to attack an outpost or town occupied by the opposite faction, or in 'battlegrounds', areas designated for factions to compete in mini-game activities such as 'capture the flag' (a form derived from games designed for smaller LAN groups). It is within raids, PvP or PvE (Player versus the Environment), that player-led game tactics which are likely to increase a sense of player agency come strongly into play. When conducting a PvP raid on territory belonging to another faction, an automatic message is displayed in a localised zone stating that a place is under attack, acting as a call to arms to those players who wish to protect that area. Often such raids will be undertaken in waves; an initial attack followed by withdrawal to regroup, by which time the opposing side has time to gather forces and place various players in strategically advantageous positions (rogues, who can become invisible, might be placed outside the town to pick off healers working from the sidelines of the main action, for example). In other cases, a group of low-level players might taunt and then attack a bunch of higher level opposition players, who do not see hidden from view higher level players who jump in once the skirmish begins.

Raiding can be exhilarating and help forge bonds between players but it can be maddening (less exciting perhaps when you've done PvE raids, for example Molten Core, 30 times). Deaths are frequent, the risks involved create a greater sense of intensity as well as providing visual spectacle through the numbers of players that are often involved (although not quite as spectacular as cinematic battles found in films like *Ran* (Kurosawa, 1985) or *The Lord of the Rings* trilogy (Jackson, 2001, 2002, 2003), but in relation to small group action raids can seem visually impressive). Unlike PvE raids, PvP raids do not lead to more experience points and loot is minimal, as such, most players combine raiding with small group activities and quests. The raid facility might require players to choose to participate, but it is part of the game's text, linked to the fictional-historical context. It potentially offers players a carefully crafted opportunity to regard themselves at the level of make-believe as heroic agents whose deeds will be written into the world's history and to test their skills against other players (often the subject of discussion in chat).

Questing, gathering valuable items, taking part in raids and becoming increasingly efficient agents in the game-world combine the striving to complete set game goals with the opportunity for make-believe and to be playful in a social context; each has a role in creating a greater sense of agency and identity for players within the context of the game. Relationships with other players, whether they are comradely, romantic, cheeky or aggressive, are important factors in increasing the sense of being a social agent in the gameworld. In order to explore more fully what it means to experience acting as a mediated social agent in the game-world entails getting to grips with the complex and dynamic ways in which interpellation and identity operate.

Interpellation/identity

Sherry Turkle (1995), Alec McHoul (1997) and Richard Bartle (2004) argue in, and under, different terms that participation in online communities transforms identity. Turkle claims that the Internet is fundamentally an 'identity technology', providing a space within which it is possible to create and sustain fictional personas and that this tallies with a new and positive definition of identity as fluid and multiple. McHoul takes a more complex philosophically-informed approach, arguing for a state of 'cyberbeing' in which registers of the 'as' and the 'as if' are blurred: 'the cyber's unique equipmentality flick(er)s or hovers between the actual and the virtual, between the "as" and the "as if"' (1997: 5). Both these authors make claims which key into the notion that participation in digital cultures is part of a general 'post-modern' change in the way that identity is defined. Their claims suggest a seismic shift and are focused on broader cultural trends brought about by digital culture rather than on the particularities of playing games. Bartle's claims are made in rather less abstract terms and relate specifically to multiplayer games. He argues that being a participant in an online virtual game-world is at base a form of identity play and that the experience of being immersed in a virtual world hinges on a blurring between the boundaries between character and player: 'the player is the character. You're not role-playing a being, you *are* that being; you're not assuming an identity, you are that identity...' (2004:155–156). As with McHoul, the 'as' and the 'as if' are merged, providing thereby the condition for identity transformation. Bartle stresses the role played by the structured, textual nature of game worlds: 'Virtual worlds, armed with a potent combination of environment and fellow players that's unavailable to other online applications, are able to present people with a stream of challenges; an individual's response to each challenge helps define that individual ... your reactions to these causes you to acquire insights, which in turn lead to minor adjustments in your understanding of yourself (that is, your identity)' (2004: 161). Unlike McHoul and Turkle, he does not claim that there is a profound shift in the way that identity is defined or experienced in a general context, however, but that transformation occurs in the very specific act of playing.

I regard the work of these three authors to be important in beginning the complex task of thinking through the way that 'play' might be conceived of within the specific context of multiplayer online games, particularly those games that utilise a fantasy modality for adventure-based role-playing. I want to test out the claims made by these writers about 'identity play' in relation to my own experience of playing *World of Warcraft*. This comes out of a suspicion that their conception of identity is bound into a desire for identity itself to be more malleable than in fact it is, and that they are co-opting the types of thematic and dramatic transformations to identity upon which a lot of fantasy-based narrative fiction depends. The post-modern conception of identity is indeed very seductive and theatrical; it suggests that we can never know ourselves fully and are in a perpetual state of becoming. In these rhetorical terms, this conception of identity potentially keeps us more interested in ourselves, acting as a kind of narcissistic impetus. But, might it not be the case that identity—the way we regard ourselves as well as how we wish to appear to others – has core features that inform the way we 'play' in a virtual world? I am not suggesting that identity is always fixed or indeed 'hard-wired', but rather that one of the pleasures of playing games such as *World of Warcraft* might be located in the 'shoring up' of a player's existing identity rather than changing it in any profound sense, and that this might work with or against the way the game seeks to interpellate the player. My contention here is that an examination of the interplay between identity, play, the game as structured 'text' and fantasy modality holds the key to understanding massively multiplayer online role-playing games (MMORPGs) as a cultural and social phenomenon. The attraction of the *illusory* notion that we are agents of our own identity keys very neatly into the attraction of role-play, and indeed it might be this that makes games – and MMORPGs in particularly – so very appealing.

Is this enthusiasm just about 'having fun' or is there something more complex and psychologically and culturally potent going on? Games are powerful and deterministic agents, but it is likely that our game personae are in fact extensions of existing characteristics of our identity (some aspects more than others perhaps), and that playing in a socially oriented virtual world like *World of Warcraft* is more likely to reinforce some of the ways we already see and express ourselves. Rather than making fundamental changes to core attributes of identity or facilitating a completely different mode of being, it is far more likely that more subtle changes are in play, particularly given the fact that games like *World of Warcraft* are likely to be played over an extended period with people who we come to know well. Fantasy personas cannot be maintained over an extended period if they diverge too much from real world personas. Aspects of real persona normally inhibited by physical or social limitations when given free rein can *appear* to make a change to identity, as an act of play or otherwise.

Assessing what impact playing a social and fantasy-based game like *World of Warcraft* has on personal identity is not easy, particularly as identity is performative and has playful aspects. As well as personal differences in taste and investments in particular cultural artefacts, awareness of changes to identity can be somewhat allusive. Identity is a complex thing; small subtle changes occur in response to a gamut of factors, with the occasional bigger change. Within a psychoanalytic model of the psyche, identity is not at base a stable construct, even though it is experienced mainly as such. Jacques Lacan, for example, claims that the sense of being unified is an illusion that protects against psychological fragmentation and alienation. Identity, as an expression of the 'I', is *apparently* coherent but is composed of fragments, projections and introjections, bound together by a necessary fiction of unity (Lacan 1989). Text-based introjections of an ideal kind are also likely to prop up our desire for agency (which may in part explain the 'magical' appeal of fantasy role-play), even where they conflict with real conditions (indeed role-play might be seen as a response to the limitations and determinisms of such). While it is attractive to conceive identity as a highly protean entity, it is nonetheless the case that many of us experience certain roles imposed upon us that clash with the way we regard ourselves. This suggests that at least some aspects of identity are not quite as malleable as post-modern and some psychoanalytic accounts construe. What we choose to consume in conspicuous ways is often a means of expressing and reinforcing existing identity with its concomitant tastes; this applies to the games we buy and play for any length of time.

In my case, playing *World of Warcraft* feeds into things that I regard as core to my identity, which pre-existed entry into the game. I have a strong investment in fantasy media, magic and game design, as well as enjoying role playing strong, adventurous, female characters. These factors informed my initial purchase of the game, as it did with other games that I played for any length of time, such as *Buffy the Vampire Slayer*, *Primal*, *American McGee's Alice* and *EverQuest*. In most of these games magic is deeply tied to agency and determination, which in turn tie into the games' thematic and gendered concerns. The video footage used to market *World of Warcraft* showed a female Night-Elf druid transforming in mid-run into a black panther – the particular qualities of movement and image of which I found captivating. As Louis Althusser suggests, the process of successful interpellation into an imaginary frameworks rests on calling ('hailing' as it is translated) to us in personal terms (2001: 115); if we are to be drawn in then we must be made to feel that what we are offered is important to us in some way, which presupposes an identity. Games do this by using various codes and conventions that seek to speak to aspects of that identity (which extends into the types and expressions of agency – real or in fantasy – that we are inclined toward). Obviously not everyone is called to the game in the same way as myself, although the use of certain player-character names that relate to other magic-based texts suggest that I am not alone (names, whether intertextually derived or not, often speak not just of character but also often signal aspects of a player's identity). Those people who do not have a personal investment in fantasy rhetorics are unlikely to find a game like *World of Warcraft* attractive (the gap between existing identity and the identities offered by the game is too wide). It is, however, clearly not the case that those of us who are 'called' by the game believe it is real (as Althusser argues is the case with ideology). The attraction of *fantasy* is that it is precisely not real; its pleasures rest on fantasy *as* fantasy. It offers the scope to play at being something we are not (quite), be something that we cannot easily be in real life, something we would not wish to be in real life perhaps, *but* what we chose to play at being, our willingness to buy into certain commercial fantasies, is nonetheless embedded in our sense of who we are. If a role-playing game does not accommodate this then it is unlikely that we will play for very long.

Althusser's concept is useful because it enables us to talk about the way that a game-text constitutes us as players, as game agents and game subjects, as an effect of the game's structure and its sometimes abrasive relationship to the identities we bring with us to a game. This relationship can be seen in the following example. *World of Warcraft* assigns titles derived from the conventional army as a 'reward' for honour kills; my name currently appears on screen to other players as Private Sorelcei. This addition to my self-generated name I experience as a horrible intrusion of real life army nomenclature on the 'fantasy' nature of the game and I regard it as galling that the game 'text' interferes with the way I use my character and her name to express to other players something of my identity. What this example demonstrates is that we bring ourselves to a game and that game designers need to be sensitive to the fact that many players use role-playing in a social context as a way of expressing aspects of their real-life identity (this raises some sticky questions around gender and the way it is figured representationally in games, but I do not have the space to explore these here).

World of Warcraft offers three different types of servers ('normal' (PvE), 'PvP' and 'RP (role-play)'). Each accommodates and encourages different game-play styles: the RP servers, in particular, promote greater depth of identity play (even if role-play goes unrewarded by the game in any direct way). It is expected that those playing on the RP servers will adopt more pervasively the speech and behaviours associated with the character played. The nature of general chat is quite different to that of 'normal' servers, with far less non-game related conversation. By contrast, on the normal servers, in-guild and in-game chat is frequently unrelated to the game. When playing on the normal server, when I ask how another player is I am asking the player and not the character, although they are related in some way in the act of choosing and playing character. Even playing on the RP server, the type of role-play engaged in is based on aspects of identity that already exist, albeit mediated through fantasy-style rhetorics. Within my 'main' player-character's guild, sited on the normal server, chat is divided between that which is related to game tasks and more general things pertaining to real life; discussions about the impact of game design and upgrades are also common and rapid shifts between referential registers occur frequently. The nature of in-guild chat does depend on the 'culture' of a given guild; some guilds reserve the guild-chat for more game related tasks, for example. In the guild chat to which my main player-character belongs, conversation is largely spoken from the position of real-life identity, rather than character identity, yet too much personal speech is often policed in subtle and not-so-subtle terms (requests to shift to whisper mode perhaps). It is also apparent that players within this guild tend to use their game characters as agents for expressing their real-life characters; this may be affected by the fact that many of us know each other in a real-life context, however.

Players who stay with the game for any length of time invest in it a great deal of time, money, desire and emotion. The game, therefore, clearly offers for some a powerful experience. Identity play is only one aspect, however, and for many it tends to tail off after a while as it is harder to maintain the more you play. Transformational elements do not simply operate in terms of identity play; becoming more skilled at playing the game, making for a greater sense of agency and acting as an *apparent* foil to the forces of determination, is also a form of pleasure-generating transformation. In my experience most players play regularly because they have become competent and skilful, enjoy the game's high fantasy milieu and have forged meaningful relationships with others. These aspects may well affect some transformation in the way we regard ourselves and the way others regard us, but what is more important is whether one regards being a gamer as core to one's identity rather than playing a given character, particularly when character choice is already an expression of one's existing identity. Becoming a competent player, for example, may compensate for real-life difficulties, but this is grounded in the ways that players make use of material that they bring to the game. Games can and do facilitate what appear to be transformatory experiences, but I am not convinced that identity play promotes any significant shift in core aspects of one's identity. Indeed because identity is in itself operational in the registers of both the imaginary and the real, the textual and the performative, it could be said to already exist between the 'as' and the 'as if'; *World of Warcraft* works with this rather than creating it. Given that the game plays artfully with a dynamic between agency and determination it is therefore inevitable that existing aspects of identity, which are embedded in broader currents of agency and determination, come into play and operate as textual themes; these aspects should therefore be regarded as core to the experience of playing a game like *World of Warcraft*.

Works cited

Althusser, Louis (2001) *Lenin and Philosophy and Other Essays*, New York: Monthly Review Press.

Bartle, Richard (2004) *Designing Virtual World*, Indianapolis: New Riders.

Benjamin, Walter (2003) *The Origin of German Tragic Drama*, trans. John Osborne, London: Verso.

Eco, Umberto (1986) *Travels in Hyperreality: Essays*, London: Picador.

Jakobsson, Mikael and T.L. Taylor (2003) *The Sopranos meets EverQuest: Social Networking in Massively Multiplayer Online Games*, Melbourne DAC – the 5th International Digital Arts and Culture Conference, School of Applied Communication, Melbourne, http://hypertext.rmit.edi.ac/dac/papers/index.html, accessed 18 May 2005.

King, Geoff and Tanya Krzywinska (2006) *Tomb Raiders and Space Invaders: Videogame Forms and Contexts*, London: I.B. Tauris.

Kolo, Castulus and Timo Baur (2004) 'Living a Virtual Life: Social Dynamics of Online Gaming', *Game Studies*, November 2004, www.gamestudies.org/0401/kolo/, accessed 18 March 2005.

Lacan, Jacques (1989) 'The mirror stage as formative of the function of the I as revealed in psychoanalytic experience', in *Ecrits: a selection*, London, Tavistock/Routledge.

Martin, George R.R. (2001) *Introduction* in Karen Haber (ed.) *Meditations on Middle-Earth*, London: St. Martin's Press.

McHoul, Alec (1997) *Cyberbeing and ~space*, available at www.mcc.murdoch.edu.au/ReadingRoom/VID/cybersein.html, accessed 21 March 2005.

Stern, Eddo (2002) *A Touch of Medieval: Narrative, Magic and Computer Technology in Massively Multiplayer Computer Role-Playing Games*, in Frans Mäyrä (ed.) *Computer Games and Digital Cultures: Conference Proceedings*; Studies in Information Science 1, Tampere, Finland: Tampere University Press.

Turkle, Sherry (1995) *Life on the Screen: Identity in the Age of the Internet*, New York: Simon and Schuster.

Games

American McGee's Alice (2000), Rogue, Electronic Arts.
Buffy the Vampire Slayer (2002), The Collective, Electronic Arts.
EverQuest (1999–), Sony Online Entertainment.
Primal (2003), SCEE/SCEA.
Ultima Online (1997–), Electronic Arts.
Warcraft 3 (2002), Blizzard.
World of Warcraft (2004–), Blizzard.

Notes

1 See Richard Bartle (2004) for a succinct and authoritative 'history' of the development and industrial context of online games.
2 'Fantastic Neo-medievalism' is the term used by Umberto Eco to describe the ways in which many forms of popular culture 'dream the Middle Ages' (Eco 1986: 64).
3 For more on functional realism see King and Krzywinska (2006: 143–152).

7

Female *Quake* players and the politics of identity

Helen W. Kennedy

This chapter considers the ways in which female *Quake* players and female *Quake* clans have developed and enunciated a particular gaming identity and technical competence within a gaming culture that is heavily coded as masculine. Videogame and computer game play *and* the cultures that have emerged around these practices in the form of web pages, websites and other means of supporting and displaying playing preferences and practices are a critical site for both the development and display of technological prowess and virtuosity. It is also clear that technical competence is a key marker for gender differentiation in a culture that increasingly privileges a playful relationship with technology. Analyses of games and gaming practices such as those which surround *Quake* – the practice of 'skinning' which is enabled through the sharing of software to produce your own 'in game' persona; the formation of clans to compete with others in multiplayer versions of the game; the creation of web pages and web rings to support and maintain the clan communities – provide rich material for examining the relationship between technological competence, gender identity and play.

These female clans and individual players are knowingly engaged in a form of gender play and technoplay which operates counter to dominant notions of femininity, female play preferences, play styles and technical prowess. Furthermore, through their clan memberships the players form strong social bonds which enable the affirmation and articulation of an individual and collective identity based on technicity,[1] pleasure and gender insubordination. A feminist perspective developed from the work of Donna Haraway and Judith Butler, alongside theories drawn from play and performance studies, is used to examine the ways in which the identities that are articulated through these online sites are both a reflection of their liminality within the dominant gaming culture and an active attempt to carve out a space for a specific female gaming subjectivity within this apparently hostile and excluding context.

There have been relatively few explicitly feminist analyses of popular videogame or computer game playing as a cultural practice and very few which engage positively with existing female players, their pleasures and their communities. The Cassell and Jenkins edited collection *From Barbie to Mortal Kombat* (1999) is still the only volume focusing on the issue of gender and computer game culture and largely deals with the issues of how to make *better* games for girls and how to improve female access to game playing rather than engaging with the games and players that already exist (or existed then). T.L. Taylor's (1999, 2003) research into female players of the highly popular massively multiplayer online role playing game (MMORPG) *Everquest* is a significant exception to this general tendency. The feminist response to female players of first person shooter games (FPS) has been either to condemn them for their adoption of masculine values (as evidenced by bell hooks (Marriott 2003)) or to largely dismiss these players as of little interest to feminism and to privilege instead the creative practices of female game artists (Flanagan 2003). However, by locating these female play practices within a technofeminist framework and by drawing on play and performance theory it is possible to see that computer games can afford many moments of the creation of oppositional meanings and further can allow for the elaboration of an oppositional identity.

In the discussion that follows I will be drawing from a case study focusing on the consumption and production practices of individual female *Quake* players, female *Quake*-playing clans, and the ways in which they have separately and collectively represented themselves to the rest of the online game-playing community that has formed around *Quake*. This case study is part of an ongoing study of female game players and the communities which have developed through their play and play related practices. Here I will be drawing from the online material produced by individual players and particular play communities (web pages, web sites and other more specifically game-related creative practices) and interviews and correspondence with individual players. This research began in 2000 and the interviews were conducted over an 18-month period between 2001 and 2003 during which time I also learnt to play the games in single player mode and played with other female players online. I also draw from earlier online archive material on specific female gamer websites such as www.grrlgamer.com. Firstly, however, it is necessary to sketch out the specific context of these practices in order to better understand the ways in which these players and producers are required to negotiate and subvert particular meanings around appropriate feminine behaviour and appropriate feminine pleasures.

Quake (and its sequels) is an enduringly popular example of the 3D first person shooter genre, making use of an innovative game engine which offered new possibilities in terms of the 3D representation space of the game and the speed of gameplay. *Quake* also offered multiplayer capabilities and eventually the possibility for it to be played online via dedicated game servers[2] *Quake* was initially released on 24 June 1996 as a shareware version with the release of the official version following a few months later in August. The shareware ethos and the possibility of making changes to the game allowed fans access to the production and distribution of new game content for others to share (this process is know as modding – short for 'modifying') and in the process spawned an online community based around these practices.[3] These fan activities have also enabled new forms of relationship between producers and consumers where power relationships between them may become less fixed, less predictable and less easy to control.

These factors have allowed for the emergence of highly *visible* participatory cultures where there is a collapse of distinction between the dominant culture (the games industry) and the subculture (games players and modders) not typically associated with cinema-going or television viewing (Giddings and Kennedy 2006a). There are two critical aspects of this fan/subcultural activity which are important for the discussion of female *Quake* players that follows – shareware has also been a cultural driver in so far as it facilitates the display and delight in technical virtuosity that characterises and maintains certain sub-cultures which are often predominantly male. Technical expertise provides the means of exchange in communities of expert consumers, hackers and modders which are usually highly gendered. The oppositional force of the examples which are to be discussed here derive precisely from the fact that female players have often been entirely excluded from the communities that form around these practices.

Frag everything that isn't you

To play a computer game you have to master the interface in order to engage with the game at any level, from loading the game through to making the settings suit your play style. This means that a very basic level you have to be able to make use of a mouse and operate a keyboard simultaneously – these games require that you are adept at the handling of these controls and are incredibly unforgiving of the absolute novice. The moment that you click the mouse to signal your readiness for play you are immediately thrown into a noisy, chaotic, confusing 3D environment filled with computer generated characters whose sole function is to destroy your avatar as quickly and as efficiently as possible – even on the easiest setting in the game (there are several levels of difficulty available ranging from the novice 'I Can Win', through 'Hardcore' to the hardest level 'Nightmare!') the speed and pace of the game has to be adapted to very quickly in order to make any progress. This description provided by one female player neatly captures some of this complexity:

> you have to be able to use the mouse for more than just point and click you have to sort of be able to use it around in space which is a bit different and its easy to end up looking at the ceiling or getting stuck in corners and becoming frag bait. Oh, yeah, and your left and right hands are doing totally different things, you've got to really know where all the keys are ... at first I couldn't get it all sorted out, changing weapons, jumping, moving around and shooting it was all a bit much and my mouse hand would be doing one thing and I'd have to look at the keyboard to try and find the right keys ... then after a while it all sort of clicks and you're just staring at the screen and your hands are going like crazy and you just sort of do it all on automatic and you feel like its you in there, sneaking round corners and fragging that poor little eyeball on legs to bits ... (Interview with author, Xena, *Quake Interviews*, December 2001)

This extends to the processes of modification which will require some facility with operating sub-programs, understanding game code and operating graphics packages. Even without engaging in modding practices, in order to play online you will have to be able to navigate through the web to find a server and choose a level to play that is active, each step requiring you to operate the computer with some skill and proficiency.

The complex technical, legal and cultural interplay between players, player/creators and developers is wonderfully exemplified by Sue Morris's account of the steps she goes through to play *Quake III: Arena*. (Morris 2003). The Gamespy server which she uses to access the game engine was originally developed by Joe Powell, a *Quake* gamer, but is now a commercial portal, using voice software developed by gamers using venture capital. The latest update is downloaded from another portal developed by gamers in 1996 to organise LAN tournaments, in turn this update includes anti-cheat software originally developed by a team of gamers but now commercially deployed by a range of online game companies. Morris then finds a local server running games that may either be commercial or enthusiast-run, there she can choose from any one of 1600 player-created environments made for *Quake*

III: Arena. Once there again she may choose to play as a ready-made avatar or choose a skin made by another gamer or indeed by herself. Before play commences she will choose customised configurations for her machine that 'optimise the game's performance and appearance to my liking'; these configurations might be unique to her or learnt from online player community forums.

> In a multiplayer FPS game such as *Quake III: Arena*, the 'game' is not just a commercially released program that players use, but an assemblage created by a complex fusion of the creative efforts of a large number of individuals, both professional and amateur, facilitated by communication and distribution systems that have developed out of the gaming community itself. As a cocreative media form, multiplayer FPS gaming has introduced new forms of participation, which have led to the formation of community structures and practices that are changing the way in which these games are developed and played. (Morris 2003)

This assertion of games as 'cocreative' is a critical one and Morris's account here helps to underscore the complexity of these processes as engagement with different kinds of technology (hardware and software). Morris also draws attention to the formation of community structures and practices around the preferences that develop through these activities.

Gameplay as masculine technoplay

Game design, content, packaging and marketing all serve to demarcate games playing as a specifically masculine activity. This remains as true today as it was in the early 1980s and this is despite the numerous attempts, both commercially and politically motivated, to undermine this notion. Brenda Laurel is one of the few female games designers to be recognized in the wider culture and she was one of the key players in the games for girls movement. Laurel confirms this gendered lineage of the computer game and computer game culture:

> Computer games as we know them were invented by young men around the time of the invention of graphical displays. They were enjoyed by young men, and young men soon made a very profitable business of them, dovetailing to a certain extent with the existing pinball business. Arcade computer games were sold into male-gendered spaces, and when home computer consoles were invented, they were sold through male-oriented consumer electronics channels to more young men. The whole industry consolidated very quickly around a young male demographic –

all the way from the gameplay design to the arcade environment to the retail world. (Laurel 1998)

The majority of research and writing around female computer game players has to date tended to suggest that there exists a 'feminine' set of computer game pleasures and preferences – something which is vehemently resisted by many female players:

> I keep reading about articles and studies where experts say girls don't like shooting and blasting games but instead prefer quiet, contemplative games with well-rounded characters and storylines that stimulate their imagination. I'd venture to say, however, that these studies are a reflection of how we condition girls to be passive. The image of a woman with a gun is too shocking, too disruptive and threatening to the male dominant order of things. (Aliza Sherman aka Cybergrrrl) (Cassell and Jenkins 1998: 335)

'The notion that some forms of activity and entertainment are more appropriate to men and some to women, that some genres can be called "masculine" whilst others are labelled "feminine", has a long history.' (Tasker 1993: 136) Whatever the intention, these studies of 'feminine' play styles and play preferences contribute to the construction of appropriate feminine tastes and behaviours that cannot help but inform the ways individuals understand their preferences as either 'normal' or 'abnormal'. Female *Quake* players have to live with and reconcile the fact that their pleasures have been deemed unfeminine and inappropriate. The players themselves are quick to articulate a critique of normative femininity: 'People say it's not ladylike to sit in front of a computer or want to play a game where you run around with a shotgun, but why not? I get insulted a lot and told I'm like a boy, but I'm not. I'm just a different kind of girl' (Stephanie Bergman, *Quake Interviews*, January 2002).

Gameplay as cybernetic

Videogame play works through feedback between user, hardware and software. It has been argued that the circuit of game and player in the act of playing is literally (for the duration of the game at least) cybernetic. In one of the most influential works on computer games Aarseth makes two critical points which enable us to understand the game as cybernetic. The first is to offer a conceptualization of early text based adventure games (which remains analytically useful in relation to all videogames and computer games in general) as machines:

> the text is seen as a machine – not metaphorically but as a mechanical device for the production and consumption of verbal signs. Just as a film is useless without a projector and a screen, so a text must consist of a material medium as well as a collection of words. The machine, of course, is not complete without a third party, the (human) operator, and it is within this triad that the text takes place. (Aarseth 1997: 21)

The second critical point is that this relationship between text/machine and user/player is cybernetic:

> Cybertext ... is the wide range (or perspective) of possible textualities seen as a typology of machines, as various kinds of literary communication systems where the functional differences among the mechanical parts play a defining role in determining the aesthetic process ... cybertext shifts the focus from the traditional threesome of author/sender, text/ message, and reader/receiver to the cybernetic intercourse between the various part(icipant)s in the textual machine. (Aarseth 1997: 22)

This understanding of gameplay as a cybernetic loop in which player and game are inseparable for the duration of the game is a compelling literalization of the ontology of the cyborg – a subjectivity that depends precisely on this collapse of boundary between the human and the machine. This notion of player as cyborg has taken root in many of the most recent articulations of player subjectivity but has also been present in some of the earliest work on computers generally and computer games specifically. (Lister et al. 2003; Lahti 2003; Giddings and Kennedy 2006). In the lived enactment of gameplay there is no player separate to the interface and game world, there is a fusion of the two into a cyborgian subjectivity – composed of wires, machines, code and flesh. For the duration of the gameplay 'a new physiological entity is thus constructed from this network of organic and technological parts' (Lister et al. 2003: 374) which although temporary is a meaningful embodied experience.

By understanding gameplay as cybernetic, issues of interactivity and player agency are recast in terms of networks and flows of energy which are entirely interdependent:

> we do not see here two complete and sealed-off entities: the player on the one hand and the game on the other. Rather there is an interchange of information and energy, forming a new circuit ... Through the tactile and visual interface with the machine, the entire body is determined to move by being part of the circuit of the game, being, as it were, *in the loop* (Lister et al. 2003: 370)

The cybernetic nature of gameplay and the interdependency of game and player is perhaps the feature that distinguishes gameplay most clearly from other kinds of textual consumption or play. Videogames and computer games produce the gameplayer *as* cyborg. This 'new physiological' entity – avatar, machine and player – 'a wholly constructed creature composed of biological and technological components is exactly what we mean by the cyborg' (Lister et al. 2003: 375). For Haraway (1991), the cyborg is a means of conceptualizing subjectivity which disrupts the myth of the concrete stable and boundaried subject of the Enlightenment tradition; we see this cast in light of the dissolution of the boundary between player and game – in gameplay there is only player *and* game inseparable and irreducible.

The complexity of the circuit of machines, code and bodies is further increased when engaging in multiplayer games whether console based or online. Playing *Quake* as a clan in multiplayer mode with shared skins developed to provide a collective in-game identity or collectively working together on a quest in *Everquest* are compelling examples of the cybernetic circuit described above. The complexity of this human/machine circuit is startling; the individual players respond to each others' actions within the game and the process of feedback through which play advances. These instantiations of gameplay invoke Haraway's (1991) notion of 'networked and collective selves' (this notion has been taken up by many feminists working specifically in the area of cyberculture – most notably Plant (1993a), an idea she offers in recognition of affiliation and collective identity developed through technological circuits). During the gameplay there is no separation of individuals and machines but only a collective process of engagement where action and reaction flow in a circuit of technologized bodies and their pleasures.

Cyborgian pleasures

Playing *Quake* is therefore a means for displaying or performing technological competence and a form of technological embodiment but is also the means through which technological competence can develop further *beyond* the game itself, as we shall see. When describing what they enjoy about *Quake*, female players (both those who have participated directly in my own research and those who have posted online) use terms such as 'athleticism', 'balance', 'coordination' and 'taking risks' in such a way as to suggest that the cyborgian nature of gameplay is experienced as a set of embodied pleasures. Although it is the avatar that performs these feats of athleticism or coordination within the game space, it is the player's skill in controlling the interface that shapes this performance. The dizzy pleasures of FPS gameplay – the racing pulse, sweating palms, the adrenalin rush and the feeling of exhaustion all suggest a set of pleasures associated with movement, abandonment and risk. The sense of agency the (competent) player experiences is doubled; the player experiences a freedom of movement and sense of authority and mastery within the game alongside a sense of empowerment through their skill in mastering the technology. These two responses indicate the double nature of their pleasure:

> I really like the way the other bots in the game respond to how well you are doing – they get really narked if you win and say things like 'lets all gang up and kill "tankgirl" next time' or the machine says 'excellent' when you frag a couple of bots in a row. I know it sounds a bit, I don't know, but it makes me feel really good and I feel like I'm really there. (, tankgirl, interview with author)

> I loved the challenge with Hunter – she's so beautiful, and she says all this sort of spiritual stuff and she's really hard to beat one on one and I felt really proud when I won when playing on 'hurt me plenty' mode which is quite hard. (supergirl, interview with author)

In my own play I have taken perverse pleasure in the practice of 'camping' in a safe place and using a powerful weapon to pick off the NPCs without fear of being fragged myself. I have enjoyed observing how the NPCs articulate a disapprobrium at my behaviour in the textual version of 'their' speech. Camping in this way was also the means through which I experienced my first 'Perfect' when playing *Quake III* – 20 NPC kills without dying myself. These examples also demonstrate the delightful confusion and ambiguity of our relationships with these *other* participants – how we assign intention and emotion to characters that are wholly computer generated.[4]

Many of these women have articulated a strong sense of pleasure in surprising male players with their competence and skill when playing online or over LAN (local area networks such as those found in Internet cafes) connections. They are aware that they are not expected to be good at these games and gain enormous satisfaction in flouting convention. In this typical response, the player has first encountered *Quake* with a group of male friends at a cybercafe, become hooked, bought the game to practice at home and then subsequently had the opportunity to play against the same group of male players. 'Next time we played together over a lan connection I held up my end and I could see that the blokes were really surprised and even a bit fed up that I was "fragging" them so successfully … I LOVED IT!' (Amanda/ Xena *Quake Interviews*, November 2001). These female players – who take pleasure in the mastery of a game which is seen as requiring skills which are clearly demarcated as masculine – are aware of the transgressive nature of their pleasure.

The figure of the cyborg as developed by Haraway (1990) offered us the idea that our new intimate connection with machines could create a space for identity affiliation and agency which would destabilize conventional relationships between body, machine and nature, challenging the 'command, control and conquer' logic of state/corporate digital domination. Instead of critiquing technology solely on the basis of its embeddedness in both a colonialist, teleological and capitalist set of processes, the dawning of the cyber age was met with a sense of new opportunities – the figure of the cyborg was offered by Haraway as a way to move beyond the potentially essentializing association of women with nature. Haraway offered the cyborg as a new metaphor for subjectivity which could potentially avoid the problematic binaries which pervade around nature/culture, male/female. In doing so she promoted the cyborg as a 'site of possible resignifications ... to expand the possibilities [of subjectivity] ... to enable an enhanced sense of agency' (Butler 1992: 16). Crucial to this new sense of agency was a rally call for those who were deemed to be marginalized by technoculture to embrace their affinity with technology and to offer new symbols, new uses and practices through which to 'code' this new subjectivity. Female *Quake* players, their creative practices and the community they have developed should be understood to be relevant to a technofeminist agenda that seeks to offer both new images of technologised embodiment *and* to foster an active engagement with technology amongst women. Haraway argues that 'Cyborg imagery can suggest a way out of the maze of dualisms in which we have explained our bodies and our tools to ourselves ... [and provide] a powerful infidel heteroglossia. It is an imagination of a feminist speaking in tongues to strike fear ... It means both building and destroying machines, identities, categories, relationships, spaces, stories' (1990: 223).

Skinning and pimping – from player to creator

> Skinning is the art of creating the images that get wrapped around 3D player character models in 3D games. These images are what give the 'mesh' a solid, realistic look. A good analogy is if you think of the skin as the paper that goes around the bamboo frame (mesh) of a chinese lantern. You paint what you want on the paper and the game wraps it around the frame for you based on the mapping the model has with it. (Chiq/Milla, female *Quake* player and skin artist, www.chiq.net)[5]

A particularly adept skinner may eventually see her skin being included in the range of characters on offer to other players through online communities and may receive prizes and acclaim for their art (http://www.planet quake.com/polycount is a site that monitors and nominates particular skins as well as providing guides and downloads of recommended skins and mods). Skinning is not an easy process – some taking as much as 60 hours to complete – like other art forms it is a process requiring a great deal of commitment and engagement. Camilla Bennett is a skin artist whose consumption/play practices have developed into more professional/creative activities.[6] A self-taught skinner since 2000, Milla has developed a high degree of competence and has moved on from designing her own skins to a professional role as a texture artist in the development of the skin for the heroine of Betty Bad (WildTangent) a web-based game, developed skins for *Unreal Tournament* and produced artwork for the company Liquid Development. Milla has also won a number of awards for her skins, and features prominently on the key web site which operates as a trading post for 'skinners' and players (Polycount). Milla also operates as a role-model for other female *Quake* players:

> I found this one skin artist 'Milla' and I thought – 'I want to do that'. Her website is the most beautiful and has this lovely front page with this line 'skin is armor' which I just loved I don't know why and she's really doing stuff and even getting awards and things for her skins. I like spent ages following all the links and there was like this whole community out there of other women producing really great images … and I followed up all the links on the *Quake* sites and taught myself how to download different 'skins' for me to play around with and I even tried to make some of my own – not successfully though … (buff-e-girl, *Quake Interviews*, January 2002)

This player is just one example among many for whom their gameplay becomes the jumping-off point for a greater engagement with technology in general:

> It really made me want to learn a how to use graphics on the computer – I had never thought that I could or that I would ever be interest[ed], I'd done some online chatting, used the computer for emails and played some free web games and stuff but I had [not] thought of myself as any good with computers … A friend is teaching me how to use Photoshop on his computer and when I'm okay I'm going to try to do a really good skin and stick it up on the web. (supergirl, *Quake Interviews*, December 2001)

Chiq/Milla describes her own personal skin: 'Woodswoman/warrior in a post-apocalyptic context. She's flaking rust, greasy and has these damn pesky hoverblades stuck to her feet.' The imagery used draws heavily from fantasy/ science fiction as well as closely resembling the type of female subject that often crops up in feminist cyberpunk literature. 'Female skinners sample elements from the pre-existing female character lexicon and add new flavours into the mix, resulting in fem monsters better suited to their female inhabitants' (Schleiner 1999). These fantasy constructions of identity offer an exploration of alternative subjectivities in which being feminine does not necessarily equal being a victim or needing rescuing.

Producing skins for their own use or to 'pimp' out to others allows players to engage in the production of images and symbols through which to articulate their own identity, tastes and agency. The skins often become the means through which a player will express aspects of their identity to other members of the community either through its inclusion in a web page or during online tournaments. The material produced through these practices become resources for other players who are either entering the world of online gameplay or seeking evidence that they are not alone in their play preferences.

In her feminist analysis of women's leisure Betsy Wearing has drawn on Foucault's notion of heterotopias: '[i]n contrast to "utopias" which are fictional critiques of society, without any actual locality, "heterotopias" for Foucault can be 'real' existing places of difference which act as counter-sites or compensatory sites to those of everday activity' (1998: 146). Wearing argues the importance of these 'counter-sites' as a means of experiencing alternative subjectivities and forms of self-empowerment not readily available in other aspects of daily experience and they 'provide spaces for rewriting the script of what it is to be a woman, beyond definitions provided by powerful males and the discourses propagated as truth in contemporary societies' (1998: 147). The creative practices which surround this playful consumption allow for gender play as these gamers explore aspects of their identity which are not recognized or legitimated in other contexts. The requirement for technological competence which is so central to these activities can lead to enhanced employment prospects (as exemplified in Camilla Bennett) but can also lead to more general forms of reward and acclaim in the larger community of players.

Female *Quake* communities

The online capability of these games has allowed for the emergence of 'clans' (teams of players who compete against other teams in tournaments) who may also develop their own particular clan 'skins'.[7] A number of communities have formed through these play practices – some are clan specific, while others are more open.[8] 'Network shooters like *Quake* and *Unreal* enable social grouping into clans that coalesce both locally among friends, workers and family, and also long distance over the Internet. The female clan offers a powerful support structure to female gamers, a place where knowledge can be shared and friendship bonds strengthened that extend outside the scope of the game' (Schleiner 1999). This is particularly significant in relation to the 'offline' representations and constructions of game culture, whether this is television programmes that may feature a female presenter but clearly address a male audience, or in the numerous magazines – official and unofficial – which through their style, layout, content and tone indicate their address directly to a male (and frequently adolescent) audience. Scantily clad female bodies are used in advertising promotions for many games; games industry gatherings feature a preponderance of 'booth babes' who are there to entice the 'putatively' male professional (developer, designers, writers, reviewers). As a financially significant player in popular culture, videogames and computer games remain the most resolutely sexist in their advertising, marketing and promotions. Yet in the heterotopic world of online game culture, female gamers and game reviewers have found a context which enables them to enunciate their identity, declare their existence and to find others of their kind. Through the creation of web pages, web sites, and web rings these women are able to recognize and affirm each other's identity as 'gamer' in opposition to an offline context where they are invisible, marginalized and frequently demeaned. This is of particular significance to players who may feel isolated as a female:

> I was the only female I knew who played and then one day I went on the web and discovered all these sites and women and art and chat about games and I just thought 'wow' – there weren't just loads of other women out there playing *Quake* but they were making stuff with the game as well, new 'skins' for the female game characters, sharing them out with other women and even playing together online in what they called 'clans'.
> (Xena, *Quake Interviews*, November 2001)

The female *Quake* playing community demonstrates a playful use of names to demarcate a specifically oppositional female identity within the online community. This is true both of the naming of individuals and the naming of clans or communities such as Chiq, Hellchick, Supergirl, Geekgirl, Clan PMS (Psycho Men Slayers), Da Valkyries: The Women of Quake, Clan Crack Whore, Nimble Little Minxes, The Coven and Hell's Warehouse. The names appropriate female subjectivities and identities that are drawn from real or mythical monstrous female identities (these names are also evocative of the kinds of radical feminist re/mis-appropriation of previously pejorative terms). In doing so they demonstrate their perception of themselves as countering hegemonic representations of femininity as well as the masculine representation of games culture and games players in general. Female *Quake* playing personae are chimeric, cyborgian and disruptive, they appropriate the demarcation of the female body as always already monstrous and redeploy these images as a 'tactical assault' on the normative construction of this identity. The images and names clearly draw from a long history of transgressive feminist informed femininity countering notions of femininity as passive or nurturing. By foregrounding both their 'femaleness' and their skill in the game they offer a different set of meanings to computers, computer games and technological competence. By bringing their own bodies or their fantasized bodies to the play arena they disrupt the assumption of a white male heterosexual player and avatar. They also problematize the dominant image of games playing as a masculine retreat from the 'feminized' body and make the female body figure as an agentic force in this relationship with technology. In doing so they offer compelling representations of cyborg subjectivity.

> Lethal female body architecture, deft combat moves and an organized female affront in the form of female gamer clans are shifting the gender topography of the shooter. Working the keyboard and mouse behind these female fighting machines are the women players who have dared to cross a rigid gender boundary into a violent gamer culture often understood by men and women alike as a boys' world, (embraced by men affirmatively, often disparaged by women). (Schleiner 1999)

This celebration and reappropriation of the monstrous feminine cannot be dismissed as simply 'aping' masculinity – as already suggested their performance of skills which have been deemed masculine can be read as undermining the assumption of a 'male body' as the site of these competences (Butler 1992).

These personae and the interventions made through the female gaming websites cannot be considered other than as a response to the very particular context in which there exists a dominant discourse within which their voice is largely silent or absent. 'Any voice within a community is heteroglossic, combining others' voices in individualized ways. In so doing, speakers position themselves relative to other voices in their communities.' (Bakhtin in Morris1994: 89.) Nancy Baym in her analysis of online fan practices also draws on Bakhtin to suggest that individuality 'gets defined in and by the effects of appropriating, transforming and resisting particular discursive practices in particular ways' (Baym 2000: 182). Nikki Douglas here takes direct issue with the statements made about gendered pleasure; she is responding to the claim that *Quake* and other action games are good for male players as they are a means of relieving stress: 'Lord knows we, as women, don't need to relieve stress. We just go shopping or eat or color code our underwear drawers, right? And I want all my gaming to be … just like my life is, not some escape. Oh, no, why would I want to temporarily escape all the stress and problem solving that I'm faced with every day? Why would I just once like to answer some insipid question like "I thought you were going to make dinner?" with a spray of automatic gunfire? There's your dinner, baby!' (Douglas in Cassell and Jenkins 1998: 293)

Feminism *in* and *at* play in female games culture

As well as challenging dominant notions around appropriate feminine behaviour, pleasures and competences, the female *Quake* playing community has also provided the means and support through which to contest and critique sexist behaviour amongst players and discussion list contributors. In 1998 a 'green ribbon campaign' was launched in response to the harassment experienced by a British female player known in the community as Hellkitten. Images that she had posted on her website were hacked and altered to include pornographic imagery to the dismay of many within the community. The campaign involved displaying modified (and green) version of the *Quake* logo on web pages and web sites as a symbol of support for both the individual victim of this attack and as support for tolerance and respect amongst players. The campaign served to raise awareness of the frequency of online harassment and its damaging consequences for players and for the community.[9] The campaign was not accepted wholehearted by all of the community, however, and it became a particular site of vociferous and visible contestation of dominant but unspoken ideas about gender and games. These moments of disagreement and debate, however fleeting, are important in challenging dominant discourses about gender and for the participants they are the hallmark of community as norms, prohibitions and sanctions emerge around particular behaviour.

In taking up space and answering back, these feisty, fearless and transgressing female gamers perform a kind of gender insubordination which may not be feminist in its intentions but may be feminist in its effect upon themselves as subjects and within the wider community. These online personae or avatars provide us with representations of performed subjectivities where the boundaries of what is acceptable are potentially different to those experienced in the offline setting. The web pages, web sites, and online personae can be viewed as enunciations of identity that are directed at particular discourses which are important to them. These performative spaces enable the living out (however temporarily) of imaginative heterotopian identities or playful representations of self which may be limited and constrained, but in very different ways to the offline context they regularly inhabit.[10] Certainly, the successful repetition of these performances appear to have direct consequences on the offline subjectivity in that in the examples given here they also achieve a different status within the culture as they access a producerly mode of engagement with technology.

The female *Quake* playing community makes no specific claims to a feminist agenda or a feminist politics, yet it is clear from the practices of the community that their activities are at least implicitly informed by issues which have been central to feminist critiques of technology and of popular culture. They have deployed a sometimes contradictory feminist discourse in the articulation of their relationship to the game culture in general; they have produced web sites, web pages and formed clans through which to enunciate their outsider status in the naming of these clans and the imagery which inspires their skins. Their activities are analogous to other kinds of feminist practice where separate space is deemed important for the critical work of developing a network and supporting other women. They make use of language derived from feminist debates through which to describe their experiences and to critique the representation and treatment of women in computer games and computer games culture. I would argue that women who take pleasure in and contribute to popular games culture contribute significantly to the democratization of technology and technological competence in a way which elitist/artist interventions can rarely hope to achieve. Popular games culture is made up of a heterogeneous range of players, practices and pleasures and it is *the* crucial site where dominant notions of technology, gender and technological competence are both constructed, negotiated and contested.

Works cited

Aarseth, Espen (1997) *Cybertext: Perspectives on Ergodic Literature*, Baltimore: John Hopkins University Press.

Baym, Nancy (2000) *Tune in, Log on: Soaps, Fandom and Online Community*, London: Sage.

Butler, Judith (1997) *The Psychic Life of Power: Theories in Subjection*, Stanford:

Stanford University Press.

——(1992) 'Contingent Foundations: Feminism and the Question of "Postmodernism"', in Judith Butler and Joan Scott (eds) *Feminists Theorize the Political*, London: Routledge.

Cassell J. and H. Jenkins (eds) (1998) *From Barbie to Mortal Kombat: Gender and Computer Games*, Cambridge, MA: MIT Press.

Douglas, Nikki (2006) 'The Future of Games Does Not Include Women', April 2006, www.grrlgamer.com/article.php?t=futureofgames, accessed April 2006.

——(2000) 'Uncommon Me', in www.grrlgamer.com, available at www.grrlgamer.com/gamergrrl04.html, accessed February 2002.

Dovey, Jonathan and Helen Kennedy (2006) *Game Cultures: Computer Games as New Media*, Milton Keynes: Open University Press/McGraw Hill.

Flanagan, Mary (2003) '"Next Level": Women's Digital Activism through Gaming', in Gunnar Liestol, Andrew Morrison, Terje Rasmussen (eds) *Digital Media Revisited: Theoretical and Conceptual Innovations in Digital Domains*, Cambridge, MA: MIT Press.

Giddings, Seth and Helen Kennedy (2007 forthcoming) '"Little Jesuses" and "Fuckoff Robots": Aesthetics, Cybernetics, and Not Being Very Good at *Lego Star Wars*', in M. Swalwell and J. Wilson (eds) *Gameplay: Pleasures, Engagements, Aesthetics*, Jefferson, NC: McFarland & Co.

——(2006) 'Digital Games as New Media', in Jason Rutter and Joanne Bryce (eds) *Understanding Digital Games*, London: Sage.

Haraway, Donna (1992) 'Ecce Homo, Ain't (Aren't) I a Woman and Inappropriate/d Others: The Human in the Post Humanist Landscape', in Judith Butler and Joan Scott (eds) *Feminists Theorize the Political*, London: Routledge.

——(1991) 'Situated Knowledges: The Science Question in Feminism and the Privilege of Partial Perspective', in Haraway (ed.) *Simians, Cyborgs and Women: The Reinvention of Nature*, London: Free Association Books.

——(1990) 'A Manifesto for Cyborgs: Science, Technology, and Socialist Feminism in the 1980s', in Linda J. Nicholson (ed.) *Feminism/Postmodernism*, London: Routledge.

——(1987) 'Contested Bodies', in Maureen McNeil (ed.) *Gender and Expertise*, London: Free Association Books.

King, Brad and John Borland (2003) *Dungeons and Dreamers: The Rise of Computer Game Culture from Geek to Chic*, San Francisco, CA: McGraw Hill/Osborne.

Kushner, David (2003) *Masters of Doom: How Two Guys Created an Empire and Transformed Pop Culture*, London: Piatkus.

Lahti, Martti (2003) 'As We Become Machines: Corporealized Pleasures in Video Games', in Mark J.P. Wolf and Bernard Perron (eds) *The Video Game Theory Reader*, London: Routledge.

Laurel, Brenda (1998) Keynote Address given at CHI 98 conference 'New Players

New Games', available online at www.Tauzero.com, accessed 20 March 2004.

Lister et al. (eds) (2003) *New Media: A Critical Introduction*, London: Routledge.

Marriott, Michel (2003) 'Fighting Women Enter the Arena, No Holds Barred', *New York Times*,15 May 2003.

Morris, Pam (ed.) (1994) *The Bakhtin Reader: Selected Writings of Bakhtin, Medvedev and Voloshinov*, London: Edward Arnold.

Morris, Sue (2003) 'Wads, Bots and Mots: Multiplayer FPS Games as Co Creative Media', *Level Up – Digital Games Research Conference Proceedings*, Utrecht: University of Utrecht/DIGRA (CD ROM).

Plant, Sadie (1993) 'The Future Looms: Weaving, Women and Cybernetics', *Broad Sheet*, 22: 3, 12–16.

Schleiner, Anne-Marie (1999) 'An Underworld Game Patch Router to Female Monsters, Frag Queens and Bobs whose First Name is Betty', available at www.opensorcery.net/mutetext.html, accessed 11 September 2003.

Tasker, Yvonne (1993) *Spectacular Bodies: Gender, Genre and the Action Cinema*, London: Routledge.

Taylor, T.L. (2003) 'Multiple Pleasures: Women and Online Gaming', *Convergence*, 9:1, 21–46.

——(1999) 'Life in Virtual Worlds: Plural Existence, Multimodalities, and Other Online Research Challenges', *American Behavioral Scientist*, 43:3, 436–449.

Wearing, Betsy (1998) *Leisure and Feminist Theory*, London: Sage.

Games

Quake (1996), id Software.

Quake II (1997), id Software, Activision.

Quake III: Arena (1999), id Software, Activision.

Unreal Tournament (1999), Epic Games, GT Interactive.

Notes

1 The concept of technicity is used here to encapsulate taste, technological competence and the use of technology as a means through which to form and express individual and group identities. For a fuller discussion of this see Dovey and Kennedy 2006.

2 (*Quake III: Arena* and *Quake III Gold* are the most popular iterations offering this online facility with *Quake IV* yet to establish a particularly large online following.)

3 For a useful account of the shareware ethos of early games distribution see King and Borland (2003). For an account of how this ethos specifically informed the practices at *id* see Kushner (2003)

4 See Giddings and Kennedy 2006b for a fuller exploration of these processes in

relation to playing *Lego Star Wars*.

5 Camilla Bennett was interviewed via email over the period between January 2001 and August 2002.

6 See her work online at www.chiq.net, accessed April 2006.

7 An amusing example is The Partridge Family *Quake* Clan, www.geocities.com/Area51/Cavern/2690, accessed April 2006.

8 Planet *Quake* www.planetquake.com is perhaps the most important example of the latter.

9 I am grateful to 'Xena' for drawing my attention to this campaign and for providing links to archived responses that were sparked by the campaign. Unfortunately most of these links are broken.

10 See Taylor (2003) for a discussion of this in relation to *Everquest* players.

8

Of eye candy and id: the terrors and pleasures of *Doom 3*

Bob Rehak

Let's start with a claim often heard about *Doom 3* (2004): that it is 'just' a remake of the 1993 original, the same stuff packaged in prettier graphics. That, although separated by 11 years and profound changes in the cultural, technological and aesthetic dimensions of videogaming, *Doom 3* – like all of *Doom*'s versions – boils down to a single conceit, recycled in the contemporary digital argot:

> First, people are taken over, turned into cannibal Things. Then the real horror starts, the deformed monstrosities from Outside ... Soon, brave men drop like flies. You lose track of your friends, though sometimes you can hear them scream when they die, and the sounds of combat echo from deep within the starbase. Something hisses with rage from the steel tunnels ahead. They know you're here. They have no pity, no mercy, take no quarter, and crave none. They're the perfect enemy, in a way. No one's left but you. You ... and them. ('The Story Continues', *Doom II Instruction Manual* 1994: 1)

Here the second-person voice does to readers what *Doom* so famously did to players, isolating them in a substitute self, an embattled, artificial *you*. The original *Doom* had its shareware release on 10 December 1993, marking the popular emergence of the first person shooter or FPS.[1] Less a game than a programming subgenre all its own, *Doom*'s brand of profane virtual reality was built around a set of graphical hacks – an 'engine' of specialized rendering code – that portrayed navigable, volumetric environments from eye-level perspective. Players peered over shotgun barrels at fluidly animated courtyards and corridors, portals and powerups, and 'deformed monstrosities' like the fireball-hurling Imp, the elephantine Mancubus, and the Cyberdemon ('a missile-launching skyscraper with goat legs').[2]

Technologically, *Doom* depended on advances in computer sound and imaging, themselves a result of newly affordable memory and speedy processors. Psychologically, the FPS stitched the human body into its gameworld double with unprecedented intimacy. Gone were the ant-farm displacements of third-person videogames, the god's-eye steering of *Pac-Man* (1980) and the sidescrolling tourism of *Super Mario Brothers* (1985). *Doom* fully subjectivized the avatar – the player-controlled object around which action centres – turning it into a prison of presence whose embodied vulnerability (*they're coming for me!*) deliciously complemented its violent agency (*take that, you bastard!*)

Shooters that followed – *Unreal* (1998), *Half-Life* (1998), *Deus Ex* (2000), *Halo* (2001) and countless others – deepened the FPS formula with narrative and strategic refinements, not to mention improvements in multiplayer, artificial intelligence and level design. But to judge by its latest iteration, the *Doom* series didn't bother to evolve at all – except in terms of technical execution. In *Doom 3*, the player is once again a marine stationed at the Union Aerospace Corporation's research base on Mars; once again, errant science opens a doorway to Hell, unleashing beasts and spectral forces; once again, the player must gun his or her way through level after level of bloody onslaught. Shotgun and chainsaw, Imps and Hell Knights are all present and accounted for. Even its creators acknowledge that the scenario is essentially unchanged. 'It's a retelling of the original *Doom*,' said lead designer Tim Willits, 'like the first game never happened.' (Smith 2002: 60.) Not so much a new chapter, then, as an update – Doom 3.0.

Critics, whether they liked or disliked the game, agreed on the inverse relation between its sophisticated graphics and crude play. *PC Gamer* wrote

> The visual stylings are so palpably creepy, the lighting so subtly realistic, and the sound composition so bristling with pinpoint accuracy that you'll come for the name *Doom* and stay for the dread that the gameplay delivers. There's no redefining of gameplay here: quite the contrary, *Doom 3* is a classic (traditional/established/expected) run-and-gun action game. (Smith 2002: 58)

'*Doom 3* is filled with graphical eye candy,' echoed *PC Magazine*. 'The use of bump-mapping and lighting effects provides an entirely eerie setting, and one that has never looked better. [But] the retro-styled game play is another story, and one that might leave you longing for much more. The actual plot is built around a far too linear quest that, while true to the original, feels dated.' (Suciu 2004.) The *Ottawa Sun* (Tilley 2004) summed it up this way: 'It's a very, very, VERY good-looking game, and initially it's also extremely scary as well. But peel back the incredible graphics, character animation and overall production values, and there's really nothing we haven't seen done before.'

These perspectives share certain assumptions, chief among which is that *games are conceptually separable from their technologies.* Invoked in this sense, 'technology' is a catchall for sound and imagery, sensory surface – in a word, graphics. Mark J.P. Wolf has defined the difference using 'the two criteria present in the name of the medium: its status as "video" and as "game".' (Wolf 2001:14.) In the *game* column Wolf places attributes such as conflict, rules, player ability, and outcome. The prefix *video*, by contrast, specifies a display, be it cathode-ray tube, vector graphic, or liquid crystal; by extension, the term designates a historically specific articulation of hardware and software, the game's material platform, from home console to mobile phone to fully tricked-out PC.[3] The notion that games possess timeless formal qualities which remain recognizable from one instance to another is, of course, common both to vernacular and academic discourse. It is what enables us to trace the venerable *Space Invaders* (1978) through countless iterations in spinoffs, sequels and ports, stipulating that they are all *Space Invaders* 'at heart' no matter how great their apparent difference; or assert that the 3D makeover of *Centipede* (1998) is the same game 'in principle' as its arcade-cabinet forbear. Wolf's point is that there is no videogame without a display of some kind – no videogame without graphics. One can imagine a silent videogame; one cannot imagine an *invisible* videogame.[4]

A related assumption is that, in determining a videogame's overall quality, *graphics are secondary to play.* In some cases they can even lessen its entertainment value. Richard Rouse argues that although lavish graphics may be appropriate to the FPS, their widespread adoption amounts to 'fancy window dressing' and 'a pointless distraction'. He writes, 'a 3D engine will not necessarily enhance the play of every game it is applied to, sometimes making a game worse by adding distracting fluff on top of an otherwise solid game' (Rouse 1998). In a critique that smacks of the Frankfurt School, Rouse connects the pursuit of sophisticated graphics to the dumbed-down aesthetics of a culture industry intent on squeezing money from the largest possible audience.

> It is hard to communicate 'compelling storyline' or 'highly refined gameplay' on the back of a box, while a hot 3D engine communicates easily via glitzy screen-shots. Having your game be 3D is a 'money in the bank' sort of guarantee that makes investors feel more comfortable, just as a film's financial success seems more likely if it has a big-name star attached to it, or a new book's potential profitability greater if John Grisham were to praise it on the dust jacket. (Rouse 1998)

All of these views contain elements of truth. But taken together, they explain away *Doom 3* – and the FPS phenomenon – too easily. *Doom 3*'s ink-shadowed metal hallways, dusty Martian caverns, and magma-puddled landscapes of Hell are haunted not just by forces of evil but by paradoxes of time and technology inherent to the videogame medium. In one sense, the game is tremendously advanced; in another, hopelessly primitive. The contradiction speaks not only to the evolution of digital computers, game design and programming subculture but to the manner in which those histories interweave. Moreover, the competing forces in *Doom 3* are crucial to understanding the experience of playing it – indeed, of playing any first person shooter – reliving the mingled terrors and pleasures of a traumatic stage in our avatarial relations.

To begin with, we must confront the dilemma posed by *Doom 3*'s apparently opposed extremes. Is the game a breakthrough masquerading as a throwback, a throwback masquerading as a breakthrough, or something else entirely? How might we best frame its strange heterogeneity? And how might such a perspective – one that rejects tidy teleologies and the ideological comfort of the commonsense – modify the premises of academic game studies?

A friend of mine likes to say that 'id doesn't make games; id makes engines'.[5] He means this, I think, both as praise and criticism. Praise because the software company formed by John Carmack, Adrian Carmack, and John Romero in 1991 has so consistently pushed the limits of computer technology with imaginative and unorthodox programming. Criticism because the results so consistently fall short of the imaginative involvements achieved by other, less graphically sophisticated and hardware-intensive games.[6] On an industrial level, his statement could be taken to refer to the company's habit of licensing substantial portions of its code to other developers, as was the case with the modified *Quake II* engine used in *Half-Life*. The circulation of prefab VR toolkits has implications for videogame theory that I will explore in more detail later on; for now, suffice it to note – with Geoff King and Tanya Krzywinska – that the practice makes good business sense, 'permitting shorter and less expensive development time and enabling the developer to benefit from the status of engines that have already earned a good reputation in the gaming community' (King and Krzywinska 2002: 27).[7]

But on an aesthetic level, my friend is really saying that id's shooters (*Doom* in 1993; *Doom II* in 1994; *Quake* in 1996; *Quake II* in 1997; *Quake III: Arena* in 1999) were created mainly to showcase their engines. Under this interpretation, the pared-down gameplay of classic FPSs – construed by some as failing to draw players into a narrative or tantalize them with puzzles

– is, in fact, intentional and necessary; too much "depth" would get in the way of the graphics. Instead, story developments and action beats are motivated by the tools and capabilities each new engine makes available to programmers.

As evidence of this relationship, consider *Doom 3*'s system of unified lighting. Heavily promoted in pre-release publicity, this aspect of the engine combines dynamic light sources, shading, and textures to produce a host of chiaroscuro environmental effects. These effects feature prominently in sequences involving the pursuit of a solitary light source moving through a darkened environment. In one, the player tracks an alien specimen in a glowing canister suspended from a conveyor belt, and in another, follows a scientist who carries a swinging lantern. More than once, a sentry bot (a dog-sized metallic spider) leads the player on a brisk march through the cavernous darkness, interrupted by sudden firefights with attacking monsters. In these moments, *Doom 3* arguably invites us to appreciate itself as pure technological achievement, following an alternative mode of game 'spectatorship' described well by Andrew Mactavish.[8] Far from garnering applause, however, the chase-the-light sequences draw attention to themselves as failures of a different order. Except for the fact that the player is always rushing to keep up, they unspool with the dreary automaticity of cutscenes, like spliced-in chunks of hamhandedly noninteractive exposition.

The engine/game distinction, then, whatever actual differences in the architecture of videogame code it implies, serves rhetorically as a measuring stick by which we sort good gameplay from bad. It serves, that is, an *ideological* function, constructing a technological 'outside' to the videogame experience (as though videogames were not technologies through and through). This is especially evident with regard to an element that drew noisy complaint from *Doom 3*'s audience. Navigating the zombie-filled environment, players may use a flashlight to illuminate their path, but cannot hold a weapon at the same time. The choice – *see where you're going* versus *defend yourself blindly* – leads to much panicked toggling back and forth between gun and flashlight and is suspenseful or annoying depending on your disposition. As graphic bravura, the flashlight succeeds brilliantly, making the game effectively into one long 'chase the light' session. To many players, however, it is a game-disabling error on the level of a bug. There soon appeared a software patch – not of id's making – that allowed flashlight and weapon to be used simultaneously.[9]

Doom 3 demonstrates that the difference between *game* and *engine* is hard to untangle. But how long has this been the case? Did it begin with *Doom 3*? With the original *Doom*? Did videogames undergo a sudden upheaval in the early 1990s, a moment of punctuated disequilibrium in which graphics 'took over' gaming? At what point did videogames manifest engines – and more importantly, when did the concept of 'engine' emerge as a discursive figure, a tool for conceptualizing videogame content? For answers, we must delve into the genesis of the first person shooter, through id Software and the two figures who have come to represent contentious but productive polarities of game design: John Carmack and John Romero.

> Carmack didn't so much care about the accoutrements of the game as he enjoyed Romero's passion for showing off what his engine could do. Romero *got* what [Carmack] was doing – trying to make a sleek, simple, fast game engine. And he was the one who dreamed up the sleek, simple, fast game to go with it. (Kushner 2003: 97)

Both Romero and Carmack first appear in David Kushner's *Masters of Doom* as 'fourth-generation' hackers: teens in the late 1970s and early 1980s enjoying the explosion of arcades, homebrew computing culture and increasing availability of computers in classrooms and at home that marked the flowering of popular computing in the US. These forces were crystallized in the videogames – arcade favorites such as *Asteroids* (1980) as well as programs for the Apple II – that the boys avidly played. Each was inspired by these examples to create his own games, but while Romero's passion centred on the visceral thrills of combat and the sensory lushness of the game surface, Carmack was fascinated by the engineering side – the challenges of coding. Videogames, for him, were a virtual-world technology bridging the paper-based *Dungeons and Dragons* originated by Gary Gygax in the early 1970s and the Holodeck foreshadowed on *Star Trek: The Next Generation* (Kushner 2003: 25). Working with the PC, Carmack developed ever-more sophisticated ways of making the videogame screen mobile and dimensional, first with side-scrolling, then with rudimentary 3D (see Wolf 2002: 51–75). His skills complemented Romero's in almost archetypal fashion:

> Carmack was most interested in programming the guts of the game ... Romero enjoyed making the software tools – essentially the palette they would use to create characters and environments or 'maps' of the game – as well as the game design – how the game play would unfold, what action would take place, what would make it fun. It was like yin and yang. While Carmack was exceptionally talented in programming, Romero was multitalented in art, sound, and design. And while Carmack had played video games as a kid, *no one* had played as many as Romero. The ultimate coder and the ultimate gamer – together they were a perfect fit. (Kushner 2003: 40–41)

This 'perfect fit' expressed itself throughout the late 1980s and early 1990s in games developed for software magazines and the company at which Carmack and Romero worked, Softdisk. There was *Slordax*, 'a straightforward shoot-the-ships descendent of arcade hits like *Space Invaders* and *Galaga*'; (Kushner 2003: 47); *Dangerous Dave*; the *Commander Keen* trilogy; and two early experiments in first-person perspective released under the id label, *Catacombs 3D* and *Hovertank 3D* (both 1991). Each marked an incremental advance toward *Doom*, requiring the step-by-step solution of graphical problems specific to the real-time rendering of videogame environments. Carmack used clever shortcuts to produce a representational system capable of maximum detail and speed with minimal computation. He tailored his code to the human sensorium, 'let[ting] the graphics engine focus on drawing only what the player needed to see' – engineering virtual reality from the bottom up (in terms of the PC's powers) and from the inside out (with the subjective space of the player centring the created vista).

By late 1991, id was at work on *Wolfenstein 3D*, a first-person update of an Apple II game that promised to be 'brutal, as originally imagined by Romero' and 'fast, as engineered by Carmack' (Kushner 2003: 95). During development, Carmack pursued consistency at all costs. Tensions flared, for example, over the issue of 'push walls' – secret portals that could be opened only when a player shoved against them. Carmack resisted push walls, which violated the tidy rule set that was both a natural consequence of his elegant and economical programming and the armature of a consistent, immersive graphical world.

> The *Wolfenstein* engine simply wasn't designed to have walls sliding back into secret rooms. It was designed to have doors slide open and shut, open and shut. It was a matter of streamlining. The simpler Carmack kept his game, the faster the world would move, therefore, the deeper the simulation. (Kushner 2003: 109)

After *Wolfenstein*, id's direction was clear. For their next game, *Doom*, Carmack added diminished lighting and texture-mapped floors and ceilings. Solving problems of lighting and perspective, as well as having walls of variable height, enabled the virtual construction of new kinds of rooms and passages; alterations in the engine directly determined gameplay, setting conditions of possibility for the player's existence in, and exploration of, a three-dimensional environment (Kushner 2003: 121). The nuts and bolts of the graphics system enabled specific types of 'contested spaces' to be built (Jenkins and Squire 2002, 64–75). But even while putting the finishing touches on *Doom II* (not so much a full-fledged game as a new set of levels running on the *Doom* engine), production moved ahead on the followup, *Quake*. By that time – the mid-1990s – the Internet and its associated communities of connectivity were becoming a driving force in the industry. Networked gaming, or multiplayer, had been a clumsily executed feature in *Doom*, but dominated development priorities in *Quake*. Accordingly, Carmack built the new engine in order for its two strengths – environments shareable by more than one person, and consistent rule sets – to support, not simply augment, the gaming experience.

It seems likely that Romero's departure in 1996 – he left shortly after *Quake's* release to start up his own company, Ion Storm – marked a turning point in id's creativity. Rather, it is the point at which id *stopped* turning and settled into a single groove: that of building successively more complex graphic engines. While Romero buried himself ever more deeply in the quagmire that was *Daikatana* (2000), Carmack moved into production on *Quake II*, touted as 'the most cohesive and technologically impressive id game yet' (Kushner 2003: 237), taking advantage of the specialized graphics accelerator cards then becoming a standard add-on for PCs and Macs. In the late 1990s, faced with the option of pushing ahead into the territory blazed by massively multiplayer online role-playing games (MMORPGs) like *EverQuest* and *Ultima Online* – persistent virtual worlds with capacity to accommodate thousands of players, monsters, and quests – id opted instead to return to old favourites, such as *Wolfenstein* and *Doom*, using updated engines. *Doom 3* in particular would enable Carmack to 'incorporate ideas he'd been kicking around for a next-generation graphics engine, something that could dynamically exploit the world of lights and shadows' (Kushner 2003: 283–284).

Viewed one way, the development of the FPS does indeed signal a shift in programming priorities, with a corresponding increase in size and complexity of game code – irrevocably changing the way in which videogames are made, as well as the experience they provide players. King and Krzywinska characterize the trend as one in which

> The production of a compelling game world, in three-dimensional graphics, often appears to be privileged over dimensions such as narrative and gameplay. Game developers, designers and programmers often appear to devote more energy to the creation of spectacular, coherent and (in their own terms) believable worlds than to the quality or variety of gameplay itself. (King and Krzywinska 2002: 28)

While the authors allow that 'play' is a concept elastic enough to encompass the pleasures of the engine ('The appeal of being able to explore spectacular 3D virtual worlds in real time should not be underestimated' (29)), their perspective threatens to reinscribe the simplistic gameplay/graphics divide that stops us from taking full account of *Doom 3*'s complex nature. The problem is that *any* formulation such as "the relationship in games between narrative and qualities such as spectacle, sensation, and kinesthesia" (29) implies that these categories are irremediably opposed – that we recognize narrative precisely because it is *not* spectacular or sensational, and recognize spectacle because it lacks narrative or ludic elements.

But *Doom* – one of the most profitable, popular and influential videogames in history – was never about story or ludological complexity, beyond a few paragraphs of setup. Its appeal is more often described in terms of the way players engaged its world as a product of its graphical presentation. 'The pace and fluidity of motion are astounding, the aesthetics those of corporeal disintegration, nightmare monstrosity, extraordinary velocity, bewildering disintegration, and extreme fear.' (Kline, Dyer-Witheford and de Peuter 2003: 145.) Fear and its emotional kin also anchor J.C. Herz's analysis, though for her, the control we exert over our technological recreations adds a crucial ingredient of pleasure:

> *Doom* has invoked the kind of horror that you only experience as a small child when the lights go out and the monsters in the closet and under the bed come to life. Ultimately, you know you're safe –you can always race for the door. You can always turn off the computer. But for a moment, you're exquisitely frightened. It's the kind of fear that turns us on and makes us feel alive and sends us on skydiving expeditions and roller-coaster rides. *Doom* gave you a way to get the same thrill from your very own dorm room. (Herz 1997: 88)

If graphics were nothing but window dressing over an 'actual' game, *Doom* would be no scarier than any other title based on the same premise. But in videogames, graphics do not merely illustrate a world – they constitute it. Such has been the case since the dawn of the medium in the late 1950s and early 1960s. What we call 'engines' are simply enormously metastasized sub-routines of the type that used to switch pixels on and off, animate shape tables and sprites, or play buzzing tones through a speaker. Rendering, physics, sound, AI and networking modules generate every layer of the phenomenological playing field: from frame rate and resolution to 'perspective, camera angles, lighting and shadows' to the way in which 'characters or objects exist or move within the game, simulating qualities of gravity and solidity' (King and Krzywinska 2002: 27). The process can be seen as kind of activated *mise-en-scène*, an image that is itself an environment (perceived through another image – an ongoing representation of our own senses). In what David Myers labels 'technology-driven design', 'the id graphics engine and the relationships it establishe[s] among signs and symbols within the Doom environment [is] the game'. As a consequence, 'Everything else – levels, plots, characters – provide[s] extended opportunities rather than vital necessities for play.' (Myers 2003: 104–105, italics in original.)

The partnership at the heart of id demonstrates that technologies of gaming have always been inseparable from aesthetics of play; the company's games evolved through continual dialogue among the team and other staffers. Furthermore, the story of Doom and Quake is not one of sudden breakthroughs, but gradual stages in increasing graphic sophistication tied to the capacities of whatever platform happened to be in use at the time. In this sense, the 1990s were no different from the 1980s and 1970s. Carmack and Romero's work extends consistently from the milieu of the Apple II and arcade cabinets to the first PCs and Macs, through the second wave of home consoles (Doom was released for Sega's PlayStation, the Nintendo 64 and the GameBoy Advance), to contemporary processors.

Neither was it the first time that a 'coder' and a 'gamer' came together to produce something greater than either might have alone. In 1980, Ken and Roberta Williams developed a game along a partnership model with similarities to id's. Roberta, inspired by the text adventures of the time, was developing a murder mystery for the Apple II. Ken, sceptical about the game's prospects, suggested that it needed an angle of some kind. Roberta proposed that perhaps the text could be illustrated by graphics, and Ken wrote a routine to store and display these images – eye-catching for the time – during the game.

> The secret was not storing data for entire pictures, but using assembly-language commands which stored coordinates of the individual lines in each picture; as each new picture was due to appear, the computer could follow the commands to draw the picture. It was a dazzling program bum that characterized Ken's facility for top-level hacking. (Levy 2001: 298.)

Roberta, like Romero, was transported by the idea of the game. The more technically inclined Ken 'pitched in and added a graphical element that pushed the boundaries of Apple II display technology beyond anything that had been done before' (King and Borland 2003: 46). Like Carmack ten years later, Ken found an elegant way to unite visual representation with game 'plot'. The result was a hit – Mystery House, also called Hi-Res Adventure #1 – which, based on its graphic appeal, led to the creation of Sierra On-Line.

Indeed, one can glimpse in the very origins of the videogame – Spacewar! (1962) – this pattern of game development. Steve Russell's love of the Lensman space opera series led him to produce a core game which was then modified by other hackers, such as Peter Samson, whose 'Expensive Planetarium' provided an accurate starmap as backdrop for the action. Over time, other programmers added hyperspace, invisibility, black holes and gravity.[10] It seems hardwired into the medium: code cultivated by multiple authors, their work disappearing seamlessly into a whole.

We are now a step closer to understanding the contradictions and currents running under the surface of *Doom 3*. But a mystery remains: the game's failure – in the eyes of critics – to convincingly deliver the same experience as its predecessors. The game starts off well enough: 'Darkness hangs like a thick fog in this first-person shooter, shrouding your vision and adding a nearly unbearable sense of dread.' But, this reviewer goes on, 'by the end, my fear had been a bit numbed by a familiar pattern: enter darkened room, wait for monsters to spawn all around you, kill them all, go to next chamber, repeat' (Slagle 2004). Perhaps it was the narrowness of the tightrope id set up for itself. 'Change the old demons too much, and the fanatical, old-school crowd will say that id didn't stay true to the original vision', worried a making-of text released concurrently with the game. 'Should the demons of *Doom 3* not evolve enough, critics will complain that id has not kept up with the times.' (Kent with id Software 2004: 72.) From weapons to monsters, id laboured to maintain the iconic brand associated with *Doom*, using an engine more advanced by an order of magnitude.[11] But they could not recreate its mood, any more than Gus Van Sant's shot-for-shot remake of *Psycho* (1998) could recapture the impact of Alfred Hitchcock's 1960 original. Why is this? The answer, I suspect, has to do with a self-sabotaging paralysis at the heart of the *Doom* experience – a repetition compulsion hinging on the inherent timelessness and self-referentiality of the videogame medium.

Early in *Doom 3*, the game seems to remark on its own heritage. On a computer terminal at the UAC research lab, players can access an informational clip on base security. The animation shows a cartoon maze from first-person perspective; graph-paper tunnels in which schematic monsters leap out from sliding sections of wall. By its very crudeness, the maze recalls id's prior shooters. At the time of their release, those forerunners looked terrific, but held up against what's out there today (that is, *Doom 3*), they seem about as cutting-edge as tic-tac-toe. And it is not the only time that an id game has commented on its own past. 1994's *Doom II: Hell on Earth* contains two hidden levels, 'Wolfenstein' and 'Grosse', which transport the player into the world of *Wolfenstein 3D*, released in 1991. Here, as Angela Ndalianis notes, the shock derives not from attacking monsters but from the juxtaposition of contrasting visual aesthetics, tied inseparably to styles of play.

> After the hyperrealism of *Doom II*, we find ourselves in the rigidly angular, monotonously decorated and colored corridors of *Wolfenstein 3D*, where we battle against two-dimensional images of soldiers that all look exactly the same. This shift of game experience is both a treat and a disappointment. It is hysterically funny and quite jolting. The atmospheric game play of *Doom II* is suddenly replaced by a type of game play that had, before the emergence of *Doom*, been quite innovative and exciting. (Ndalianis 2002: 513)

The easter-egg reference to prior id titles does double duty, prompting nostalgia for games past while reinforcing the sense that the videogame we are *now* playing is truly 'state of the art'. But videogame history feeds on itself in more subtle (and perhaps unconscious) ways. As I have argued, Carmack and Romero represent a bridge between modern gaming and the era that preceded it. Without exception, their FPSs preserve the black-and-white morality and haiku simplicities of the arcade machine – *Shoot everything that moves* is not so different from *Avoid missing ball for high score*. Id's history is dense with echoes of the past and prefigurations of the future: the company's first major success, after all, was based on an Apple II game a decade old.

That *Doom 3* intentionally reproduces the rudiments of original *Doom* is clear. The frustration this provokes, however, has little to do with the gap between advanced graphics and simple play – for id has always been about those things. Instead, by so closely following in the tracks of its 1993 incarnation, *Doom 3* returns us to a premultiplayer past when the technical constraints of VGA displays and 386 processors created a singularly claustrophobic experience, reflected in the profound isolation of its avatar: *No one's left but you. You … and them.*

Doom 3 insistently revisits a stage in videogame evolution when the pleasures of avatarialism attained full and terrible flower. The birth of the FPS was the moment when the puppet through which we experience gameworlds sharpened its senses and, correspondingly, its dynamism. Assigned scale by its surroundings, it could inhabit gamespace more closely – we learned how it felt to walk through a doorway, or gauge an opening to decide if our 'body' would fit through it. As the world perceived by the avatar came into higher resolution, the avatar itself acquired a more fine-grained sense of control. Which is all, ultimately, an avatar *is*: a perceived world and a sense of control; a moving map, like a projection on the inside of a sphere, and outside it the intention, attention, urgency and passion we bring to our virtual pursuits. It only makes sense that the first-person/detailed world apparatus, once established, became a kind of standardized software wizard, an interface to other types of gameworld – including, in chase-cam mode, elaborately social and graphical MMORPGs. It spread quickly to other games, which, in refining it, distanced us from its essential solitary uncanniness. Only *Doom* remained proudly (and perversely) unchanged.

That critics of *Doom* distinguish so easily between gameplay and graphics in the FPS should not shock us. More alarming is the tendency of academic game theory to reproduce that opposition without stepping back to question its premise or implications. Espen Aarseth preaches the gospel of dualism in his analysis of 1970s text adventures. Running on teletype terminals connected to mainframes (or on personal computers with limited powers), games such as *Colossal Cave*, *Adventure*, and *Zork* used textual descriptions and typed input to convey the sense of a navigable environment populated with characters and objects. In Aarseth's view, the text adventure's 'demise' coincided with the development of improved processing and rendering capability (Aarseth 1997: 101). 'Computer graphics became better and cheaper,' he writes, 'and so the adventure game genre, with its spatially oriented themes of travel and discovery, gradually migrated from text to pictures and, eventually, to three-dimensional 'virtual reality' games like *Doom*.' (101–102)

> The ergodic structures invented by [Will] Crowther and [Don] Woods twenty years ago are of course far from dead but instead persevere as the basic figure for the large and growing entertainment genre called, by a somewhat catachresic pleonasm, 'interactive games' … It is a paradox that, despite the lavish and quite expensive graphics of these productions, the player's creative options are still as primitive as they were in 1976. (102–103)

A similar notion that videogames consist of timeless structures wrapped in graphical skins underpins the conventional wisdom that all games can be described as representations of other processes. '*Mortal Kombat* is a representation of hand-to-hand combat, *Go* is a representation of territorial conflict, and *Pong* is a representation of Table Tennis', state Katie Salen and Eric Zimmerman (2004: 364) crisply. The dominant perspectives in game studies may differ in their particulars, but all agree that games possess certain timeless qualities (themes, situations, procedures) which are instantiated, with greater or lesser success, in concrete 'versions'.

Such conventions hinge on the belief that games can be generalized beyond their superficial disparities. Clearly, it would be foolish to deny the power of this conceptual tool. But it seems equally foolish to assert that categories of gameplay remain eternally fixed, like Platonic ideals, with only their graphic shells to distinguish one instance from another. To do so leaves little room to analyze the way videogames evolve over time, tied to the dizzying exponential sweep of Moore's Law. How then do we account for their growth and change? Their specific cultural meanings? (Consider *Grand Theft Auto 3* (2001) alongside *The Simpsons: Hit & Run* (2003) – more or less identical in terms of their 'ergodic structures', but vastly different in social signification and corresponding political impact.) How do games negotiate their kinship with ancestors and descendents, pre- and post-texts kept alive through emulation? How do they mediate the shifting forces of aesthetics, technology and commerce, and thus participate in a much older tale of western culture's ideological transformations of vision?

The formalist approaches of game studies tend to produce synchronic snapshots rather than diachronic descriptions of videogames' material existence. This lack of historical perspective is related to the tendency to downplay graphic surfaces as simple cosmetic overlays for the scaffolding of interactive hails, Proppian oppositions and labyrinthine flowcharts of options and obstacles that Espen Aarseth calls 'cybertexts' and Janet H. Murray terms 'multiform stories'.[12] The simulationist school, whose basic principles have been articulated by Gonzalo Frasca (2003: 221–235), opposes simulation to representation, downplaying the fact that one cannot exist without the other – and that both are forged in the graphic engine's cyclings.[13] When theorists of new media do discuss computer graphics, they fixate on philosophical problematics of realism versus illusion and the erosion of photographic truth by digital manipulation, rather than engaging with the diverse ways in which games stylize their worlds. Lev Manovich (2001: 178) may be correct in arguing that 'The quest for a perfect simulation of reality drives the whole field of VR', but this does not shed much light on the contrast between two titles released for the GameCube in 2003, Nintendo's cel-shaded *Legend of Zelda: The Wind Waker* and the sportscast-mimicry of EA Sports's *Madden NFL*. The teleological notion that games and their players constantly pursue 'better' graphics also fails to explain the enshrining of prior games in emulators, nostalgic web sites and the host of commercial products that constitute the retrogame movement. And while our bodies – organic and avatarial alike – never vanish entirely from such arguments, they are reduced to mindless and involuntary relays in a circuit of sensation, a 'twitch' state linked to the narratively-impoverished attractions of motion-simulator rides, music videos, and special-effects films.

All of this leaves traditional approaches with a substantial blind spot when it comes to matters of messy corporeality and sensate (as opposed to cognitive) videogame experience. Perhaps this avoidance is due to a lingering elitism or aesthetic unease on the part of game studies toward the FPS, a genre that in its purified form resembles the penny dreadful or snuff film; perhaps it is because *Doom* and its ilk have drawn the ire of mainstream media and moral guardians in a maddeningly circular debate whose basic premises remain undertheorized. Whatever the cause, the effect is that important phenomena are going unremarked. Id's work in particular, and videogame history in general, suggest that our virtual realities become genuinely gripping only when avatarial 'lives' are at stake. We accept dual embodiment only when that second body is at risk. (Otherwise, VR just provides us with the World's Most Boring Kitchen.) If this is so, then videogames are not a subset of virtuality, but vice-versa – the graphical pleasures of digital fantasy *Doom*ed in the first instance to solipsistic agonism.

Works cited

Aarseth, Espen J. (1997) *Cybertext: Perspectives on Ergodic Literature*, Baltimore: Johns Hopkins University Press, 1997.

Brand, Stewart (1972) 'Spacewar: Fanatic Life and Symbolic Death Among the Computer Bums', *Rolling Stone*, 7 December 1972.

Frasca, Gonzalo (2003) 'Simulation versus Narrative: Introduction to Ludology', in Mark J.P. Wolf and Bernard Perron (eds) *The Video Game Theory Reader*, New York: Routledge, 221–235.

Herman, Leonard (1999) *Phoenix: The Fall & Rise of Videogames*, 2nd edn, Union, NJ: Rolenta Press.

Herz, J.C. (1997) *Joystick Nation: How Videogames Ate Our Quarters, Won Our Hearts, and Rewired Our Minds*, Boston: Little, Brown and Company.

id Software/GT Interactive Software (1994) *Doom II Instruction Manual*.

Jenkins, Henry and Kurt Squire (2002) 'The Art of Contested Spaces', in Lucien King (ed.) *Game On: The History and Culture of Video Games*, New York: Universe, 64–75.

Kent, Steven L. with Id Software (2004) *The Making of Doom 3*, New York: McGraw-Hill/Osborne.

King, Brad and John Borland (2003) *Dungeons and Dreamers: The Rise of Computer Game Culture from Geek to Chic*, New York: McGraw-Hill.

King, Geoff and Tanya Krzywinska (2002) 'Introduction: Cinema/Videogames/ Interfaces', in Geoff King and Tanya Krzywinska (eds) *ScreenPlay: Cinema/ Videogames/Interfaces*, London: Wallflower Press, 1–32.

Kline, Stephen, Nick Dyer-Witheford and Greig de Peuter (2003) *Digital Play: The*

Interaction of Technology, Culture, and Marketing, Montreal: McGill-Queen's University Press.

Kushner, David (2003) *Masters of Doom: How Two Guys Created an Empire and Transformed Pop Culture*, New York: Random House.

Levy, Steven (2001) *Hackers: Heroes of the Computer Revolution*, New York: Penguin Books.

Mactavish, Andrew (2002) 'Technological Pleasure: The Performance and Narrative of Technology in *Half-Life* and other High-Tech Computer Games', in Geoff King and Tanya Krzywinska (eds) *ScreenPlay: Cinema/Videogames/Interfaces*, London: Wallflower Press, 33–49.

Manovich, Lev (2001) *The Language of New Media*, Cambridge, MA: MIT Press.

Murray, Janet H. (1997) *Hamlet on the Holodeck: The Future of Narrative in Cyberspace*, Cambridge, MA: MIT Press.

Myers, David (2003) *The Nature of Computer Games: Play as Semiosis*, New York: Peter Lang.

Ndalianis, Angela (2002) 'The Rules of the Game: *Evil Dead II* … Meet Thy *Doom*', in Henry Jenkins, Tara McPherson and Jane Shattuc (eds) *Hop on Pop: The Politics and Pleasures of Popular Culture*, Durham, NC: Duke University Press, 503–516.

Rouse, Richard III (1998) 'Do Computer Games Need to Be 3D?', *Computer Graphics*, 32:3, www.paranoidproductions.com/gamingandgraphics/first.html, accessed September 2005.

Salen, Katie and Eric Zimmerman (2004) *Rules of Play: Game Design Fundamentals*, Cambridge, MA: MIT Press.

Slagle, Matt (2004) '"*Doom 3*" a Terrifying Experience', Associated Press, 10 August 2004.

Smith, Greg M. (1999) 'Introduction: A Few Words about Interactivity', in *On a Silver Platter: CD-ROMs and the Promises of a New Technology*, New York: New York University Press, 1–34.

Smith, Rob (2002) '*Doom III*: The World Exclusive', *PC Gamer*, 9:12, 58–74.

Suciu, Peter (2004) '*Doom 3*', *PC Magazine*, 14 September 2004.

Tilley, Steve (2004) '*Doom 3* Looks Great', *Ottawa Sun*, 15 August 2004.

Wolf, Mark J.P. (2001a) 'Space in the Video Game', in Wolfe (ed.) *The Medium of the Video Game*, Austin: University of Texas Press, 51–75.

——(2001b) 'The Video Game as a Medium', in Wolfe (ed.) *The Medium of the Video Game*, Austin: University of Texas Press, 13–33.

Games

Asteroids (1980), Midway, Atari.
Centipede (1998), Hasbro Interactive.
Daikatana (2000), Ion Storm, Eidos.

Deus Ex (2000), Ion Storm, Eidos.
Doom 3 (2004), id Software, Activision.
Doom II (1994), id Software.
Grand Theft Auto 3 (2001), Rock Star North.
Half-Life (1998), Valve, Sierra.
Halo (2001), Bungie, Microsoft.
Legend of Zelda: the Wind Waker (2003), Nintendo.
Madden NFL 2003 (2003), Electronic Arts.
Myst (1993), Broderbund/CyanWorlds.
Pac-Man (1980), Namco.
The Simpsons Hit and Run (2003), Radical Entertainment/Vivendi Universal Games.
Space Invaders (1978), Taito.
Super Mario Brothers (1985), Nintendo.
Unreal (1998), Epic, GT Interactive.
Wolfenstein 3D (1992), id Software.

Notes

1 Subjective-viewpoint videogames, of course, existed long before *Doom* came along, the most celebrated example probably being *Battlezone* (1980). *Doom*'s explosive online release attracted so many users that at first id was prevented from uploading the game to the FTP server at the University of Wisconsin. Once system administrators solved the problem, the overloaded server promptly crashed (Herz 1997: 84; also excitingly retold in Kushner 2003: 150–153.). The story of *Doom*'s release carries interesting resonances of another mythic moment in videogame history: in 1972, the *Pong* cabinet at Andy Capp's Bar in Sunnyvale, California stopped working after two weeks. Upon investigation, Atari engineer Al Alcorn discovered the problem – the popular game's coin reservoir was jammed by quarters (Herman 1999: 14–15).

2 'The Enemy', *Doom II Instruction Manual*, 14.

3 At the time of writing, flat-panel LCD monitors are already squeezing out the traditional CRT; coming years will surely see the emergence of new display methods that render the *video* in 'videogame' as anachronistic as the *dial* in 'dial a phone number'.

4 An increasingly common tactic is to elide the question of *screen* altogether through the use of labels like 'interactive games' or 'digital games', the latter being the preferred usage of the Digital Games Research Association (DIGRA). While I agree that the games under discussion are all interactive as well as digital – and appreciate the desire to tidy up the categories – it seems plain that ignoring videogames' highly mediated nature won't make that mediation go away, or relieve academics of the responsibility of critically investigating it.

5 I am sincerely grateful to Dan Weible, programmer, gamer and friend of long

standing, for his generosity, insight and assistance. Our many hours of conversation on the topic of videogame graphics and metaphysics – as well as his loan of the gaming system on which I played *Doom 3* – were vital to this project.

6   Comparing *Doom* to *Myst* (1993), Greg M. Smith suggests that the FPS's graphic versatility *curtails* player freedom – a tradeoff of 'choice depth' for high-speed engagement. '*Doom* actually offers a relatively limited choice of action: basically we can move in various directions, and we can shoot at demons using different weapons. There is less of the sense of infinite possibilities for action at any one time [than in *Myst*]. However, because the demons come at us so rapidly, forcing us to respond, the interaction between player and [game] object is highly charged. The pace of the action helps boost *Doom*'s interactivity.' (Smith 1999: 28.)

7   The authors add that licensing engines 'is also a way of ensuring that troublesome "bugs" have already been eradicated' (27).

8   Mactavish writes that 'we oscillate back and forth between immersion in the game's world and astonishment at the technological performance' (Mactavish 2002: 42).

9   The mod, rather than functioning as a simple cheat, preserves in subtle ways the intended mood and logic of the *Doom 3* experience. The accompanying text at http://ducttape.glenmurphy.com reads 'Under the crazy presumption that a roll of duct tape has to exist *somewhere* on the Mars facility, the Duct Tape mod sticks flashlights to your machinegun and shotgun. In order to preserve the atmosphere, these new lights are much narrower (and a little brighter) than the standard flashlight, and are only available on the basic weapons. The pistol is not equipped with a flashlight, so as not to spoil the early sections of the game.'

10 The saga of *Spacewar*'s origin has been told many times, but nowhere as authentically as in Brand 1972.

11 *Doom 3* contains 785,000 lines of source code, compared to the original's 54,000 (Kent with id Software 2004: 180).

12 Aarseth characterizes videogames as instances of *cybertext*: a kind of machine that generates meaning in concert with an active, goal-seeking reader whose choices shape the final work. Cybertexts differ from the invariant structures of Hollywood cinema or traditional novels by virtue of their *ergodic* qualities – the 'nontrivial effort' required of users to navigate branching pathways, overcome obstacles and reach a destination that is by no means preordained (Aarseth 1997: 1). For Murray, videogames are best described as a type of 'narrative that presents a single situation or plotline in multiple versions, versions that would be mutually exclusive in our ordinary experience' (Murray 1997: 30).

13 To be fair, Frasca acknowledges that simulation and narrative share a representational base – including 'the characteristics of objects and characters, backgrounds, settings, and cut scenes' (2003: 232) – but slips frequently and symptomatically into a more pronounced antithesis. 'Certainly, simulation has

its limitations, just like representation. Simulation is only an approximation and even if narrauthors may feel threatened by it, it does not announce the end of representation: it is an alternative, not a replacement' (233). The problem is one of throwing out the baby with the bathwater. In its strident critique of the narrative/dramatic paradigm, simulationism is forced into the logically untenable position that 'modeling reality and fiction' (233) is not first and foremost an act of representation – that, again, the 'real' of the videogame is some secondarily-inferred complex of inner workings, not its immediately apprehensible outer surface.

9

Second Life: the game of virtual life

Alison McMahan

> I don't want the public to see the world they live in while they're in the park. I want them to feel they're in another world. (Walt Disney, in Imagineers 1996: 90)

> Virtual Reality is basically nothing new. We have been creating Virtual Reality around here for more than forty years. (John Hench, Senior Vice President, WED Enterprises, *ibid*.: 91)

Walt Disney's theme parks contain two key elements of virtual reality: high levels of engagement and of immersion. Physically, the 'guests' are almost fully immersed, as they are completely removed from their real world while in the park. Psychologically, they are immersed by story: each themed area is built on a myth (the myth of the American Frontier for Adventureland, or the utopian concept of technological progress for Tomorrowland, for example) and each ride is based on a story that might be familiar from storybooks or films (for example, the Indiana Jones Ride, based on Steven Spielberg's 1981 film *Raiders of the Lost Ark*) or similar enough to a familiar story that we can quickly grasp the story from the ride itself (the Pirates of the Caribbean Ride, based loosely on novels like Robert Louis Stevenson's classic *Treasure Island*, and later the inspiration for a Hollywood film). To a certain extent, Disney's theme parks are also interactive. As guests queue for a ride they are often addressed by characters (enacted by humans, whether live or pre-recorded, or by Audio-Animatronic automatons) from the storyworld of the ride as if the guests were characters in the story. Most of the rides are voyeuristic (travelling through the Haunted Mansion) but some attractions involve more direct participation (exploring Adventure Isle). Furthermore, games and events or performances within the world, like the shooting gallery or a sing-along in the Golden Horseshoe saloon in Frontierland, go further in strategically engaging the guests in the world of the park.

The quote above by John Hench invites us to compare Disneyland to virtual worlds in cyberspace. Persistent Worlds (PSWs) like *Second Life* could be described as 3D virtual theme parks. In *Second Life* there is no one story or myth set, as there are in graphic medieval fantasy worlds such as *Ultima Online* or in text-based Multi User Domains/Dungeons (MUDs) such as *Genesis* or *Angalon*, all of which owe a considerable debt of inspiration to *The Lord of the Rings* (1954–55) trilogy of novels by J.R.R. Tolkien. Instead, there are a number of areas with different themes, such as the area set in the world of Ridley Scott's film (and Philip K. Dick's original novel, *Do Androids Dream of Electric Sheep* (1968)), *Blade Runner* (1982) or an area based on the various worlds contained in J.M. Barrie's novel *Peter Pan* (1911), as well as various areas based on real life clubs, amusement parks, museums, art galleries, bars and restaurants, to name just a few. *Second Life* might not provide the same sensation one can get from a roller-coaster at Disneyland, and a 3D world accessed via a desktop or laptop computer is certainly not as physically immersive as a theme park, but the level of interactivity is much higher: visitors are not just 'guests', they are 'residents'. Residents automatically become members of a virtual familial group (when they choose their name), and their first task is to design their own appearance in the world, an appearance they can alter at will, including their gender.

In other words, the difference between Disneyland and *Second Life* is the difference between meatspace (that is, the physical world where the player's flesh and bone body resides) and cyberspace (the virtual reality space where the player's avatar, or digital, manipulable alter-ego resides). Persistent worlds represent a different kind of digital play from the better known first person shooter games, adventure games, or even massively multiplayer online games (MMOGs). They offer interesting opportunities to test out various theories about interactive narration and gaming and what creates a strong sense of presence (the feeling of really 'being there') in the user. Finally, they can serve as an excellent and affordable teaching tool for teachers working with students from various backgrounds in issues involving non-linear narrative, gaming and virtual reality.

This paper describes a second year undergraduate course I taught at Vassar College in Poughkeepsie, New York, in the autumn of 2003 (course syllabuses available at www.alisonmcmahan.com). The course challenged students to develop and confront their assumptions about virtual reality (VR) and to understand what constituted authentic virtual reality experiences of different types. They were asked to think about VR in both theoretical and practical terms, and then apply and test their new knowledge in their mid-term and final projects. For these they created a virtual reality environment for their peers to enjoy, using one of several technologies: a MUD or MUD Object Oriented (MOO), QuickTime VR, a gaming engine such as the *Unreal* engine, a mini-CAVE (computer automated virtual environment) system or in *Second Life*. In the process, we learned a great deal about how immersion and engagement are achieved in virtual environments, and what factors affect them. Some of the conclusions we reached were surprising.

Virtual worlds and films

> Until this time, Walt [Disney] knew little of the three-dimensional side of the entertainment fence, where fairs, amusement parks and the like could be found. But he did know movies and television. Driven by the desire to take his passion for storytelling far beyond the confines of two-dimensions, he landed on the idea that visitors who stepped in to this new park should feel as though they stepped into a movie. Every inch of the place should be part of a story, as in a movie or television show.
> (*Imagineers* 1996: 11)

On the first day of class I asked my students to tell me how they under-stood and defined virtual reality. As they gave their answers I made a list on the board. Most of their assumptions were wildly inaccurate (except for one or two who had some computer programming experience), reflecting what they had seen in the movies. The final list was wide ranging, but it boiled down to a few widely accepted myths about VR: that the technology for a holodeck-type VR (as depicted in *Star Trek: The Next Generation* (1987–94) television series) already exists, but is used, mostly secretly and for nefarious purposes, by powerful institutions such as the military; that these purposes include brainwashing and possibly torture; that the same technology could be used for intensely hedonistic purposes such as 'safe' drug trips and in-tense but remote sex; that extensive VR use for work or play could lead to brain damage; that one could lose one's soul to the VR machine or become a 'ghost in the machine',[1] that is, that their personalities or souls would get trapped in the computer generating the virtual reality environment and never be able to escape. Clearly, this reflected a misunderstanding of how artificial intelligence works as well as how virtual reality works. As part of the course I encouraged the students to distinguish between the two as well as to understand each one better. There was little understanding, except amongst some of the computer programmers, of the different types of VR that were possible. For example, most of the students did not see hypertext, text-based adventure games or even 3D computer games as forms of VR; in their minds VR had to include stereographic projection. And almost no one thought of the VR tools used for telepresence, such as the tools used to control the Mars Rover or for microscopic surgery, as forms of VR.

To encourage students to get to know and to collaborate with each other, as well as enabling them to understand how the myths and urban legends around VR had come into being, they were asked to do the following assignment. In groups of two, they were to watch a fiction film that featured extensive VR sequences, discuss how that film represented VR, then write a 500-word paper summarizing their findings which they also presented in the class. A selection of films had been put on reserve for them, but they were free to choose a different film if they wished.[2]

It was easy to see, in the ensuing discussion, how most of the urban legends around VR were an outgrowth of a general set of political and cultural anxieties. The political anxieties were focused around the militarization of American culture, polarization within the group on the value of the US invasion of Iraq, and the global social aftermaths of 9/11, an event that was very present in students' minds since Vassar is only forty miles from Ground Zero.

The cultural anxieties focused on the predominance of machines in our lives, our inability to understand them, and our fear that many of these machines could be used against us. Conceptual and practical mastery of the technology was presented as the solution for such anxieties, starting with an exploration of an easily accessible type of VR world: text-based multi-user domains.

MUDS

For their next assignment, students were asked to work in groups of three or four. Each group selected a different text-based MUD from the list on www.mudconnect.com and spent some time in it. I illustrated navigation by having the entire class join me in Angalon, an LPMud (that is, a MUD programmed in such a way that players can add on to the world) where I had spent a fair amount of time.[3]

A few students found this exercise enjoyable, especially because they had fun working in a group, but most of them, especially the gamers (there was a large number of PC and Xbox gamers in the class, plus a few that had grown up with Nintendo) found the text-based nature of multi-user-domains, or MUDS, off-putting, though by this point in the course we had read most of *Narrative as Virtual Reality* (Ryan 2001). The students felt that Ryan's narrative-based analysis of MUDS was misleading: perhaps the level of immersion in the MUD fiction that she described was possible for highly experienced Mudders who could alter the environment as well as exercise high-level powers and skills, but not for a casual visitor who only wanted to put in about twenty hours over the course of one week. In other words, the mudding experience failed for them because it wasn't enough like the 3D games at which they were more adept.

This was not simply a problem coping with text instead of the graphics they were used to, but it also reflected the fact that the narratological approach, when applied to game analysis, is insufficient for describing the degree of experience that the average user or player brings to the environment. The narratological approach focuses on the degree of immersion an ideal player will experience in the story world of an interactive environment. However, this approach, though necessary for a certain part of a game analysis, does not account for the player's previous experience and personal preferences that have evolved as a consequent of that experience. As a result a purely narratological analysis cannot give us a complete picture of how gameplay works, even for a virtual environment as story-oriented as a text-based adventure. A ludological approach takes into account the pleasures that result from game strategy and from the non-diegetic chat that usually accompanies play (especially in games like first person shooters). We quickly realized that narratological analysis helped us assess the degree of immersion a virtual environment could offer, but a ludological analysis was more important for analyzing engagement. The next assignment aimed at helping students distinguish between immersion and engagement.

Historical overview of VR

A fairly large number of the students had become disheartened by what struck them simultaneously as the 'excessively technological' and 'dated' demands of Mudding. In order to help them get some distance from technology, the next assignment was research oriented: working alone, they were asked to pick an early (pre-1990) VR technology, such as stereographic images (two dimensional images that appear three dimensional when you cross your eyes and look at them again), early 3-D projection systems such as Friese-Greene's stereographic system, 3D Hollywood films, OMNIMAX (the stereographic projection of IMAX movies which requires viewers to wear goggles), 3D television experiments, the transition from two dimensional graphics to isometric and then to three dimensional graphics in computer games, or any other 3D application. In their research papers the students were asked to describe the technology to demonstrate their understanding of how stereo works, and, more subjectively, assess the impact of that particular technology on the artistic content.

Many students were very creative about finding out-of-the-way applications of 3D technology, from the 1953 experimental television broadcasts in the US, to a reception study of the film *Friday the 13th: 3D*, to autostereoscopic displays, to Omnimax projection technology and its attendant interface, and 3D movie attractions in theme parks like Disneyland and Universal Studios, to name just a few. The overall impact of this exercise was that students learned that the earliest filmmakers and many visual artists experimented with stereographic images in pursuit of what they called realism but which would later be defined as an increased sense of presence; that though many forms of virtual reality include three-dimensional images, not all of them do, nor it is necessary requirement for an application to be 3D to be virtual reality.

The elements of presence

I have previously summarized my findings on presence in the article 'Immersion, Engagement and Presence: A Method for Analyzing 3-D Video Games' (McMahan 2003). 'Presence' is a term that covers elements of immersion and engagement. Scholars who analyze presence in a virtual environment (VE) are looking at the VE's immersive and engaging elements. My article surveyed the literature on presence and immersion (two terms that are often mistakenly used interchangeably, especially by humanities scholars working in game studies and film studies who adapt the scientific terminology for their own uses), and an update and clarification, based on my own research, on what VR specialists mean by these terms. Following Janet Murray (1998: 98–99), immersion is defined as the sense the player has of being involved in the story of the game – the kind of involvement that Ryan analyzed in her book. Engagement refers to the non-diegetic level of involvement with a game (the involvement with aspects of the game that do not have to do with story, such as strategic planning, hoarding of gold or health potions, etc.) Both diegetic immersion and non-diegetic engagement are aspects of what researchers in virtual reality have labelled *presence*. Many elements, some overlapping, some fairly incompatible with each other, go into making up a sense of presence; researchers Lombard and Ditton (1997) have summarized these elements into six characteristics, summing up their findings as follows: 'Because it is a perceptual illusion, presence is a property of a person. However it results from an interaction among formal and content characteristics of a medium and characteristics of a media user, and therefore it can and does vary across individuals and across time for the same individual' (Lombard and Ditton 1997: 10).

An increased sense of presence can result from a combination of all or some of the following factors:

1　Quality of social interaction (how the avatars are programmed and how much creative control users have of their avatars; how well the world's backbone facilitates inter-player communication; how the communication interface is designed).

2　Realism in the environment, which is further broken down into social realism (how well the virtual world interactions line up with the user's expectations based on their real-world experience) and perceptual realism (how closely the visual, audio, and game physics within the world match those of the real world).

3　'Telepresence', that is, the degree of immersiveness generated by the interface design. Telepresence systems use specific interfaces to place one or more users (the 'teleoperators') at a remote or inaccessible location for the purposes of accomplishing a specific task such as operating the Mars Rover.

4　The user's ability to accomplish significant actions within the environment (a result of how well the interface is designed as well as the in-world physics).

5　The social impact of what occurs in the environment.

6　The user's responding to the computer itself as an intelligent, social agent.

Students were encouraged to apply this terminology and identify the six elements of presence when discussing or writing about various VR applications, including their own midterm and final projects such as the play they staged in *Second Life*. Forms of virtual reality we studied in class included the panoramas and dioramas we saw at the Museum of Natural History in New York, the early virtual technologies they had researched, and the VR applications we looked at in class, such as surgical and space applications of VR, the work of artists like Zoe Beloff, Char Davies and Jeffrey Shaw, 3D environments ranging from Quick Time Virtual Reality (QTVR) environments (cylindrical panoramas created by stitching together photographs or drawings of a location), to game environments ranging from the vector spaces of *Battlezone* to first person shooter games like *Quake* and *Unreal*. We had no access to an actual CAVE but we did have a demonstration of a mini-CAVE setup by Dave Pape, the creator of the CAVE computing language, and Josephine Anstey, the designer of *The Trial, The Trail*.[4]

Putting theory into practice

For their midterm and final projects, on which the bulk of their grade would be based, the students were asked to form new groups of three or four and build virtual reality environments themselves. Everyone had to work on a QTVR in their group for the midterm project; for the final the students could choose from a variety of technological formats, based on what we had available at Vassar at the time. The choices included: writing an in-depth research paper, designing another QTVR, or adding to the one they had built for their midterm project; using Director MX to build 3-D environments; using a game engine to build their own mod or game level (in fact, one very adept student used the *Unreal* game engine to build his own little *Night of the Living Dead* kind of world); doing graphic design for one of the environments in the CAVE project which was the focus of my research (McMahan 2003b, McMahan and Tortell 2004) or designing an experience for the entire class in an online graphic world called *Second Life*.

For the play the students were required to secure a performance space in *Second Life*, advertise it to other *Second Life* residents, and design the play in such a way (it could be a play they wrote or a play they found and modified) that members of the audience were pulled into the action.

About *Second Life*

We have chosen to use the title Persistent State World or PSW to describe these online experiences. Also used are the terms: virtual world, multi-user domain or multi-user dungeon (MUD), massively multi-player (MMP) game, massively multi-player online game (MMOG) and massively multiplayer online role-playing game (MMORPG). The sheer variety of acronyms and the inadequacy of them all are indicative of the young age of this industry. In particular the authors point out that the growth of the persistent worlds market is almost predicated upon its moving away from its origins in fantasy role-playing type games. (IGDA 2004: 6)

At the time of our group exercise in the autumn of 2003, *Second Life* was in its version 1.1. The world was directed at the 18–24 year-old student and the over-45 year-old demographic. However most players were 19–44 and 70% male. Since our exercise in 2003, the demographic has changed somewhat. According to a news item posted on the *Second Life* website on June 29, 2005, 40% of players are female, average player age is 32, and average playtime is 16 hours a week. The world is now supported by 1,000 CPUs (computer processing units) (Takahashi 2005) and covers 12,000 acres with 20,000 owned plots of land ('What is *Second Life*' 2005).

Second Life is available by downloading from secondlife.com with a free seven-day trial. In 2003 membership was available for $15 a month or $135 a year. In 2005 the subscription level is 32,000. Players only need to pay the $9.95 monthly fee if they want to own land. For a $9.95 one-time fee players can travel through the world, interact, build objects such as their own avatar, clothes and art, keep these objects in an inventory, and build larger objects in free-zones or "sandboxes".

For an even more voyeuristic approach to entering the world visitors can watch *Second Life* TV, a live video stream from the virtual world available on the home web page. It is random in its selection of images and is accompanied by a live music track, making it reminiscent of Big Brother TV.

The hardware requirements of 2003 still apply today: Windows XP/2000; 800 MHZ computer or higher, 256 Mb of RAM or more; broadband internet connection (DSL Cable modem/LAN), a graphics card (NVIDIA Geforce 2 or ATI Radeon) with 32 Mb of RAM or more).[5] In 2003 these hardware requirements represented state of the art computing which was hard to obtain. At Vassar we needed access to the most sophisticated computer lab on campus, normally used by chemistry and physics students, for our *Second Life* experience.

Second Life: the game metaphor

Unlike a MUD or a MMORPG, a persistent world is not a game, though it incorporates games within it. Persistent worlds have some codes of behaviour as well as strategic guidelines, but these rules are not story-based as they are in MUDS (in a MUD you build up your skills by belonging to a clan and training in the clan's guild hall, for example). The most obvious way to describe the difference between a world and a game is the difference in their metaphors.

Players of computer simulation games such as *The Sims* are aided in their gaming by a simple metaphor the designers put forward to help the player get an initial grasp of the game. So *SimCity* is likened to a train set and *The Sims* (2000) to a doll's house. However, game metaphors, much like the philosophical theme in a film, are not always reducible to a single concept. As players develop a better understanding of the game dynamics, they discover that the metaphor they started with is not very accurate, and that more complex underlying metaphors exist that can only be grasped as the game is being played, for example, 'gardening' for *SimCity*.

Game designer and theorist Chris Crawford (1983: 8) refers to mental models as the philosophical core, as well as the *raison d'être* of the historical game. Players also carry mental models in their heads, and this model changes according to circumstances. For example, Microsoft was pressured to remove the player's ability to fly between New York's Twin Towers and even crash into them in *Flight Simulator*, after the Twin Towers were destroyed in just that way by terrorists on 11 September 2001. But during the 1991 war on Iraq players demanded that flight simulator companies sell add-on Iraq war scenario disks to already existing flight simulator games (Dunnigan 1992: 249). Clearly, simulation games are not just about competing against other players, or a computer, at computation (though this describes most puzzle games). Simulation games are also about the mental models of a simulation in the player's head. The player's models and the designer's models can come into conflict with each other. The playing out of these simulation games results in 'simulation narratives', that is, the player's gameplay adds up to the story of their game experience (Ryan 2001: 110–114).

A persistent world is not a game, but it still has an overall metaphor. For *Second Life* the metaphor is clear from the very title: your participation in this world is much like your participation in your real world; it's your Second Life. You are expected to take it seriously and make a considerable emotional investment. You are expected to respond officially (through a rating system) to the spaces and games built into the world by other 'residents' (note that they are no longer called 'players'). You need to earn money and you pay taxes. You are only allowed one avatar; among other things that you can do, you can virtually marry another resident from *Second Life*.

Gaming in *Second Life* today

The designers of *Second Life* have built in an open source development model into the world. Players can develop apps (applications) and products inside the game; it is a great introduction to computer science for children and young people.

Residents have developed games within the persistent world of every size and style: multiplayer and solo play, dozens of in-world games, first person shooters, fantasy role-playing games, puzzle and strategy games, races across the world to find scavenger items, and solo board games and story-driven adventures. Residents can also socialize in nightclubs, participate in fashion shows, art openings, fancy dress balls and other kinds of social events. Scripting is empowered by Havok™, and is compatible with Poser, Photoshop, GIMP, Quicktime movie, .mov, .wav, .bvh, .tga and .mp3. There is a wiki (web site that can be changed by anyone) that gives an overview to all of the games in *Second Life*, which are constantly changing (wiki.tinypirate.com/tiki-index.php). Competitions are held regularly for the best game design.

Probably the most unique thing about games in *Second Life* is that residents retain all the intellectual property (IP) rights to their own creations. This means that game developers can charge admission, franchise their idea, become a scriptor for hire and trade Linden dollars on third party sites for real-world dollars. Several resident game developers have already exercised their rights to sell a cross-platform version of their in-world game to a real-world publisher, or rented out their in-world game settings for commercial use.[6] This means that the best game in *Second Life* is the game of making money. Anshe Chung from Germany made $150,000 in 2005 buying land in *Second Life*, developing it and selling it (Au, 2005a). *Second Life* CEO Philip Rosedale says 'residents spent $1.5 million Linden a month in buying and selling from each other. Hundreds of thousands of those dollars are converted into real world money.' (Au 2005b.)

Staging a play In *Second Life*

Putting on a play for one's community is a very social act. In addition, the students were charged with building some form of interaction between performers and audience. They found this a rather difficult thing to do. It might have worked better if they had chosen to stage a more 'street theatre' or improvised kind of play, where some of the play involved more interaction with the audience; their plan was to engage the audience as wedding guests at the end of the play. But it is of interest that though a 'street theatre' option was available to them, the organizer students, who were drama majors at Vassar, chose to put on a traditional play; in fact they chose one of the most traditional plays around, Shakespeare's *A Midsummer Night's Dream*. Their choice was partly motivated by the 'play-within-the-play' aspect, which they thought would be interesting to experiment with in a persistent world where residents have already designed an avatar to begin with, adding a further layer of performance to the performance (McMahan 1999). Their first task was to shorten the play, taking only a selection of scenes, most of which focused on setting up Theseus and Hypolyta's wedding plans, the play within the play, and the marriage at the end. Once scenes were selected, cuts were made in the dialogue.

Music and sound effects are not required for gameplay in *Second Life*, though some use of sound is possible. Physical sounds relating to objects and the player's avatar are available. Short sound clips can be attached to objects. Sounds can be synchronized to the avatar's gestures. There is also a music synchronizer for those who want to make music, or players can download their own music on the sliders of the mixing board. However, it is not possible for residents to voice their comments to each other; these have to be typed in and read from the screen.

The students tried not to modify Shakespeare's language, but simply to cut out some of the dialogue strands. They discovered the hard way during rehearsal that no one could type their lines fast enough, nor could the audience 'read' the lines fast enough to keep a sense of performance going, even when the lines were pre-entered and just had to be cut and pasted in to the chat line. Many students, especially those who hadn't mastered the cut and paste and couldn't type fast enough, ended up simplifying their lines on the fly.

In addition to their traditional approach to play selection and performance, the students also chose to stage the play in a very traditional way, in a theatre with a proscenium stage and space for audience to sit. No one had the programming skills to build a proscenium stage but by negotiating with other residents in the *Second Life* space the students rented a piece of land (everyone contributed to the rent) and borrowed a theatre that someone else had built and had in their inventory of objects. We discussed staging the play in a *Second Life* forest, but most of the students felt the audience would not be able to find or follow the performance under those circumstances.

On the day of the performance, the audience, about twenty strong, sat everywhere in the proscenium space except in the space designated for them – many of them sat on ceiling beams or on the chandelier. Some would arrive in *Second Life* right in the middle of the stage and had to quickly be escorted off. No one seemed to mind this, and the play performance continued without interruption.

At a certain point, about a third of the way into the play, there were too many people on stage, between audience and performers, and the memory allocation for that portion of the grid was exceeded. This caused *Second Life* to reset and we were all kicked out of the world and had to sign on again. To help solve this during the performance, students who were not actually onstage began to sign off and watch the performance of their peers on the large classroom screen, making comments along the way, giving the players a meatspace audience as well as a cyberspace audience. Even with these precautions we had several resets. What astonished me most is that the audience was very faithful and kept signing back on after each reset.

The range of programming skills (and interest in programming) among the students showed in their character avatars. The student playing the lion wanted to look like a lion for the play-within-the-play, but in the end just gave himself a mane of golden locks; however the wall did make himself look just like a wall, but with arms and feet sticking out. Often the character in *Midsummer* and his character in the play of *Pyramus and Thisbe* within *Midsummer* were played by different students, adding another interesting layer of performance.

The actors assembled a list of gestures, and they experimented with various combinations of gestures until they achieved a kind of pantomimic set of moves that they used to convey various emotions. For example, the Lion used a combination of gestures such as the 'Boo' gesture, the bow gesture and the clap gesture to depict his roaring visually.

At the end of the performance the actors came down from the stage and invited the audience to join the dance to celebrate Theseus and Hypolyta's wedding. Most of the audience did not know how to use the gesture commands and so the performers spent some time teaching them. Then everyone danced wonderfully until the next reset ... This felt like the most successful part of the exercise.

All of this, especially the interesting problems encountered by the students in their staging of the play, sheds a new light on the ludology versus narratology argument. (For an in-depth treatment of this issue see Marie Laure Ryan's Chapter 1 in this volume.) The students aimed to test the limits of classic narration in a virtual world. Their dramatic presentation worked, but it seemed terribly limited in such an interactive medium. What we discovered as the result of our performance is that a persistent world like *Second Life* offers heightened possibilities but also limitations for presenting classical narrative. The limitations, as we have seen, included the inability to speak or type as quickly as Shakespeare's dense language required and the limitations on physical performance. The possibilities included the immense range of design choices and graphic possibilities for props, and the numerous ways the avatars could move or be used, including the ability to 'fly', the possibility that several humans could invisibly play the same character in the play, and the heightened possibilities for interaction.

Using the terminology for presence, we found that the quality of social interaction in *Second Life* is very high, as is the impact of that interaction (the students had entertained a large audience, taught the audience how to use gestures, and had networked with other residents to make the performance possible). The interface was intuitive enough (learning it came naturally because we were already so familiar with the PC interface), but psychological immersion was sometimes interrupted by technical problems such as the resets. Students experienced the world as intelligent primarily in how the *Second Life* engine enabled their avatar and character designs, a process that they enjoyed so much that they would re-do their avatars over and over again. Students experimented with an extended definition of telepresence during the play and during rehearsals by taking over each other's characters for short periods of time. Students were especially thrilled by the newness of the experience, of doing something very traditional (putting on a play) that they usually only did in meatspace, in cyberspace.

We concluded in the end that classic narrative, even that of a dramatic presentation, can work in a persistent online world, but seemed terribly limited in such an interactive medium, a limitation that was brought home to us by the audience's choice of seating. By hanging from the chandeliers and venturing onto the stage, whether wilfully or accidentally, the audience was reminding us of the limitations of meatspace rules in this world, which are also the limitations of classical narrative.

The IGDA 2004 white paper on persistent worlds (PSWs) predicts that PSWs will do better as they move away from the adventure games format. This almost seems to predict that games within PSWs will lead to more interactivity and sense of presence than something with a narrative – even a loose overall narrative that simply unifies the design and dictates the nature of player interactions as it does in *Ultima Online*.

For our play, the diegetic immersion required by classic narration was the least important aspect of the experience (admittedly the choice of a narrative that is very well known to everyone made it less important); instead, the engagement in the non-narrative elements were what really heightened the feeling of presence.

At one end of the immersion scale are theme parks like Disneyland, where rides, buildings and themed area are all designed based on classical narratives that the audiences know well, where physical immersion is complete, but where interactivity is fairly low. At the other end are persistent worlds, with *Second Life* very similar to Disneyland in that it is a space where people can play in differently themed environments, and even go on rides; but the level of interactivity is much higher, though physical immersion is of course much less – the ultimate difference between cyberspace and meatspace. The principal similarity between theme parks and computer games and even themed areas in persistent worlds is their reliance on classic narratives better known to us from film as a shared world reference. Games have an added element of game metaphors, which the player may or may not understand; and understanding of the metaphor can also be at the conscious or subconscious level. Finally, the player's previous experience is an increasingly important factor, with a generation gap appearing in choice of genres: few of my students had the patience to master the skills required for a text-based world; but they had a high level of skill in 2D and 3D gaming which made an online 3D world more appealing.

Works cited

Au, Wagner James (2005a) 'Anshe at the Gates', http://secondlife.blogs.com/nwn/2005/03/anshe_at_the_ga.html, accessed July 2005.

——(2005b) 'Greenspanning the Globe – Philip Linden Interview, Part I', http://secondlife.blogs.com/nwn/2005/01/greenspanning_t.html, accessed 4 July 2005.

Crawford, Chris (1983) *The Art of Computer Game Design*, Chapter 1, www.vancouver.wsu.edu/fac/peabody/game-book/Coverpage.html, accessed July 2005.

Dunnigan, James (1992) *The Complete Wargames Handbook: How to Play, Design and Find Them*, revised edn, New York: Quill.

IEDA (International Game Developer's Association) (2004) *Persistent Worlds Whitepaper*, IGDA Online Games SIG, www.igda.org/online, accessed June 2005.

Imagineers, The (1996) *Imagineering: A Behind the Dreams Look at Making the Magic Real*, Foreword by Michael D. Eisner, New York: Disney Editions.

Lombard, Matthew and Theresa Ditton (1997) 'At the Heart of it All: The Concept of Presence', *Journal of Computer-Mediated Communication*, 3:2, September 1997.

McMahan, Alison (2003a) 'Immersion, Engagement and Presence: A Method for Analyzing 3-D Video Games', in Mark Wolf and Barnard Perron (eds) (2003) *The Video Game Theory Reader*, New York and London: Routledge, 67–86.

——(2003b) '*Memesis*: A Prototype in Biofeedback and Virtual Reality Narration for CAVEs', in Hal Thwaites (ed.) Proceedings of the Ninth International Conference on Virtual Systems and Multimedia, *VSMM2003: Hybrid Reality: Art, Technology and the Human Factor*, Montreal: Hexagram Institute, 694–702.

——(1999) 'The Effect of Multiform Narrative on Subjectivity', *Screen*, 40:2, 146–157.

McMahan, Alison and Rebecca Tortell (2004) 'Virtual Reality and the Internal Experience', paper given at the VR2004 Workshop, Virtual Reality for Human

Consumption (co-located with Haptics Conference) Chicago, 27–31 March 2004.

Murray, Janet (1998) *Hamlet on the Holodeck: The Future of Narrative in Cyberspace*, Cambridge, MA: MIT Press.

Ryan, Marie-Laure (2001) *Narrative as Virtual Reality: Immersion and Interactivity in Literature and Electronic Media*, Baltimore and London: Johns Hopkins University Press.

Shermans, Bill and Alan B. Craig (2003) *Understanding Virtual Reality: Interface, Application, and Design*, San Francisco, CA: Morgan Kaufmann Publishers.

Takahashi, Dean (2005) A+e Mercury News Interactive, www.typepad.com/t/trackback/2709692, accessed June 2005.

'What is *Second Life*?', on the *Second Life* web site, www.secondlife.com, accessed June 2005.

'Tringo Fever – Catch It! Resident-made in-world game licensed to Real Life new Media company', *The Second Opinion*, 3 March 2005, http://secondlife.com/newsletter/2005_03_05_archive.php, accessed 20 June 2005.

Games

Flight Simulator (1983), Psion.
Sim City (1989), Maxis/Maxis.
The Sims (2000), Maxis/Electronic Arts.
Ultima Online (1998), Electronic Arts/Electronic Arts.

Notes

1   The phrase 'The Ghost in the machine' was coined by Gilbert Ryle in his 1949 *The Concept of Mind*, as a derogatory way of referring to Cartesian Dualism. The phrase was further popularized by Arthur Koestler's 1967 book *The Ghost in the Machine*, which linked the possibility of nuclear war to primitive human brain functions that overwhelm our 'logical' minds. Most university students are familiar with the manga (1991) and anime franchise (began 1995) *The Ghost in the Shell*, in which a policewoman is all robot, except for her brain and spinal cord.

2   The films included: *Johnny Mnemonic, Jumanji, Lawnmower Man, The Matrix, Virtuality, Fugitive Mind, The Cell, Dark City, Virtual Encounters, Contact, Simone, Final Fantasy, Star Trek First Contact, Total Recall, Tron, Future Shock, What Dreams May Come, The 13th Floor, eXistenZ*, and *Minority Report;* television episodes from series such as *Star Trek: The Next Generation, The X-Files* and *Lois and Clark*.

3   The regular members of Angalon had given me permission to bring in a class at an agreed upon time. I am grateful to all of the members of Angalon, especially

Maguest, who helped the students get oriented.

4   For more on Pape and Anstey's work see www.resumbrae.com.

5   *Second Life* opened up to Mac users on 24 November 2005. System requirements: 1Ghz G4 or better, with 512 Mb of RAM, Mac OS 10.3.8 or higher,
same graphics card and internet connection as PC.

6   From the *Second Life* webpage for game developers, www.secondlife.com/games/
game_dev.php. See also 'Tringo Fever – Catch It!'

10

Playing to solve *Savoir-Faire*

Nick Montfort

Emily Short's 2002 *Savoir-Faire* is a quintessential work of interactive fiction (IF), an all-text adventure game that draws on the substantial history of the form but also contributes its share of innovations.[1] The basic conceit is that of the treasure hunt – a classic organizing principle for interactive fiction. *Savoir-Faire* is set in a novel IF world, however, where an unusual sort of magic is possible. The game works in what Short calls a 'simulationist' way.[2] This term is meant to indicate a richer environment in which puzzles may have multiple solutions, where magical and physical effects are simulated even when they are not directly relevant to solving puzzles.

Savoir-Faire is clearly the sort of program that asks to be understood as a game (a play experience), as a sort of puzzle or riddle (an experience of solving), and as a textual exchange that has literary qualities (a reading experience). The relationship between play and reading in another piece of interactive fiction, Adam Cadre's *Varicella*, has already been explored (Montfort and Moulthrop 2003), and the figure of the literary riddle has been introduced as a way to connect the literary nature of interactive fiction with the process of solving it (Montfort 2003). In this chapter, I will focus on the remaining connection: on how the activities of playing and solving interrelate in the form generally and, more specifically, in *Savoir-Faire*.

It is also important to consider how several interactors may be simultaneously at work, or at play, in the same session. By all appearances, interactive fiction presents a one-player experience, but one perspective on interactive fiction is that games in this form are inherently cooperative – it's stereotypical for a single person to play alone, but if more than one person plays, the structure of the game means that they'll naturally work together. *Savoir-Faire* provides an opportunity to see, in the context of a particular interactive fiction work, how different types of cooperation might be accomplished and how the nature of the game might support such activity. Considering how individual or cooperative interaction can be both play and solving can also help to explain how interactive fiction can be a complex system powerfully resolved into sense by a solution, while, at the same time, it is fun and can be enjoyed in other ways.

A capsule history of interactive fiction

The category of interactive fiction, to which *Savoir-Faire* makes one elaborate and well-written contribution, was originally defined by Will Crowther and Don Woods. Their *Adventure* – first programmed by Crowther, then expanded and cleaned up by Woods, working independently across the country – was released in its canonical form onto the Internet's ancestor Arpanet in 1976. It became extremely popular. Since then, a wide array of programs have been developed that are known variously as text adventures or text games, or sometimes as 'works of interactive fiction'. The early game-makers, many of them academics, worked in their spare time to develop programs such as *Zork* (at MIT), *Haunt* (at Carnegie Mellon) and *Acheton* (at Cambridge), usually making their programs freely playable and freely available, at least to the limited few who had access to computers at that time.

When the home computer first took off in North America and Europe in the 1980s, a market for entertainment software arose. A huge number of commercial works of interactive fiction were developed. The major IF company in the United States was Infocom; elsewhere in the world were Level 9, Melbourne House and Magnetic Scrolls. Some commercial interactive fiction works were adaptations of earlier 'mainframe' games; some had simple graphics added in; some were based on books; and some were designed and written with literary care by authors who included Robert Pinsky (*Mindwheel*), Tom Disch (*Amnesia*), and Douglas Adams (*The Hitchhiker's Guide to the Galaxy, Bureaucracy*). By the mid-1990s, buyers did not seem as eager to play all-text or text-based computer games – their other options around that time included engaging spectacles such as *Doom* and *Myst* – and the once-bustling market for interactive fiction was shuttered. Around the same time, however, tools became available to allow individuals to easily create complex works of interactive fiction that rivalled the best commercial productions. A community of developers and players began to gather online. Today, individual authors, including many academics, once again work in their spare time to develop interactive fiction programs, usually making them freely available to anyone who has Internet access. Some see this as a disappearance into non-commercial obscurity, but interactive fiction actually seems to have returned to its roots, and innovation in the form continues.[3]

The making of *Savoir-Faire*

'Emily Short' is the pseudonym of a University of Pennsylvania doctoral candidate in classical studies. She is one of the leading authors and programmers of interactive fiction active today. Her entry in the 2000 IF Art Show, *Galatea*, won Best of Show and became a model for the rich simulation of a character in interactive fiction. Her *Metamorphoses* took second place in the 2000 IF Competition and won the Best Writing XYZZY Award.[4] Her major releases in 2001 were *Pytho's Mask* and *Best of Three*; in 2003 she released the text-and-graphics interactive fiction *City of Secrets*. She has written and collaborated on numerous other projects, is a prolific reviewer of interactive fiction and is the editor of the volume *IF Theory*.[5]

Savoir-Faire was the winner of four XYZZY awards in 2002, including Best Game. It takes place in what Short calls a 'somewhat mangled version of the early 1780s'.[6] The player character, Pierre, in search of an emergency loan, returns to the house where he grew up, only to find that everyone is gone. So the player must direct him in a search for valuables, one that is aided by Pierre's ability to perform the magic of the 'lavori d'Aracne'.

The game was written (as with Short's other interactive fiction) in Inform, a freely available language that was created by Graham Nelson specifically for the development of interactive fiction.[7] *Savoir-Faire* is a Z-code program, which means that it runs in a virtual machine called the Z-machine. The nature of the Z-machine is important because it both enables massively cross-platform access to interactive fiction and places austere constraints on the size of programs. The Z-machine, developed by Infocom's Joel Berez and Marc Blank in 1979, is in some ways like a media 'player' or document 'reader', except that it is a complete software computer and can execute programs, not just play time-based media or displaying data. One important feature of such a system is that a Z-machine interpreter only needs to be implemented once on each target platform (for instance, Microsoft Windows, Macintosh OS X, or Linux). After this is done, a developer can write a single Z-code program and that program can immediately be 'played' or 'read' on all the platforms that have interpreters. This virtual machine concept was first commercialized by Infocom in the Z-machine. Later, it became a central idea in Sun's Java.

Because *Savoir-Faire* is a Z-code program, and because many Z-machine interpreters remain available for modern computer platforms, the game runs on all common desktop and notebook computers, on the Internet in a Java applet, on many handheld computers and PDAs, and on many uncommon systems.[8] However, even version 8 of the Z-machine – the most capable version – is a very underpowered virtual computer by today's standards. *Savoir-Faire* was originally developed for the even more limited version 5, although since release 5 the game has used version 8. Version 5 files can be at most 256 KB; the original release of *Savoir-Faire* reached the absolute limit of that version of the Z-machine: 'Yes, it really truly does fit in a z5, though my compiler produced this curious message at the end: >0 bytes free in Z-machine' (Short 2002). While the format provided strict constraints, it is notable that Short chose to make her IF world as intricate as it could be within those constraints.

A sketch of the world

The 'IF world' is not just a literary setting, nor is it just a carefully arranged virtual space. It does include a space that can be represented on a map, as well as the atmosphere evoked in the generated text. But the IF world also contains existents – some of them inert 'objects' and some called 'non-player characters' and capable of action, with motivation, emotions, and knowledge. The IF world includes, as well, a system of physical laws. Sometimes (as in *Savoir-Faire*) this includes magical or other unusual variations on the laws of our world. Even the capabilities, memories, and preferences of the player character – to the extent they are defined by the program rather than being suggested by the player's commands – are part of the IF world. The only aspects of an interactive fiction that are not part of the world are at the level of interface and at the level of the IF program outside this fictional, simulated world: the player's ability to restart the game, for instance, or to read a license statement or a help text of some sort that is not part of the IF world.

In *Savoir-Faire,* the player character, Pierre, begins in the 'Kitchen Garden'. Five other areas in and around the kitchen are initially accessible. After working some of this world's magic, linking objects together so that actions performed on one will affect the other, Pierre can get into the main house, where eight more areas can be accessed. A few more above-ground areas become accessible as the player makes progress, but the overall space of the two-storey house is not that expansive or confusing, and many can navigate it without bothering to draw a map, as was traditional in early interactive fiction. The thirteen underground areas include a puzzling wine cellar whose linked coloured doors must be opened by Pierre in his quest for loot. They are more perplexing, but the real difficulty here also lies in negotiating and recognizing relationships among objects, not in mapping some *Adventure-like* maze.

This *Savoir-Faire* transcript shows the solution to one puzzle and gives a hint of what interaction with the game is like:

Kitchen Garden

West is the wall of the kitchen. Most of the space along the wall is planted with herbs – bay, parsley, stalks of mint – left of the open doorway. To its right is only a drainage ditch, catching the outflow of a pipe that comes through the wall.

In one corner of the plot is the well, drilled many deep feet; in another is the antique sundial.

A tangle of climbing roses covers almost completely the wall and door of a shed to the southeast.

>*link the chocolate rose to the roses*
Bending your will, you form the link between the chocolate rose and the roses.

>*cut the chocolate rose*
What do you want to cut the chocolate rose with?

>*knife*
(first taking the butcher knife)
(putting the hinge-lidded teapot into the sack to make room)
The chocolate rose cuts partway through, then splits of its own accord in rough surfaces, becoming a pile of small bits.

The roses split into a pile of small bits.

[Your score has just gone up by three points.]

The player finishes solving a puzzle by creating a magical link between similar-looking objects and cutting up the one which can be easily cut. Trying to cut the climbing roses directly will not work, and won't allow Pierre access to the shed.

By using the special commands *link* and *unlink*, and another magical command that the player must learn in the course of play, the player can cause Pierre to form or break magical connections between similar-looking objects. While Pierre supposedly knows how linking works, the player must discover this and figure out how magically connecting objects can unlock more of the house, providing access to loot and access to information about why the house has recently been abandoned. Another special command, *remember* (which can be used with or without a direct object), allows for some events from Pierre's past to be narrated. These provide clues about the nature of the house, about Pierre's missing adoptive family, and about how the lavori d'Aracne works.

Again, this is most usefully illustrated with a transcript:

>*examine model*

Fitted out with tiny planets on arms, and the major moons of the planets, revolving around a center. There is no sun, however; there is only a sort of holder designed to contain something spherical.

Most of the planets are ordinary balls of solid metal, except for Jupiter. They stand still.

Oddly, the contraption also seems to be linked, and quite unsubtly, to something in the foyer, to the south. You can feel the pull of it.

Something about the model universe tickles your recollection.

>*remember model*

...

The Count was standing in the library, tinkering with the model; Marie was bent over it as well, instructing him about what to connect where. 'I will never understand,' he remarked to you, 'how it is that she has such a mechanical mind. Not the least interest in diplomacy ...'

'It is my cold heart, Papa,' she replied, tossing aside her clockmaking tools.

'It is done?' he asked her.

'Put the light in,' she said, 'and then make it go.'

You turned away. 'Stay and see how it works!' Marie called after you.

'Sorry, infant, the road to Paris is long ...'

...

The 'remember' command allows backstory to be narrated while also providing hints about how to solve the puzzles that Pierre and the player immediately face.

Savoir-Faire is difficult; while recourse to hints or a walkthrough can help one through the game in less time, Short estimates on her home page that it will take between 10 and 20 hours of play to solve.[9] This level of engagement is required by most commercial interactive fiction from the 1980s and by some of the intricate early works from before the home computer era, but only a few of the many interactive fiction works that have been released in recent years are 'long games' of this sort.

Play and solution

In announcing *Savoir-Faire*, Short (2002) wrote that 'It is an old-style game, with a score and a large number of inventory items; it probably takes longer to play than anything else I've written, despite the compact game size.' A capsule review calls it 'a real joy to play, and the kind of game that you'll keep toying with after you've finished it' (Muckenhoupt 2005). What did these two mean by 'play', and what do others mean when they say that they are playing *Savoir-Faire*? Game designers Katie Salen and Eric Zimmerman (2004: 302–304) distinguish thirteen senses of the word 'play'. Several can be quickly dismissed as irrelevant: people who say they are playing *Savoir-Faire* do not mean that they are gambling, stalling, or creating music.[10] It is most likely that self-proclaimed players are simply referring to what Salen and Zimmerman call 'game play', which the two define (recursively) as 'the formalized interaction that occurs when players follow the rules of a game and experience its system through play'. Other senses of 'play', such as the dramatic one, may be applicable to *Savoir-Faire*, but do not seem to be intended. There is no record online of anyone discussing how he or she 'played Pierre' in a dramatic sense for instance, although some players may enjoy that the game is focalized through this character. Salen and Zimmerman's most general definition of play, however, is particularly helpful for the critic, even if it is not intended by players: 'free movement within a more rigid structure'. This is meant to include 'game play' and cover ludic activity and general playfulness as well.

In considering different types of interactive fiction play, it is worthwhile to look to Richard Bartle's (1996) typology of Multiple User Dungeon (MUD) players. Two player types are directly applicable to interactive fiction, the form which the MUD is a multiplayer version of: achievers, who seek 'game-related goals, and vigorously set out to achieve them', and explorers, who 'try to find out as much as they can about the virtual world' and progress to 'experimentation with physics'. The other two player types, socalizers and killers, require communication with others through the game itself and the ability to 'PK' (kill other players' characters), neither of which are provided by *Savoir-Faire* or other interactive fiction works that are 'single user' and present one prompt at a time. But interactive fiction certainly allows more goal-focused, achiever-style play and more exploratory and ludic play. Rather than characterizing players themselves and placing them within these categories or on an interest graph, it is useful to consider how these two styles of play – whether carried out by a single person at different times or by different members of a team that are interacting in the same *Savoir-Faire* session – contribute to the experience of the game and to players' enjoyment of it.

While everything the player does in interacting with the program is determined by computational rules, and thus could be seen as what Salen and Zimmerman call 'game play', the player's activity in typing commands to Pierre may be more or less solution-oriented. It is possible in interactive fiction, as in MUDs and many computer games, to explore at random and to try silly or outrageous things without directly attempting to make progress toward a solution. This sort of 'explorer' activity could also be characterized as 'playful interaction'. When players of 3D video games try to find amusing images that are caused by clipping errors, they are playing in the same mode. In *Savoir-Faire*, this sort of play could look like this:

>kill self
That would be unhelpful.

>sing
You hum a snatch of an obscene drinking song.

>pick nose
You are fortunately too well put together for that to be an option.

>yawn
That's not a verb I recognize.

The system misunderstands 'pick nose' in this transcript as meaning 'pick up nose' – a possibly amusing discovery that sheds no light on the IF world or any puzzles confronting the player. But 'sing' does at least reveal something about the player character's personality.

In other cases, although this sort of play is not oriented towards solution, the consequences of unlikely activities may nevertheless provide hints about how to deal with puzzles and may help the player better understand the unusual nature of the IF world. Working the world's magic on objects may also simply be interesting and delightful, even for one who knows how to win. This may be why *Savoir-Faire* was called 'the kind of game that you'll keep toying with after you've finished it'.

On the other end of the spectrum from 'playful interaction' is the 'achiever' activity that can be called 'trying to solve'.[11] While trying to solve some interactive fiction, the player might give a troll every possible item, one after the other, to see if he will accept it as a bribe, or might thoroughly search the environment, examining everything that is described. The player might also search through the map that he or she has drawn, and through the player character's loot, for associations and combinations of items that may be useful. In *Savoir-Faire* specifically, this activity might involve trying to link everything held or seen to some object. Whether players are systematic and exhaustive or not, they are always consciously trying to make progress towards the game's solution when they interact in this way.

A well-crafted interactive fiction can allow playful interaction to bring the player back into its overall riddle, however, enticing the interactor to try to solve it again. When playful interaction is understood correctly and provides some new information that either enriches the experience of the fictional setting, characters and events or hints at the workings of the systems and rules of the IF world, players may find their way out of ruts that conscious 'trying to solve' would not be able to dislodge them from. These are some of the virtues of moving between these two extremes, or 'playing to solve'.

The insoluble and unplayable

There is certainly interactive fiction that the player can't solve; Short herself provides one example with *Galatea*, which has different endings, but no 'winning' one. Is there any interactive fiction that you can't play, in the sense that one can only work at solving it, and can't type commands to it playfully? Probably not. People can play with anything, even a bag marked 'This bag is not a toy'. But some playful interaction with interactive fiction is more satisfying than other sorts are; some games provide more space for free movement within their rigid structure. In the 1980 text-and-graphics interactive fiction *Mystery House* by Roberta and Ken Williams, for example, which runs on the Apple II, the player will be lucky to figure out the basic functioning of the game and the small number of commands that will work. The main thing to be enjoyed in this game is solving it and working toward the solution. *Mystery House* does not even offer a very satisfyingly systematic world. Neither does playing it reveal much about the 'mystery' situation that involves seven others who begin to turn up dead during the treasure hunt that also structures this game.[12] There are few amusing possibilities for more playful interaction in *Mystery House*; *Savoir-Faire*, on the other hand, offers objects that can be inspected, remembered, used as ingredients in a meal, and altered by being magically linked to others. While *Savoir-Faire* and *Mystery House* are quite a contrast in terms of richness of description, development of characters, overall quality of writing and narration of backstory, the interesting and more richly simulated IF world of *Savoir-*

Faire may make for the most compelling difference.

To test this hypothesis, it is useful to compare *Savoir-Faire* to a work of interactive fiction that is richly described, has rounded characters, is well-written and supplies a backstory throughout the play experience, but which does not offer a very deeply simulated world and does not require that the player express an understanding of that world by solving puzzles. One such work ('game' is not the right word, in this case) is *Exhibition,* written in TADS by Ian Finley. *Exhibition* is no straw man; it placed a respectable fifth in the 1999 Interactive Fiction Competition, received good reviews, stimulated discussion online and was nominated for three XYZZY awards. Like *Galatea,* it has several different endings but no way to win. Commands are more or less restricted to the observation and walking around that seem appropriate for an art opening. While the interactor can piece together a story – more than one story, really – and while the different perspectives of the characters are rewarding to compare to one another, *Exhibition* seems to offer more an experience of reading and choice than one of play or solution. In *Savoir-Faire,* the player can not only work to solve puzzles, but can also play around by trying unlikely actions. The result of such playful interaction may satisfy the player by being consistent with the workings of the IF world, yet also surprise the player by having some unforeseen but amusing consequence. In *Exhibition,* there's the chance to learn from characters and discover backstory, but the lack of simulation means that not only are there no puzzles, there are also no similar opportunities to actively experiment in playful ways, to alter the world and see whether the consequences are the anticipated ones. It does seem likely, then, that it is not the quality of writing or narrative elements alone, but the simulated world of *Savoir-Faire* – along with the system it forms with the backstory, space and characters of the game – that helped to make it a highly acclaimed success rather than just a compelling experiment.

The multi-player, multi-solver approach

Savoir-Faire is not explicitly set up for multiple players, as are simultaneous head-to-head games (e.g. *Soul Calibur, Super Mario Kart*), hotseat games (e.g. *Pac-Man, Galaga*), real-time and turn-based multiplayer strategy games (e.g. *Civilization, Age of Empires*), and simultaneous cooperative games (e.g. *Gauntlet, House of the Dead*). However, the form of the game allows for cooperation and collaboration in ways that other games do not. Continuous challenges to one's sense of rhythm, reaction time and physical skill, whether posed by *PaRappa the Rapper* or Activision's *Laser Blast* for the Atari

VCS, can make it difficult for more than one person to play the same game session – others cannot usefully rotate into the game or even shout useful advice. If the physical setup of the game makes it difficult for more than one player to see (e.g. Atari's arcade game *Battlezone* and games for the head-mounted Nintendo Virtual Boy), this presents a further barrier to participation by multiple players. It is plausible, on the other hand, that a 'snake expert' and an 'alligator expert' could work together to play the single-player Atari VCS game *Pitfall*, handing the joystick back and forth. Similarly, more than two players can rotate in to use the two shotguns of the arcade game *House of the Dead III*, alleviating the physical toll that repeatedly pulling the trigger takes on players. *Pitfall* is not designed for two-player hotseat play, just as *House of the Dead III* is not designed for four players to take turns at the same continuous two-player game, but these games nevertheless allow collaboration of this sort.

It was noted in print in the early 1980s that 'An Adventure game is an example of what a games theorist would call a cooperative game. If there are many players, as is often the case, they function as a team. There may be some rivalry, but that is not the purpose of this type of game' (Solomon 1984: 21). Interactive fiction generally leaves time for thinking between moves, and *Savoir-Faire* offers less 'turn pressure' than some other games, welcoming exploration and giving players room to discuss and contemplate their next move. Of course, they are also encouraged to try to solve the game, since there is always (until the end) more of the mansion to unlock, and since needs like sleep and hunger do present themselves. But several other specific features of *Savoir-Faire* facilitate collaboration.[13] The house is small enough for players to remember all the locations fairly easily, and the basic workings of the IF world's magic are not too intricate. (If there were a dozen or more spell names to remember, collaboration would be more difficult and might require the list of spells to be on hand.) Pierre can amass a tremendous inventory of objects during the game, but these are easily listed and, because many fall into similar categories, they are not as difficult to recall as a completely haphazard collection would be. A player who leaves the team for a moment to go and get a cracker and some Port Salut will probably not return to be bewildered at the current situation and unable to contribute any advice. For one thing, the current location is always named at the top of the screen, to orient players. Also, discoveries that have been made can be reviewed by referring to the scrollback buffer, which records the recent textual exchange that has transpired.

Players don't have to be physically seated in front of the same screen to work together, of course. Using an Instant Messaging or MUD bot, or using the multi-user Zinc interpreter, they can play the same game session online, taking turns at the command prompt and controlling the same player character. Or they can play their own sessions but remain in continual or intermittent communication, exploring the game together. Players' ability to share their understanding of the IF world is important in all these cases, but many things about the interactive fiction make such shared understanding possible.

Learning interplay

In corporate culture, the value of the 'real-life' treasure hunt as a collaborative learning and team-building activity has already been widely recognized. The company Dr. Clue[14] bills itself as 'the only corporate team building company in the U.S. specializing entirely in clue-based, business-focused scavenger hunts and treasure hunts', but many other organizations offer to put on similar activities. For instance, Teambonding, whose slogan is 'Where Work Meets Play', has a division called Scaventures which puts on 'treasure hunt adventures' for corporate teams. In England, the Corporate Events Division of Peak Activities Limited[15] stages similar treasure hunts. Although these companies may not suggest the next dominant business model for interactive fiction, they do show that the value of team treasure-hunting is already recognized, and that some already see how multiperson play can be more valuable than the corresponding single-player experience.

Part of the benefit of collaborative treasure-hunting, whether it is done in a national park as part of a corporate team-building activity or done by a group of friends sitting around a computer playing *Savoir-Faire*, is learning to work together, learning the abilities of different team members and who to rely on for which kinds of reasoning and insight. But team play can also help the players learn to strike the right balance between methodically pursuing a solution and more playfully exploring the environment and (in simulated worlds that differ from ours) exploring the basic laws and nature of the world. We can learn from the dogged player who attempts every combination that this tactic can sometimes work; we can learn from the more inquisitive clown that there are important things to be learned from pursuing unusual approaches.

The way in which play can be more or less solution-oriented is hardly specific to interactive fiction, of course. *Savoir-Faire*, other works of interactive fiction and computer and video games more generally can respond to playful interaction by revealing new things about the system of the game, sometimes enjoyably ushering the player back to thinking about the game's overall challenge. The formal qualities of *Savoir-Faire,* which include being able to stop and think about what command to type next and being able to undo fatal mistakes, offer adequate space for play. They also leave space for more than one interactor to work and play together at the same game session. Much of this space is present in the free-wheeling *Grand Theft Auto III* and the later games in that series, which allow the player to forgo signing up for missions to roam around and undertake exploration and random acts of violence. But, although the late games in the *Grand Theft Auto* series seem to have learned a lot from interactive fiction and adventure games that allow such freedom, they still do not offer as many affordances for team play. The real-time nature of those games and their intermittent reliance on uninterpretable performances of driving, shooting and other kinds of skill means that players can't work together as easily on their Playstation 2 as they can in front of their Z-machine interpreter.

There are lessons that *Savoir-Faire* has for other sorts of games, just as interactive fiction can learn from other computer game forms. But, just as music is especially useful for rhythm games and graphics are useful for games involving spatial reasoning and manipulations, there are also some benefits of language, the medium of input and output for *Savoir-Faire.* Players can speak complete commands to whoever is at the keyboard to communicate what they think should be done next; they can quote descriptions to call attentions to certain features of the IF world; and they can refer to characters and objects in the IF world with unambiguous phrases – the same phrases the game itself uses. While the textual realization of the IF world helps to connect the literary with the puzzling, it also helps to enable enjoyable team play.

Team-building exercises may seem like a grim destiny for interactive fiction, but a more likely commercial fate may be even less cheery, at least as far as the seldom-noticed multiplayer aspect of the form is concerned. If interactive fiction makes its way to the broader public again via the highly personal, one-player vehicle of the mobile phone, as several companies have hoped that it will, its special collaborative capability may be stifled. But, who knows, perhaps players will sit around talking about the game they are all playing on their phones, or will use them to text each other, asking for hints and gloating about having solved puzzles. Discussions of interactive fiction so far have overlooked player collaboration, but this oversight hasn't kept players of *Savoir-Faire* and other games apart. It cannot hurt to recognize that 'the player' or the 'interactor' may be several people, though, and that many different styles of play may be involved, even in a single session. Successful game designers are often those who learn the interplay of these many sorts of play, providing an environment for the playful explorer as well as a goal for the achiever, and inviting us, alone or with others, to try on these different roles and enjoy what they have to offer.

Works cited

Bartle, Richard (1996) 'Hearts, Clubs, Diamonds, Spades: Players Who Suit MUDs', www.mud.co.uk/richard/hcds.htm, accessed April 2006.

Montfort, Nick (2003) *Twisty Little Passages: An Approach to Interactive Fiction*, Cambridge, MA: MIT Press.

Montfort, Nick and Stuart Moulthrop (2003) 'Face It, Tiger, You Just Hit the Jackpot: Reading and Playing Cadre's *Varicella*', www.fineartforum.org/ Backissues/Vol_17/faf_v17_n08/reviews/montfort.html, *Fineart Forum*, 17:8.

Muckenhoupt, Carl (2005) Entry for *Savoir-Faire* on Baf's Guide to the IF Archive, www.wurb.com/if/game/1821.

Nelson, Graham (2001) *The Inform Designer's Manual*, 4th edn, 1st print edn, St Charles, Illinois: The Interactive Fiction Library.

Salen, Katie and Eric Zimmerman (2004) *Rules of Play: Game Design Fundamentals*, Cambridge, MA: MIT Press.

Short, Emily (2002) '[Announce] Savoir-Faire', news://rec.games.int-fiction>, Message-ID <emshort-1804020205020001@dialup-63.214.200.245.diall. philadelphia1.level3.net, 18 April.

Solomon, Eric (1984) *Games Programming*, Cambridge: Cambridge University Press.

Wardrip-Fruin, Noah (Forthcoming) 'Playable Media and Textual Instruments', in *Dichtung Digital*.

Games

Age of Empires (1996), Ensemble Studios/Ensemble Studios.

Civilisation (1990), MicroProse Software Inc.

Galaga (1987), Atari Games/Atari Games.

Gauntlet (1985), Atari Games.

Grand Theft Auto (franchise) (1998–present), RockStar North/RockStar North.

House of the Dead (1998), WOW & Sega/Sega.

House of the Dead III (2003), WoW/Sega.

Pac Man (1982), Atari/Atari.

Pitfall (1982), Activision/Activision.

Soul Calibur (1999), Namco/Namco Hometek.

Notes

1 *Savoir-Faire* is available for free download from the IF Archive. To play it, you

should download the *Savoir-Faire* story file http://mirror.ifarchive.org/if-archive/ games/zcode/ and a Z-Machine interpreter; one for your system can be found at http://nickm.com/if/faq.html#How_can_I_download_and_play_IF.3F. You can also play *Savoir-Faire* on the Internet at http://nickm.com/if/emshort/ savoir_faire.html, although you will not able to save your game using the Web interpreter. Those who are unfamiliar with interactive fiction will greatly benefit from reading an introduction to the form, such as Chapter 1 of *Twisty Little Passages* (Montfort 2003). Interactive fiction works simulate worlds and present them in text and they accept and understand textual input from players, to the fullest extent that 'understanding' can have any meaning for a computer system. This distinguishes interactive fiction from Choose-Your-Own-Adventure books, node-and-link hypertexts, many video games and many other cybertexts.

2 A term Short has used extensively on her own web site and on the Usenet newsgroup rec.arts.int-fiction, referring to *Savoir-Faire* and other interactive fiction.

3 Chapter 46 of Nelson 2001 provides a more detailed history, and like the rest of that book, is available at www.inform-fiction.org/manual/html/s46.html. Montfort 2003 offers even more historical detail, in chapters 3, 4, 5, 6 and 7.

4 The XYZZY Awards are considered by IF aficionados to be the Oscars of interactive fiction. Nominations and voting are coordinated by *XYZZY Magazine* and open to anyone on the Internet.

5 Including the 2005 *Mystery House Taken Over,* mainly a collaboration between Short, Dan Shiovitz and myself, with modified versions of *Mystery House* contributed by others.

6 This quotation comes from the 'About This Game' text accessible by typing 'help' at any point within *Savoir-Faire*. This chapter refers to release 7 of 6 December 2003, which incorporates a very large number of bug fixes. The changes made in different releases of *Savoir-Faire* are no doubt interesting to consider, but the basic IF world remains the same throughout.

7 Inform is a procedural language with object-oriented features; the syntax is C-like and the language is weakly typed. The Inform compiler, which is itself available for several systems, can target two platforms: the Z-machine (to which *Savoir-Faire* was compiled) or a newer virtual machine for IF, Glulx (which Short used for *City of Secrets*). The specific nature of Inform and the Z-machine may be interesting to consider in more detail, but here I will only discuss the basic nature of the Z-machine and the obvious ways in which it constrained the complexity of *Savoir-Faire*.

8 Visually, the appearance of *Savoir-Faire* depends on the interpreter and platform. If there is a visual appearance at all (the game can be played using text-to-speech systems) the screen or window running *Savoir-Faire* will just show text from the computer, text from the player (after the '>' prompt), and a status line

at the top, indicating the current location, score, and number of moves. Some of the text will be bold (for example, the name of new locations being entered) and some italic (for example, emphasized phrases) in interpreters that support this. Excerpts from transcripts, rather than screenshots, are often used to characterize interactive fiction.

9 Short has provided hints at http://emshort.home.mindspring.com/savoirhints. htm; a thorough walkthrough, with map, has been written by David Welbourn and is available at http://webhome.idirect.com/~dswxyz/sol/savoir.html.

10 It can be useful for critics and artists to group different sorts of 'playable' new media together for purposes of comparison and consideration, even if they are playable in different senses (see, for example, www.brown.edu/Research/dichtung-digital/2005/1/Wardrip-Fruin/, accessed 23 December 2006. However, it's also important to realize that when people say they are playing a game, they usually intend one specific sense.

11 We would only call this process 'solving' after we have been successful at it.

12 Although not an extraordinary literary or gaming experience on most counts, it is worth noting that *Mystery House* did make an important contribution by bringing textual descriptions and textual interaction together with graphics for the first time.

13 A strong hint that *Savoir-Faire* is 'naturally' played collaboratively is seen in a note Short provides at the end of the game, to those who win: 'The first non-beta players to finish the game (to the best of my knowledge) were Storme Winfield and Sam Kabo Ashwell, at 3:16 PM EDT, 4/19/02.' The first time the released game was solved was by two people working together.

14 See http://www.drclue.com/.

15 See the respective corporate websites at http://www.teambonding.com/, www.scaventures.com/ and www.iain.co.uk/treasure.htm.

11

Without a goal: on open and expressive games

Jesper Juul

Goals in games

According to a widespread theory, videogames are goal-oriented, rule-based activities, where players find enjoyment in working towards the game goal. According to this theory, game goals provide a sense of direction and set up the challenges that the players face.

However, the last few decades have seen many things described as 'games' that either do not have goals, or have goals that are optional for the player: *Sims 2* (2004) has no stated goals, but is nevertheless extremely popular. The also popular *Grand Theft Auto: San Andreas* (2005) is superficially a goal-oriented game, yet the game allows the player to perform a wide range of actions while ignoring the game goal. *San Andreas* is in many ways as different from *Sims 2* as can possibly be: where *Sims 2* has no goal, *San Andreas* contains an explicit goal. Where *San Andreas* is infamous for being immoral and violent, *Sims 2* is famous for its family-friendliness. Yet *San Andreas* and *Sims 2* are fundamentally similar in that they are top-selling, *open* and *expressive* games, games that let the player use them in many different ways, games that allow for many different playing styles, for players pursuing personal agendas.

These two games demonstrate that removing or making optional the goals of games can make way for new types of player experiences. While goals provide a sense of direction and a challenge in games, they can also limit the player: a goal means that the player *should* work towards the goal, rather than follow his or her personal inclinations. Based on an examination of *Sims 2*, *San Andreas*, and the arcade game *Scramble* (1981), I will argue that popular games without enforced goals generally have large expressive potential and provide a wide range of possible experiences: the *Sims*

2 player can create any kind of family and decorate the house; the *San Andreas* player can ignore the goal for a while and focus on practising bicycle stunts or exploring the countryside. Removing or weakening the goals of games affords a wider range of player experiences: where competitive multiplayer games or traditional action games force players to focus on optimizing their performance in relation to the goal, these games let players make decisions based on other criteria: the *Sims 2* player buys not the *optimal* chair, but a *beautiful* chair.

A complete theory of videogames

There is a popular theory that could be called *the complete theory of videogames*. It is a theory that describes the complete connection between the game artefact, the gameplay of the game, and the experience of the players, while allowing for variations between individual player tastes and skills. This is the theory:

1 Games have goals.
2 Goals provide challenge to players.
3 It is the mental challenge of a game that provides the fun.
4 If the challenge is right, the player is in a state of *flow*. (If the challenge is too easy, the player is bored; if the challenge is too hard, the player is frustrated.)

It is a theory that has been presented in many guises. In its most concise form, Sid Meier (designer of *Civilization* and other classics) has said, 'A game is a series of interesting choices' (Rollings and Morris 2000: 38). That is, that a game's quality hinges on it presenting interesting mental choices and challenges to the player. In a more elaborate version, Raph Koster's book *A Theory of Fun* (2005) focuses on humans as pattern matchers that seek to find the pattern in any game, and find the game boring once the pattern has been found.

The theory's focus on challenges is supported by Mihaly Csikszentmihalyi's work on *flow* (1990). Flow is a highly positive mental state that people reach when they are met with a situation with a 'challenging activity that requires skills' (49), and 'clear Goals and Feedback' (54). People in a state of flow report (among other things) a loss of self-consciousness and an altered sense of the passing of time. Csikszentmihalyi describes a *flow channel*, which is the balance between a challenge being too easy (leads to boredom) and too hard (leads to anxiety). When a challenge corresponds to a person's skill level, the person will enter a state of flow.

This theory entails the important assertion that the primary interest for players is in mastering the game rules, but that the fiction of the game is of lesser importance[1]. The sociologist Erving Goffman has described this as the *rules of irrelevance*:

> [Games] illustrate how participants are willing to forswear for the duration of the play any apparent interest in the aesthetic, sentimental, or monetary value of the equipment employed, adhering to what might be called *rules of irrelevance*. For example, it appears that whether checkers are played with bottle tops on a piece of squared linoleum, with gold figurines on inlaid marble, or with uniformed men standing on colored flagstones in a specially arranged court square, the pairs of players can start with the 'same' positions, employ the same sequence of strategic moves and countermoves, and generate the same contour of excitement. (Goffman 1972: 19)

As such, this complete theory of games describes the connection between the formal properties of a game (rules and goals), the subjective player experience, the player's use of a game over time, and variations between different players. The theory also explains why goals are so important since goals set up the challenge of the game: Without a goal, there is no well-defined challenge.

The theory indirectly points to the limits of the traditional goal-oriented game. Clear goals also mean clear failure, which may not suit a specific player since different players have different levels of frustration tolerance. Goals may also run counter to what the player *wants* to do: players may care more about the aesthetic or sentimental value of game choices than about the optimal way of playing the game. Games with goals afford certain types of experiences well, and leave less room for others.

What makes a goal

To say that a specific game *has* a goal is to say that it is an activity which contains an imperative: in a game, some of the possible outcomes are assigned positive values, and players *should* work towards these positive outcomes (Juul 2003). This means that a commercial game has to communicate its goal in some way. It also means that soccer pitches or soccer balls do not have goals, as they are not activities. *The game* of 'soccer' has a goal – we use the term 'soccer' to denote a specific activity with goals. That *Sims 2* does not have a goal means that no clear value has been assigned to the different events and outcomes of the game. *Sims 2* can be played with specific goals in mind, but 'Sims 2' refers to a game without goals: Sims 2 is like a soccer ball that can be used for a variety of goal-oriented and goal-less activities.

At the same time, games differ in the extent to which they force the player into pursuing the goal. In many multiplayer games, there is strong social pressure towards pursuing the goal as the teammates or opponents may refuse to play with a player that does not pursue the goal (a spoilsport). In single player games, the issue is more to what extent it is possible to pursue personal goals rather than the official goal. Additionally, a goal does not mean that the game can be completed. A goal can be to achieve as high a score as possible. This is the standard type of goal in the arcade game, for example in the arcade game Scramble.

Scramble: obligatory goals

Scramble is representative of the way goals were constructed and communicated in early arcade games. The Scramble cabinet states the following:

- Object of game is to invade five SCRAMBLE defense systems to destroy THE BASE.
- Use joystick to move up, down, accelerate, and decelerate.
- Use Laser and bombs to destroy rockets, fuel tanks, mystery targets and UFO's.
- Hit fuel tanks for extra fuel for AIRCRAFT.
- Bonus AIRCRAFT at 10,000 points. (Arcadedocs.com 2005)

The goal of Scramble is also indicated by way of a taunting text on the main screen: 'How far can you invade our scramble system?' As such, the explicitly stated goal of the game, to get as far as possible (destroying the base restarts the game) is unambiguous, but there is a second implicit goal, to get a high a score as possible.

The question here is to what extent is it possible to ignore the goal of the game when playing. As a first experiment, we can try invading the Scramble system not as far, but as short as possible. This is actually very easy but not terribly satisfying: the game allows us to simply drive the aircraft into the ground immediately three times, yielding a total score of 110 points.[2]

Since Scramble scrolls the screen right to left at a steady pace, the player has no option but to 'invade the scramble system' – otherwise the game will end.[3] As an alternative strategy, we can see whether Scramble accommodates a 'subversive' pacifist playing style where the player does not attack anything. This is prevented by a basic mechanic of Scramble in that the player runs out of fuel and must replenish by attacking the fuel tanks stationed on the bottom of the screen. Failing to do so renders the aircraft uncontrollable and leads to a crash. In any prolonged playing of *Scramble*, the player is forced to work towards the goal, and to some extent also forced into using a specific playing style. These are characteristic traits of the traditional arcade game, where goals have a number of recognizable features:

1 Goals are explicitly communicated.
2 There are dual goals between progressing in the game and getting a high score.
3 The game strongly punishes the player who tries not to reach the goal, ending the game.
4 The range of playing styles offered by the game is relatively narrow.

With clear goals, clear challenges and clear feedback, the traditional arcade game fits the complete theory of videogames very well.

San Andreas: optional goals

The *Grand Theft Auto* series of games nominally shares an emphasis on goals with the arcade game, but is in actual play a very different experience. The back cover of *Grand Theft Auto: San Andreas* states:

> Now, it's the early 90s. Carl's got to go home. His mother has been murdered, his family has fallen apart and his childhood friends are all heading towards disaster. On his return to the neighborhood, a couple of corrupt cops frame him for homicide. CJ is forced on a journey that takes him across the entire state of San Andreas, to save his family and to take control of the streets.[4]

The text sets up a goal not entirely unlike that of *Scramble*: the player should not 'invade the scramble system', but 'save Carl's family and take control of the streets'. *San Andreas* begins with a cutscene showing Carl returning to San Andreas and being met by unfriendly police. Once the interactive part of the game begins, the player is instructed to get on a bike and follow the radar to return to Carl's old neighbourhood. This leads to the player meeting old friends and family and beginning a series of missions. The stated goal of saving Carl's family and cleaning up the streets is achieved by completing the long series of missions that the game presents. Again, this is quite similar to the model of *Scramble*. What is not similar is the fact that the game does not force the player into pursuing the stated goal. Right from the beginning of the game, rather than following the radar to CJ's old neighbourhood, the player can choose to bicycle around town, improving our cycling skills, practising stunts, even earning money doing this. The player can also choose to explore the countryside, or even go swimming.

San Andreas is another type of game, one where the player is free to deviate from the official goal of the game and make up personal goals (improving cycling skills, for example), modify the looks of their character, or simply explore the game world. *San Andreas* is a game with goals, but the goals are optional.

Sims 2: without a goal

The back cover of *Sims 2* states:

> **The Next Generation People Simulator**
>
> They're born. They die. What happens in between is up to you. In this sequel to the bestselling PC game of all time, you now take your Sims from cradle to grave through life's greatest moments.
> Create your Sims.
> Push them to extremes.
> Realise their fears.
> Fulfil their life dreams.
> (Blurb from *Sims 2*, Maxis 2004)[5]

The game is presented as having no specific goal, but rather allowing the player something akin to complete freedom – 'what happens in between is up to you'. In actuality, the game consists of choosing a town, creating a family or using a predefined family, building them a house, trying to deal with their wants and desires, while trying to make them do what you want them to. *Sims 2* does not yield the full control over its characters, rather characters may refuse to do what the player asks them to, couples may dislike each other, and so on.

Sims 2 then pulls in several different directions: the game has no imperative, no demands on what the player *should* do, yet Sims (the characters in the game) generally become miserable if the player does nothing. The game is very open, but it also sets up a path of least resistance where purchasing more items for the Sims and trying to make their personalities match leads them to become happier, which in turn makes it easier to make money for them. Yet, a large part of the home decoration is not as much functional as it is aesthetic. Sims enjoy having chairs and tables, but players can choose between a wide range of chairs and tables, many of which will be functionally identical. *Sims 2* allows for precisely the type of consideration that Goffman denied in the quote above – the player can play based on aesthetic consider-ations. The player does not have to choose an *optimal* chair, but can choose a *beautiful* chair.

Still, the financial and character personality constraints in the game mean that as player you cannot do what the packaging promises, because much of what happens is not up to you: *Sims 2* is *not* a doll's house. During my playing of the game, I instructed a character called Cornwall to eat snacks and lunch seven times in a row. I intended Cornwall to eat all the food I had instructed him to eat, but in actuality, a fire broke out in the kitchen, which led to the nervous breakdown of Cornwall, who was then visited by a doctor.

The events in *Sims 2* are not simply up to the player, but result from the interaction between the player and the objects in the game, the whims of the characters, the characters' internal moods and the financial constraints in the game. As such, *Sims 2* is the mirror image of *San Andreas*: *Sims 2* prom-ises absolute freedom, but is a game with many constraints and resistances to the player's plans; *San Andreas* promises a clear goal, but provides much freedom and allows the player to ignore the goal entirely. *Sims 2* does have a general nudging of the player in certain directions: improving character happiness requires improving their material conditions, and as such the player is not free to play in any way he or she likes.

A beautiful chair: expressive games

As outlined, the potential problem with goals is that they may force players into optimizing their strategy rather than doing something else that they would rather do. The last few decades has seen much experimentation with goals. There is a whole class of goal-less games such as *Sims 2*, *SimCity* (1989), and many role-playing games. Additionally, many games *with* goals put no strong pressure on the player to pursue this goal. Prior to *Grand Theft Auto III* (2001), games such as *Elite* (1985) , *Pirates!* (1987), and *Super Mario 64* (1996) were among the more prominent games with non-en-forced goals.

Games without goals or with optional goals can accommodate more playing styles and player types, in effect letting players choose what kind of game they want to play. Not having enforced goals also changes the 'rules of irrelevance' mentioned in the Goffman quote earlier: when the player is not under strong pressure to optimize a strategy, the player is afforded room to play for other purposes, such as designing a house that the player finds aesthetically pleasing. If we assume that the 'complete theory of videogames' provides a reasonable explanation of game enjoyment, these new games pose a problem: if goals provide a challenge that players enjoy working towards, why would anybody want to play a game without a goal? One way to see this is to consider games as vehicles of expression: there is much indication that many players find great enjoyment in creating (and showing off) families and houses in *Sims*, and exploring and perfecting their clever manoeuvres in the *Grand Theft Auto* series.[6]

To see games as expressive devices, they can be considered as languages: a language can be said to contain a lexicon (the words) and a syntax (the arrangement of the words) (Eco 1995: 21). In this perspective, an expressive game is one that allows players to arrange and combine the elements in the game in a large number of different ways in a way that players interpret to have a wide range of meanings. A game requires an amount of flexibility and openness in order to let the players express themselves through the game. *Scramble* is not an expressive game because the range of potential events (the lexicon) is very small, and because the game forces the player into playing for the goal (a very rigid syntax). *San Andreas* and *Sims 2* feature a wide range of objects and events (lexicon), while accommodating a wide range of playing styles (syntax). As such, they are very flexible systems for producing meaning. The expressivity of *Sims 2* and *San Andreas* also comes from the fact that these games express events that are conventionally meaningful: social interaction, life and death in *Sims 2*; violence, exploration, social status, skilled performances in *San Andreas*.

As a comparison, *Conway's Game of Life* is not a game but a system that generates developing patterns based on a few very simple rules.[7] *Conway's Game of Life* technically has a very rich number of combinations (syntax), but can only produce cells that are either on or off (a small lexicon). It has a wide number of possible configurations and patterns, but has very little expressive potential because it does not look like anything; there is no conventional way of interpreting a specific configuration[8]. The language analogy also illustrates why *San Andreas* and *Sims 2* are *not* languages: while the games as they appear are the combination of a larger number of objects, the player, unlike the speaker of a language, cannot simply combine objects arbitrarily. These games offer a resistance to what the player may try to do. *Sims 2* is not a doll's house, as users of a doll's house may (more or less convincingly) craft whatever events they want to, but the user of *Sims 2* has only partial control and can only modify the house with sufficient in-game money, and can only try to push the characters to do what the player wants them to do. The characters may refuse to follow the player's wishes. The *San Andreas* player cannot simply fly a car through the air between two buildings, but must rely on the available game physics, resources and personal skills. This is the limit of the language analogy, and it raises a new question: why would players not simply prefer a 'game' where they could set up any set of events that they wanted, actually 'tell a story' as they wished? A first straightforward answer is that the resistance offered by these games is also a challenge as stipulated in the complete theory of videogames. A second answer is that though the player may not be able to make the game produce the events that he/she wants, such failure is in itself an interesting event: that is, the lack of complete control over the game events is offset by the interest that lies in trying, and sometimes failing to, control the game. Trying and failing to bring two characters in *The Sims* together is in itself an interesting event that is also worth retelling, because the failure to execute a plan is interesting in itself. The story I told about trying to make my character eat food with a fire ensuing is much more interesting than had my character simply performed to my wishes.

Yet the challenge that makes it hard to use these games as tools for expression, as languages, can be mitigated by use of cheat codes. Cheat codes are not illegitimate hacks, but semi-official game features created by the game developers and purposely 'leaked' to the gameplaying community. In *Sims 2*, typing 'motherlode' gives the player 50,000 credits to spend. Cheat codes are designed to let the player circumvent the challenges of the game and rather set up a game world in the way the player likes. As such, cheat codes can be a way of making games more like languages where the player can combine the elements of the game in the way they want. Cheat codes make games less challenging and more expressive.

Problems in the payoff

Clear goals place the player in a well-defined position, where the player is at least *supposed* to optimize his or her strategy in order to work towards the goal of the game. One way to analyze such situations is by way of the field of economic game theory (Neumann and Morgenstern 1953). Economic game theory is not the study of games, as much as it is the study of how to optimally solve certain well-defined problems. For any classic goal-oriented game, we can in principle perform a game-theoretical analysis of how to play the game, including what strategies are optimal and what strategies to avoid. However, such an analysis requires that the game has only one measurement of payoff. In game terms, such an analysis assumes that there is a 'goal', or more specifically that there is a *valorization of the outcome*; that some outcomes are officially sanctioned in the game as better than others. The goal of a game provides a 'measure of all things' in the game. In a game with no goal, there is no standard measure of the payoffs. We cannot make a general analysis of optimal strategies for which chair to buy in *Sims 2*, as there is no fixed scale to measure the strategies against. A strategic analysis can only be made for a specific personal goal such as 'maximize Sim happiness with the given resources' or 'create a cool-looking house', but not for the game as such.

We find the same situation in many role-playing games, and in online games such as *World of Warcraft* (Blizzard Entertainment 2004), where the game may have a semi-official goal of gaining a higher level in the game, but where actual playing can be a mix of social interaction, exploration, strategic planning, and aesthetic preferences on character creation. In such multiplayer games, we can in principle perform a strategic analysis for various situations such as battling monsters, but in actual play, many other considerations can intervene.

In a non-electronic example, researcher Linda Hughes has studied children playing the game *Foursquare* (Hughes 1989). *Foursquare* can be described as a volleyball/tennis variation played with a ball on four squares chalked on the ground. Players have to hit the ball so that it lands in the square of another player. Failing to return the ball to another square forces the player to leave the game and queue up for when another player fails and a square becomes available again. Hughes observed the children playing with a number of considerations such as helping friends, rather than trying to improve their performance. She concludes:

> Game rules can be interpreted and reinterpreted toward preferred meanings and purposes, selectively invoked or ignored, challenged or defended, changed or enforced to suit the collective goals of different groups of players. In short, players can take the same game and collectively make of it strikingly different experiences. (Hughes 1999: 94)

I think this broad claim needs to be supplemented with an analysis of *Foursquare*: *Foursquare* is a game without any final outcome, which means that though players may aim at performing well according to the goal of staying in the game, the lack of scorekeeping allows the players to help friends rather than try to maximize their performance. It also means that every possible action can be evaluated by several, sometimes conflicting criteria: staying in the game *or* being helpful to a friend *or* displaying mastery. What evaluation criteria are present depends on the game, and on the context. A version of *Foursquare* played with scorekeeping and cash prizes would likely see very different behaviour from the players.

Conclusions

In this chapter, I have sketched the limited, but seemingly 'complete' theory of videogames with goals, and I have pointed to how games without goals, or with optional goals can work in a different way, allowing players to play according to personal, aesthetic, and social considerations. This does not render the 'complete theory' irrelevant; it simply means that the theory has limits.

Multiplayer games tend to have an uneasy relation between what is inside the game and what is outside the game. The goal of a game can be considered a social norm for how the player *should* behave, and the magic circle (Salen and Zimmerman 2004: 95) that delineates the game has the connotation that players should not bring personal feelings into the game and should not bring what happened in the game to bear on non-game events. Two archetypical situations where this is not observed are the cases of the sore loser and of the adult who plays badly in order not to win against a child. The sore loser fails to leave the game properly, and the adult playing badly downplays intra-game goal optimization in favour of an extra-game social consideration. The *Foursquare* example illustrates a specific way of framing a game session where repetition mitigates the impact of the goal: playing the same card game or action game many times over without keeping an overall score changes the gameplaying in a direction where maximizing personal performance becomes less of a necessity. In this way, a goal-oriented game can be played as a game without a goal by replaying it numerous times.

Outside games, there are number of rule-based activities that do not work very well without goals. Rubik's Cube is only interesting when trying to complete it since it has little expressive potential. *Conway's Game of Life* is remarkably like *Sims 2* in its tension between the player having control and not having control, but *Conway's Game of Life* certainly lacks the broad appeal of *Sims 2*. As a commercial product, it is hard to imagine a goal-less abstract game. On the other hand, a number of other rule-based activities *are* interesting without goals: musical instruments, Lego, Tangram, playing sequences of games with goals without keeping score. These activities are popular because they allow for a range of discernibly different expressions to be made[9].

Games without enforced goals will not replace the classic goal-oriented game, but they open up a wide range of new player experiences as seen in the two quite similar games of *Sims 2* and *Grand Theft Auto: San Andreas*. This is the new style in videogames, and an illustration of how contemporary videogames are severing the ties to their historical roots in the arcade game, becoming something new and unique, open and expressive.

Works cited

Arcadedocs.com (nd) 'Scramble installation manual', www.arcadedocs.com/vidmanuals/S/Scramble.pdf, accessed July 2005.

Csikszentmihalyi, Mihaly (1990) *Flow: The Psychology of Optimal Experience*, New York: Harper Perennial.

Eco, Umberto (1995) *The Search for the Perfect Language*, London: Fontana Press.

Flanagan, Mary (2005) 'Troubling "Games for Girls": Notes from the Edge of Game Design', DiGRA 2005 conference proceedings, Vancouver, Canada.

Goffman, Erving (1972 [1961]) *Encounters: Two Studies in the Sociology of Interaction*, New York: Penguin.

Hughes, Linda (1989) 'Foursquare: A Glossary and "Native" Taxonomy of Game Rules', *Play and Culture*, 2:2, 102–136.

Juul, Jesper (2005) *Half-real: Video Games Between Real Rules and Fictional Worlds*, Cambridge, Mass: MIT Press.

——(2003) 'The Game, the Player, the World: Looking for a Heart of Gameness', in Marinka Copier and Joost Raessens (eds) *Level Up: Digital Games Research Conference Proceedings*, Utrecht: DiGRA/Utrecht University, 30–45.

Koster, Raph (2005) *A Theory of Fun*, Scottsdale, Arizona: Paraglyph Press.

Neumann, John von and Oskar Morgenstern (1953) *Theory of Games and Economic Behavior*, Princeton: Princeton University Press.

Rollings, Andrew and Dave Morris (2000) *Game Architecture and Design*, Scottsdale, AZ: Coriolis.

Salen, Katie and Eric Zimmerman (2004) *Rules of Play – Game Design Fundamentals*, Cambridge, MA: MIT Press.

Games

Elite (1985), Firebird.

Grand Theft Auto III (2001), Rockstar Games, Take-Two Interactive.

Grand Theft Auto: San Andreas (2005), Rockstar Games North, Take-Two Interactive.

Pirates! (1987), Microprose.

Scramble (1981), Konami.

SimCity (1989), Maxis, Brøderbund.

Super Mario 64 (1996), (Nintendo 64) Nintendo.

The Sims 2 (2004), Maxis, Electronic Arts.

World of Warcraft (2004), Blizzard.

Acknowledgements

Thanks to Nanna Debois Buhl and Jonas Heide Smith for input and criticism.

Notes

1   The relation between rules and fiction is discussed in detail in my book *Half-Real* (Juul 2005).
2   Screenshots of this experiment are available at www.half-real.net/resources/vtp.
3   This is also a reflection of the game convention that goals are harder to reach than non-goals (Juul 2005: 40).
4   The cover and screenshots from the game can be seen at www.half-real.net/resources/vtp.
5   The cover and screenshots from the game can be seen at www.half-real.net/resources/vtp.
6   Mary Flanagan (2005) has interviewed *Grand Theft Auto* players who prefer simply driving around over completing missions.
7   An online version of *Conway's Game of Life* can be seen at www.half-real.net/gameoflife.
8   The Latin alphabet can be used for expressive purposes because the combination of letters has a conventional interpretation. It is meaningful only to someone who knows how to read.
9   This also points to the reason why goal-less games can easily become steeped in controversy. The wide range of player actions – what makes the game expressive – also make it likely that the player can express something that offends someone.

12

Pleasure, spectacle and reward in Capcom's *Street Fighter* series

David Surman

Introduction

Scanning the shelves of games in a local retail store, and watching others do the same, it is clear that, like me, many players invest frugally and conscientiously in a specific type of game with which they identify. Answering 'yes' to the question of whether or not one plays videogames often belies the fact that players will exclusively play one particular mode or genre of videogame, such as the driving game, platform game, or fighting game. Likewise, audience studies have made clear that a cinemagoer does not necessarily attend films across a broad variety of genres, but rather a select few, since those film texts follow lines of convention that the audience is conversant in, and so can anticipate, as the film unfolds (see Jenkins 1992; Staiger 1992, 2000). Pleasures arising from a spectator's command of the language of film form extend, beyond the moment of viewing, into the media culture and social relations within which a given text is situated and debated. Through this connoisseurship the spectator is affirmed in their relation to both the film culture in which they situate themselves, and in their consumer choice as participatory cultural subjects.

Likewise, quality of gameplay (how well a gamer is performing in the game) determines both text and context; the matter of the game (e.g. areas unlocked, techniques achieved) and the patterns characterizing its consumption (in which cultural context one is situated as a gamer: hardcore, casual, etc.) As I have suggested elsewhere, gameplay proficiency plays a part in the structuring of gaming communities, with players electing complex systems of naming and orientation within their sphere of gameplay experience, 'hardcore', 'casual', 'otaku', and so on (Surman 2004). While the data on the mass-produced CD or cartridge remains consistent for all users, directions on how to play a game found in an official videogame manual, and an expert-player-authored 'faq' (acronym for 'frequently asked questions', published at sites like www.gamefaqs.com) could not be further apart. One could even say that through the lens of play, the novice gamer and expert gamer are experiencing different media texts, individuated by their implicit competency.

Lara doesn't go anywhere if you don't make her, as many have noted. While a film audience relates remotely to a film and takes pleasure and meaning from its exhibition without altering its form, the mastery of videogame play is central to unveiling multiple pleasure registers in the game, which are nested within one another like Russian dolls. Completing a game on harder difficulty settings may reveal new secrets, endings or avenues, otherwise inaccessible. Competency of play is yoked to the textual richness of the gameworld. To be good at the game means that the player's passage through its world is less fraught with frustration and repetition. While a player new to videogames explores the pleasures of the gameworld with the clumsy curiosity of a toddler, as one becomes a more sophisticated gamer other pleasure registers come into play, which are concerned with a literacy of sorts in which one is sensitive to the codes and conventions of the gameworld, and the panoramic experience of worldliness reduces to a hunt for the telltale graphical or acoustic 'feedback loops', confirming success in play. Still higher, as the core gameplay becomes exhausted, players end up centring on the reflexive undoing of the gameworld; pushing it to its limits, exploring and exploiting glitches, ticks, aberrations in the system. Gameplay proficiency, like cine-literacy, individuates the game text to a degree.

If the videogame comes into being *as text* in the moment of play, then to what degree does a proficiency of play affect the integrity of the game as text? A film intended to run at 25 frames per second is compromised by running at any other rate, perhaps to be reconstructed by those controlling the projection apparatus, as in Douglas Gordon's *24-Hour Psycho* (1993) in which the artist slows the frame rate, radically reorienting the meanings that have circulated around Alfred Hitchcock's classic. What of videogames, played in different ways, and eliciting different pleasures? Should the game scholar elect to study a game as it is played by a certain set of players (casual, hardcore or otherwise) to ensure textual coherence? However rhetorical they are, these questions inspire my curiosities about the cultural analysis of games.

As I child I visited the videogame arcades in the sleepy town of Ilfracombe on the North Devon coast, to watch the seasoned local gamers play *Street Fighter II* (1991), the subject of this essay. In retrospect, the enchantment of seeing them deploy secret fighting moves from the gallery of playable characters was a formative moment in my ongoing fascination with videogames. Currently spanning at least fourteen titles (see Udon 2005), the 'Street Fighter' series presents characters of exceptional strength and agility, each with their own trademark combat manoeuvres and powerful superhuman abilities. In this essay I shall consider what it means to a play a game in a series like 'Street Fighter', and what kinds of pleasure are found in that moment of revelation as one executes a 'special move' – the super-powered secret techniques of a chosen player-character. I want to think about what it means to be 'good' or 'bad' at this predominantly two-player game, and how this impacts on the shared experience of spectacle, since, as Guy Debord suggests, 'The spectacle is not a collection of images; it is a social relation between people that is mediated by images' (Debord 1992: 7). By figuring the performing gamer into a critique of spectacle I hope to foreground the spectacular potential of play. Finally, I aim to explore the relationship between the spectacular aesthetic and a sense of gratification associated with skilled gameplay, which I call the 'reward-spectacle'.

In this chapter, my thoughts are focused on fighting simulation videogames, hereafter referred to as the 'beat-'em-up' genre. Importantly, I want to present an account of spectacle as an essential aspect of the player's experience. Geoff King and Tanya Krzywinska have identified that '[s]pectacle is offered at the relative (in game terms) level of detail or consistency' (King and Krzywinska 2006: 153). Rather, relative in the differing spectacles within a single game, but also in the intertextuality of spectacle across a variety of titles. As such, in comparison to a reasonably unspectacular game like *The Sims* (2000), *Street Fighter* might seem to be largely comprised of interrelated spectacles and excesses, like Hollywood's contemporary action blockbusters, Indian Bollywood cinema and contemporary music video. However, within the topsy-turvy logic of its gameworld *Street Fighter* presents degrees of spectacular representation and play, which continually act as foil to one another, oscillating between a harmony and cacophony of spectacle.

As I will explain later, gameplay and representational assets – ranging from the meekest of punches, grand special moves, fragments of hallucinatory looping animation comprising the background, the pulse of the user interface, the acceleration of the music, and the feedback of moments of impact — form the hierarchy of spectacular gameplay (Cousins 2002). From the 'atomistic' low-level punch to the larger special move; each exists for the pleasure of interactive spectacle. I want to look through this shifting artifice to the structures that reinforce its effect, not least since games like *Street Fighter* are rarely appraised since they do not clearly express 'meaningful experience' in ways comparable to traditional media canons, and are inadvertently ignored as part of the larger neglect of the '8-bit to 16-bit' or 'console wars' era (1983–95) in game scholarship. Much of the aesthetic form of videogames developed in this historical moment; while game content is routinely celebrated for 'trashy' cyber-psychedelic palettes (as with the *Fantasy Zone* series (1986–91) and *Sonic the Hedgehog* (1991)) and ultra-violent fantasy (the *Streets of Rage* series (1991–93) and the *Splatterhouse* series (1991–93)), nonetheless these games formed a foundation from which the 'modern' videogame emerged through the release of genre-defining franchises like *Sonic the Hedgehog*, *The Legend of Zelda* and *Metroid*.

While contemporary videogames design is largely preoccupied with achieving greater photorealistic representation, spectacular aesthetics have developed as an autonomous mode of expression with its own hyper-reality of visceral pleasure across all screen media. Seigfried Kracauer reminds us of the central role spectacle plays in mass-cultural forms: 'the *aesthetic* pleasure gained from ornamental mass movements is *legitimate* (…) No matter how low one gauges the value of the mass ornament, its degree of reality is still higher than that of artistic productions which cultivate outdated noble sentiments in obsolete forms – even if it means nothing more than that' (Kracauer 1995: 79, original italics). The 'reality' of games arise from their domestic positioning and use as an everyday cultural practice, and formally through their foregrounding of innovations in hyperrealist digital imaging.

To understand the array of pleasures and meanings evoked by a beat-'em-up videogame like *Street Fighter* requires analysis of both its representational and play aspects. Broadly speaking, spectacle in videogames is divided between that which has been produced *for* the player, and that which the player produces through the performance of play. The audio-visual and representational elements of the game are largely outside of the player's creative control, whereas the quality of play, for which the player is almost always wholly responsible, can be spectacularly skilled, eccentric, or incompetent. In this division (between design and play) we find two distinct-yet-connected instances of spectacle. Importantly, the diminished role of narrative in favour of gameplay transforms the place of visual spectacle, or as King has summarized, '[t]he aesthetic of games, generally, is associated with an attenuation of narrative dynamics in favour of the production of qualities such as sensation and spectacle, among others' (King and Krzywinska 2002: 50). The sensation of *reward* that comes with the anticipation of narrative twists and turns in the cinema is remediated in videogames through the tacit reward of play, and its correspondent visualization, combined in a moment of *reward-spectacle*.

This chapter aims to contribute to an understanding of the beat-'em-up videogame through an analysis of *Street Fighter*, and to broaden the scope of work started by Leon Hunt in his essay '"I Know Kung Fu!": The Martial Arts in the Age of Mechanical Reproduction' (Hunt 2002). As such I often draw from Hunt's study, particularly in my later section on the various remediations of *Street Fighter*. While Hunt appraises the realm of three-dimensional beat-'em-ups (e.g. the *Tekken* series (Namco 1995–present)) and their relation to Hong Kong martial-arts cinema, I shall focus almost exclusively on the now largely 'retro' two-dimensional beat-'em-up, and the *Street Fighter* franchise in particular.

Street Fighter

The basic conventions of the beat-'em-up genre (incorporating the more action-adventure oriented scrolling beat-'em-up sub-genre) had been defined from 1983 to 1985 in titles such as *Chuck Norris Superkicks* (1983), *Bushido* (1983) *Karate Champ* (1984) *Bruce Lee* (1984), *Karateka* (1984), *Yie Ar Kung-Fu* (1984), *The Way of the Exploding Fist* (1985), *Kung-Fu Master* (1985) and *International Karate* (1985). These games invariably featured a player-character skilled in martial arts of some kind, set against exotic martial arts sects or cults, gang-land bosses, drug barons, street punks and the like, or set the player in the context of a larger martial arts tournament, reminiscent of the Bruce Lee epic *Enter the Dragon* (1973). As Hunt has explained at length, these games adapted the themes and conventions of the 1970s and 1980s martial-arts action movies coming out of Hong Kong. The stardom of these new Asian dynamos (Bruce Lee, Jackie Chan, Yuen Biao, Sammo Hung, Jet Li) disseminated the martial arts into pop culture, where one began to see the application of martial arts for fitness, self-defence and recreation. Each of these early videogame titles sought to present an interactive account of the blood-pounding combat and desperate scenarios of the source movies. The piecemeal development of the two player-energy bars, point scoring and timer(s) of contemporary beat-'em-ups arose in the fierce market competition and intertextuality of these first releases.

Capcom's[1] *Street Fighter* emerged in the global arcade sector in 1987. The first game in the long-running series, it made little impact both at home and abroad and drew only minor praise in the arcade videogame community for a curious system of hydraulic buttons affectively-named the 'touch response system' (Udon 2005: 141). The strength with which one pressed these buttons determined the relative power of the punch or kick executed by the on-screen character. This 'innovation' led to many machines being rendered defunct by over-zealous players smashing the control system. The cacophony of these large red buttons being bashed would come to signify the arcades which stocked a number of these first *Street Fighter* units. Such player-frenzy in turn motivated the development of the subsequent control system currently used in the majority of the series; an array of six buttons configured into three punch and three kick commands, with the respective strengths of light, medium and heavy.

In 1991 *Street Fighter II* was released, and has since been widely recognised as one of the landmark games of the 1990s, and the key text of the beat-'em-up genre to date. It enjoyed immense international success. The playable Ryu and Ken reprised their roles from the 1987 original to become the central characters in the second videogame. The image of Ryu in particular (wearing his modest karate-suit or *gi*, black belt and trademark red headband) has since become paradigmatic of not only the *Street Fighter* series but of the Capcom company in general, particularly its arcade sector. As playable characters, the karate masters Ken and Ryu are joined by E. Honda the Japanese sumo, Chun Li the Chinese kung fu detective, Blanka the Amazonian man-beast, Dhalsim the yogi, Zangief the Russian wrestler and Guile the American soldier, forming a truly international pantheon of world warriors, reflexively '... organised along lines of cultural, ethnic and stylistic difference' (Hunt 2002: 198). These eight were juxtaposed against the four boss characters; Balrog the American boxer, Vega the Spanish matador assassin, Sagat the Thai kick boxer, and M. Bison – end boss, criminal overlord and psychic super-villain.[2]

Street Fighter and its sequels significantly developed the user interface displaying two player-energy bars, a point scoring system, player characters, and culturally and geographically localized backgrounds as part of 'its global *mise-en-scène*' (198). Steven Poole describes *Street Fighter II* as 'the first of the really modern breed of fighting games', though eschews the issue of gameplay development for the sake of noting the 'visual excess' of 'enormous blue light trails from swishing limbs and fireball attacks' (Poole 2000: 45). *Street Fighter II* revolutionized the gameplay quality of the genre (sometimes called 'playability' in early games journalism) through the introduction of special moves in addition to the timing of attacks, blocking and 'combos'.[3] These gave *Street Fighter II* a unique appeal, and ensured its position as the premiere competitive player-versus-player arcade beat-'em-up. Rather than collaboratively competing against the computer AI, as was the norm in the dominant arcade scrolling-shoot-'em-up genre of the late 1980s (see Capcom's own *1942* (1985) and *Raiden* (Seibu Kaihatsu Inc., 1991)), *Street Fighter II* offered a chance to test your skills directly against those of another player. In the consequential 'tournament' culture that arose (particularly in the urban centres of Japan and the United States), it was through mastery of revolutionary special moves and attack combinations that players achieved distinction as 'hardcore gamers'.

Special moves

From the first *Street Fighter* onwards 'special moves' have been achieved through the input of a sequence of directional commands and button presses to achieve a distinctive player attack or action; a particularly challenging set of command inputs intended to deplete the opposing player's energy bar with greater effectiveness than 'regular' button commands. They are characterized by two pleasure registers; first in viewing the spectacular representation of the special move (hurling a fireball, belching a ball of flame) and secondly in a sense of reward or gratification – a confirmation of the player's successful mastery of the videogame control inputs. These moves are characterized by names integral to the cult appeal of the series, so memorable that they form the locus for many fan investments, such as www.shoryuken.com, the North American tournament site named after the Japanese moniker of Ryu and Ken's trademark 'dragon punch'.

Much like the act of typing on a keyboard, the use of the controller necessitates a separation of the hand and the eye to achieve optimal use. Proficient gameplay in *Street Fighter* is a sleight-of-hand in the sense that the place of the controller must be taken for granted to the extent that the player can focus their attention on the movements on the screen. The spectacular expression of 'doing without looking' with your hands is at the heart of the reward-spectacle of videogames like *Street Fighter II*.

As an example of reward-spectacle, consider that the reticent Ryu is able to hurl a fireball from his hands, coupled with the Japanese exclamation '*hadou-ken*', literally meaning 'wave motion strike'.[4] To achieve this, players must roll the directional controller or joystick from a downwards position through a quarter-circle toward the opposing player, accompanied by a depression of one of the punch buttons. These moves are clearly delineated from the regular punching and kicking moves of the player character by their visual spectacle, 'thrilling complexity' (Hunt 2002:198), and tactical importance to successful play. The visceral pleasure of synchronicity between play and representation is achieved and expressed in two 'performances', that of the player and that of the player-character. Capcom's executive director Noritaka Funamizu notes that the control commands for the special moves were designed to correspond to the image of the referent body in motion: 'With the Fireball, the body drops down and then becomes level and fires out the energy. So we made a command that looked like that ... We just created the commands based on the image of the techniques themselves' (Udon 2005: 280). As such, there is a performative correspondence between player actions and the representation of the action in the on-screen character.

In this moment of correspondence between the special move and the player's gameplay performance, there is a heightened sense of gratification on the part of the player as she or he 'becomes' their chosen martial arts superstar, in that peculiar subject position characteristic of videogames in general. Hunt writes that 'I first 'knew' kung fu when I brought a PlayStation specifically to play *Tekken 3* (1998) because of my love of kung fu films' (Hunt 2002: 194). To make a useful distinction between videogames and film, no matter the degree of identification, the majority of spectators recognise the status of the *filmed* subject as 'other'; an expectant desire to 'be' is not to be confused with real-time 'embodiment' per se. In videogames, a radically different system of subject association is constructed, in which players partially collapse on-screen characters with the first-person referent 'I', and (in an admittedly simplistic account) player-characters become a surrogate second self (Surman 2005). I don't want to recount the broader socio-cultural implications of this positioning, save to say that we might begin to think of embodiment as a central force in the formal analysis of videogames, a peak state or experience to which designers of gameplay aspire. The control of this immersed 'peak state' has historically had an economic implication for games designers producing for the arcade sector, as John Fiske describes:

> The same claim can be made for video games, particularly the pay-as-you-use ones, where the skill of the operator decreases the profit of the owner ... This release is through the body: the intense concentration of video games or the subjection of the body to terrifying physical forces of the white-knuckle rides result in a loss of self, a release from the socially constructed and disciplined subjectivity. The body's momentary release from its social definition and control, and from the tyranny of the subject who normally inhabits it, is a moment of carnivalesque freedom closely allied to Barthes' notion of *jouissance*. (Fiske 1989: 82)

In sum, this corollary between graphical representation and the execution of a spectacular special move is at the heart of *Street Fighter's* gaming appeal. Physical mastery of the game control forms part of a body politic in which the player incorporates the game text as part of an extended self, individuating it and partially effacing the authorial vision of the developer. These two correspondent 'performances' (of physical player and representational player-character) doubly signify the centrality of the special move within the thrill of the *Street Fighter* experience. It does so by yoking the performance of the player's hands and body with an on-screen referent, catalyzed by a dynamic collapse in the positioning of player and character that comes with this particular gaming experience. It is an exciting and momentary 'embodiment' or 'becoming'; spectacular, rewarding, though temporary in accordance with its carnivalesque spirit.

Aesthetics and contexts

Hunt notes that '[f]ight games remediate varying combinations of four media forms: kung fu films, *anime, manga* and wrestling' (Hunt 2002: 196). In his reflections on the spectacle of wresting, Roland Barthes contrasts boxing with wrestling, noting that '[a] boxing-match is a story which is constructed before the eyes of the spectator; in wrestling, on the contrary, it is each moment which is intelligible, not the passage of time. The spectator is not interested in the rise and fall of fortunes; he expects the transient image of certain passions' (Barthes 2000: 16). 'Transient passions' are the aesthetic heart of the beat-'em-up genre.

Given the 'attenuation of narrative' to a gaming event often lasting less than a single minute in duration, the repeatability of play, and the centring of spectacle around the successful execution of special moves, *Street Fighter* can be compared aesthetically with wrestling, as outlined by Barthes. While the duration of gaming matches are broadly framed by the user interface, energy bar of the player, and an overall win/lose scenario, the pleasures of the game are centred on the satisfying delivery of a special move that makes contact with the opponent; as Barthes notes, 'each moment imposes the total knowledge of a passion which rises erect and alone, without ever extending to the crowning moment of a result ... Each sign in wrestling is therefore endowed with an absolute clarity, since one must always understand everything on the spot' (Barthes 2000:16–17). In short, this 'reward-spectacle' is gratifying in the moment, a fleeting experience. The 'win' is transient since the repetitious character of play determines that no single match has a definitive significance, excluding when players externally nominate conditions separate from the diegetic suite of in-game rules, such as 'best of three', an agreed 'grudge-match' and so on.

Generally speaking, a beat-'em-up gaming session does not comprise of a single match, but typically involves a number of sessions, where initial matches are part of a 'warming-up process' as one gets into the game, then followed by 'core' gameplay, and then a series of closing matches in which players characteristically perform best, delivering virtuous special moves with accuracy and timing. In my experience, playing a session of one of the *Street Fighter* titles necessitates approximately a dozen or so matches, though this varies with the number of people involved, and the available seating space around my TV. The textual bracketing of a match provokes the play of successive matches; a victory (be it an explosive, spectacular super special move finish or spectacularly understated 'cheap' tap with a light attack) is followed by the image of the defeated opponent's bloodied face, mirrored by the victor, subtitled with an appropriately humiliating taunt. These taunts offer scant insight into the personalities of the player-characters, and are another of *Street Fighter*'s contributions to the language of the beat-'em-up genre. Speaking generally about videogame aesthetics, King and Krzywinska explain that

> [n]ew or unfolding spectacular vistas – including those supplied in the form of cut-scenes – are frequently offered as reward and incentive for the completion of particular tasks, sub-sections, levels or entire games. Spectacular vistas can offer compensation for periods in which players become stuck or are forced into repeated attempts at a task. (King and Krzywinska 2006:154)

In the same way as the special move is distinguished from regular punching and kicking through a competency of play, the super special move or 'super combo' found from *Super Street Fighter 2: Turbo* (Capcom, 1994) onwards is distinguished from the special move by an *even more* challenging series of command inputs. Mastery of the super special move initiates the player into a heightened experience of spectacle, and the successful execution of such moves will often tip the balance of the match in favour of that player. In sum, within the *mise-en-scène* of the *Street Fighter* series, from *Super Street Fighter 2: Turbo* onwards, there are three interwoven gameplay registers: 'regular', 'special', and 'super special' moves.

In terms of its representation, the super special move presents us with an image of the chosen character at the most expressive limits of their ability; a transitory moment of excess in which the true potential of their fighting spirit is manifest. As the character erupts into action, blue shadows trace their impossibly elegant movements, adding to the gravitas of the action. Should the move make contact with the opposing player and defeat them outright, the screen explodes into a flash of burning light, movements slow in a kind of bullet-time savouring of the moment of victory, and in more recent titles the flaming words 'K.O.!' fly toward the player, recalling Barthes observation of the affective staging of the wrestling match, 'a light without shadow generates an emotion without reserve' (Barthes 2000: 15). Such a sequence is then finally punctuated by the image of the fallen opponent juxtaposed against the elated stance of the victor.

Aesthetically speaking, such a play experience can be considered 'baroque'. From the outset *Street Fighter*'s 'staging' could be characterized as baroque when noting the trademark characteristics of the style; forced perspectives leading the eye into complex backgrounds, in which ingenious intertextual references are secreted. Looping animations bring life to false panoramas as cyclists pass (in parallax from left to right, and right to left) in downtown Hong Kong, and serried ranks of identical elephants salute your victory in an Indian temple. The speed through which these animations cycle connects to the speed with which the music track is played and both are representative of near-certain victory for one player or another. These motifs of excess ensure the appropriateness of *Street Fighter*'s classification as baroque. Importantly, I don't want to suggest a derogatory sense of the baroque, as it is often used, but rather celebrate it as an aesthetic philosophy underpinning the *Street Fighter* series.

Barthes talks of the baroque mode of wrestling, as a '...spectacle of excess' (15). He reinforces an understanding of the baroque as a markedly pleasurable saturation point in the overall experience: 'The rhythm of wrestling is quite different [to judo], for its natural meaning is that of rhetorical amplification: the emotional magniloquence, the repeated paroxysms, the exasperation of the retorts can only find their natural outcome in the most baroque confusion' (23). And he goes on:

> Some fights, among the most successful kind, are crowned by a final charivari, a sort of unrestrained fantasia of the rules, the laws of the genre, the referee's censuring and the limits of the ring are abolished, swept away by the triumphant disorder which overflows into the hall and carries off pell-mell wrestlers, seconds, referee and spectators. (23)

The image of the breaking of 'the limits of the ring' and the loss of temporality offered by Barthes is analogous to the baroque characteristic of the breaking of frames surrounding contemporary and seventeenth-century imagery offered by Angela Ndalianis in her study *Neo-Baroque Aesthetics and Contemporary Entertainment* (2004). She further redefines this aesthetic as the 'neo-baroque' to account for its broad re-emergence in contemporary culture and to delineate it from notions that locate it as a particular artistic 'style' or periodization. Rather, the neo-baroque is a form characterizing the shape of cultural texts, notably contemporary screen arts and new digital media, and in particular videogames.

According to Ndalianis, implicit to the pleasures of all baroque spectacles is a culture of audience participation, be it in the appreciation of Bernini's *David*, Barthes' wrestling matches, or, as I suggest, *Street Fighter* videogames. With the videogame, such involvement is not so much a preferred spectator position as a functional necessity of the medium, controller in hand. In a game series like *Street Fighter* where coherent narrative development of character is sparse to say the least, we come to know our on-screen equal through the expressive range of their movements (the iconic language of animation), as part of an affective understanding predicated on spectacle. Such movements and gestures are revealed through gameplay. When asked 'which are your most memorable characters?', animator 'Ishii' replies (in a transcribed interview between various designers and artists at Capcom) that for him,

> ... it's Blanka in *Street Fighter Zero 3* [1998], who I was in charge of animating. When I was animating him, I struggled with how to convey his emotions, then Mr. Yasuda said to me, 'He's covered in fur, so use his fur and his body language to express things.' After hearing that I felt as if I had a lot more freedom to create the animations and I grew to like that. In turn I have a strong attachment to him. (cited in Udon 2005: 279)

The foregrounding of animation performance is important in the process of representing plausible characters in supposedly non-narrative (though avatar-led) videogame experiences. As we are drawn in through the immediacy of gameplay the game breaches its confines to explode out toward us in moments of neo-baroque hypermediacy. In this thrilling moment, the discipline of structured play negotiates a path through the neo-baroque textuality, from which we make affective momentary meaning through the pleasures of the reward-spectacle.

Remediations

An essential characteristic of the neo-baroque form is its distribution of a cultural artefact across various media platforms in what Ndalianis has identified as its essential 'polycentricism' and 'seriality' (Ndalianis 2004: 31). This sentiment chimes with the widely cited work of Jay David Bolter and Richard Grusin in *Remediation: Understanding New Media* (2000) and provides a principle through which we might begin to consider the importance of other *Street Fighter* texts occurring across associated media forms. To determine the importance of the special move in the array of pleasures we get from the

Street Fighter games, I want to look at how specific adaptations or remediations choose to present and frame the motif of the special move within the specificity of live-action feature film, animated feature film, *anime*, *manga* and the boardgame. Leon Hunt has summarized the cinematic remediations of *Street Fighter*:

> *Street Fighter 2* (1991) spawned two feature films, the live-action *Street Fighter: The Movie* (1994) starring Jean-Claude Van Damme, and a more faithful *anime* version (Japan, 1994) which retained the 'special moves' from the game. Animated *Street Fighters* have also materialised on television and DVD-only releases (*Street Fighter Alpha/Zero: The Animation* (1999). Jackie Chan bought the rights to *Street Fighter 2* and included a brief parody of the game in *City Hunter* (1993), while *Future Cops* (1994) also deployed thinly disguised *Street Fighter* characters. (Hunt 2002: 196)

In *Street Fighter: The Movie* (1994), the Hollywood film adaptation, the special moves of the character emerge at the crescendo of the story arc. They are not reflexively 'announced' in the same way the player-character cries 'hadou-ken', 'shoryuken' and so on (recalling Barthes' observation of the 'magniloquence' of wrestling). Rather, the characters strike signature poses during action sequences, clearly reminiscent of the special moves and production artwork released by Capcom. Though, British agent Cammy (played by pop pixie Kylie Minogue) can be heard to 'magniloquently' announce her signature 'thrust kick' in the penultimate scenes of the film, as M. Bison's (Raul Julia) fortress is infiltrated by Guile (Jean-Claude Van Damme) and Chun Li (Ming-Na). Importantly, the performance of special moves in the movie is central to the appeal of the film to fans of the videogame. These signature poses are reserved for the closing scenes of the movie, and function as 'deciders' in these final staged action sequences. Ryu's 'hadou-ken' fireball, Ken's 'shoryuken' dragon punch, Guile's 'flash kick', Blanka's 'electric attack', Vega's 'rolling slash' and Bison's irrepressible 'psycho crusher' all make noteworthy appearances, to assure that the iconicity of the videogame is rehearsed with due thoroughness. They momentarily redeem an otherwise underwhelming film adaptation of the videogame, though it is clear that to remediate the special move and so convey the core characteristic is something of a challenge.

The limitations of working in live-action film with real actors is clear to the viewer, as these special move performances fail to capture the essence of the videogame's animated fervour. The authenticity of the game does not transfer to this particular live-action instance, though an earlier 'unofficial'

Hong Kong adaptation, *Future Cops* (1993), is considerably more successful in its expression of the special move. Rather than have the special moves express the closure of the narrative arc as in the 1994 Hollywood adaptation, *Future Cops* saturates the fast-paced action with endless performance of the trademark moves, references to their parody in fan culture, and in particular those impossibly elegant movements and reflexive distortions of the body that take place in the game. A knowing and comical use of camera undercranking, dummy substitution and *anime*-inspired visual shorthand rouse a greater sense of the videogame *and* its ancillary consumer culture.

Not surprisingly, the officially endorsed Japanese *anime* adaptations demonstrate most clearly the special moves of the *Street Fighter* cast. The special move takes centre stage as the primary storyline; in the opening scene Ryu is observed in combat with Sagat by one of M. Bison's cyborg spies, who are equipped to analyse the 'fighting potential rating' of the warriors they study. The modest 'boy' Ryu demonstrates unheard of fighting potential as he decimates Sagat with a dragon punch followed by fireball. This fireball in turn forms the titles of the movie, which explode outward in a sunburst effect. These film adaptations, whether in animation or film, seem to be entirely predicated on the viewer's pleasure of seeing the special move performed within the context of the action sequences, to the extent that they almost puncture the diegesis, speaking outward to the audience, characteristically breaking the frame as part of the neo-baroque aesthetic indicative of the videogame. Perhaps the greatest enquiry into the mystery of the special move takes place in the *anime* series *Street Fighter II: V* (1995) and second feature film *Street Fighter Alpha* (1999).

Both focus on the nature of the power '*hadou*', the spiritual force that fuels Ryu's trademark special fireball. While the *anime* series traces Ryu from his adolescence, globetrotting with Ken and training in the martial arts toward a mastery of the power of '*hadou*', *Street Fighter Alpha* shows Ryu at the end of this journey, struggling to repress the 'dark *hadou*', the evil fighting energy reminiscent of the dark powers of the Sith Lords opposing that of the Jedi in the *Star Wars* series and franchise. What these narratives portray is the struggle to attain a mastery over the power of the special move. Ryu's efforts to wrestle control of the *hadou* power, and then later to determine its polarity as either good or evil, echoes with the sentiment of the videogame and its player, where one labours to master the control system, and moreover decide what sort of player one should be: a nurturer of fellow players or ruthless powergamer. In this sense, these adaptations are more 'authentic', in that they present a narrative metaphor for a gameplay attribute, rather than solely trying to flesh out the scant narrative of the game series. Importantly, these texts constitute more successful remediations in that they maintain the *modus operandi* of the videogame, as a game; a narrative contextualization of the in-game difficulty of doing a fireball. It is a remediation of an aspect of the *played* game form rather than its ancillary narrative content.

The special move fails to appear in the 1994 Milton Bradley board game *Street Fighter II*. This game is much more reminiscent of Capcom's scrolling beat-'em-up *Final Fight* in its form, with players roaming the streets fighting with one another acquiring power from dice-roll victories, upon which they earn the right to challenge M. Bison in his cardboard fortress. Like videogame, the board game victory condition is a remediation of the narrative defeat of M. Bison from *Street Fighter II* onwards.

Conclusion

One of the most pressing problems in game studies is in the close analysis of played games. Figuring out how one determines the character of games as texts created through play, and the qualitative difference of players, require the scholar to interpret skill and mastery at a textual level. Players individuate games through play, and so the semantics of games are problematized by the lack of a wholly agreed text with a delimited beginning, middle and end. While the higher operations of a player's gameplay (their performance when completing a level for instance) might be different, there are commonalities between players in the lower levels of gameplay, and from these we can initiate a study, building up through gameplay structures to a point in which we can see how gameplay motivates the fracturing of the playing public along lines of competency. We can all usually make a character walk or run in a direction, most can make them attack, fewer can make a character hurl a fireball, and fewer still can integrate that move into a combination of attacks. It is necessary to announce the competency of the player as a context for a textual analysis of games.

The reward-spectacle is a textual motif of games design and play. Competency of play is confirmed in the positive feedback loop of a representation or sound. If the gameplay executed is deemed challenging, then the image and sound feedback can be thought of as a reward of sorts, affirming the player's physical control over the game system. Not all positive feedback loops are reward-spectacles, and they are distinguished by a sense of gratification arising from the player-driven evocation of a certain image. In its neo-baroque design, *Street Fighter* embodies the principle of the reward-spectacle to the fullest, in both its low-level and high-level gameplay. The special move is the most succinct example of the beat-'em-up genre's refinement of the reward spectacle down to a momentary peak experience. Split-second controller inputs give rise to a simultaneous representation on screen of a fantastic referent. While this representation might not correspond to the action of the player's hands in later beat-'em-ups, in the *Street Fighter* franchise part of the bodily gratification felt as a gamer arises from the doubling of the movement of player control and on screen player-character referent. While the writer Steven Poole cites the complex controller activity as something that throws the player out of the gameworld, I suggest that a game like *Street Fighter II* utilizes control (and the synchronicity of reward-spectacle) to reflexively comment on the bodily doubling of the performing player and the performing player-character.

When studied independent of one another the form and meaning arising from either *play* or *representation* leave us bankrupt. To create a picture of a player's textual experience, we must try to elect criteria within game design and gameplay where these aspects intersect. My observations on the reward-spectacle of *Street Fighter II*'s special moves are an attempt to initiate a move toward this method.

Works cited

Barthes, R. (2000) *Mythologies*, London: Vintage.

Bolter, Jay David and Richard Grusin (2000) *Remediation: Understanding New Media*, Cambridge: MIT Press.

Cousins, B. (2002) 'Mind Your Language – Unlocking The Secret Formula of Games Design', *Develop*, August 2002.

Debord, Guy (1992) *Society of the Spectacle*, London: Rebel Press.

Fiske, John (1989) *Understanding Popular Culture*, London: Routledge.

Hunt, Leon (2002) '"I Know Kung Fu!" The Martial Arts in the Age of Digital Reproduction', in G. King and T. Krzywinska (eds) *Screenplay: Cinema/Videogames/Interfaces*, London: Wallflower Press, 194–205.

Jenkins, H. (1992) *Textual Poachers: Television Fans and Participatory Culture*, London: Routledge.

King, Geoff and Tanya Krzywinska (2006) *Tomb Raiders and Space Invaders: Videogame Forms and Contexts*, London: I.B. Tauris.

——(eds) (2002) *Screenplay: Cinema/Videogames/Interfaces*, London: Wallflower Press.

Kracauer, S. (1995) *The Mass Ornament: Weimar Essays*, London: Harvard University Press.

Ndalianis, A. (2004) *Neo-Baroque Aesthetics and Contemporary Entertainment*, London: MIT Press.

Poole, Steven (2002) *Trigger Happy: The Inner Life of* Videogames, London: Fourth

Estate.

Staiger, J. (1992) *Interpreting Films: Studies in the Historical Reception of American Cinema*, London: Princeton University Press.

——(2000) *Perverse Spectators: The Practices of Film Reception*, London: New York University Press.

Surman, D. (2006) 'Style, Consistency and Plausibility in the *Fable* Gameworld', in S. Buchan (ed.) *Animated Worlds*, London: John Libbey Press.

——(2005) 'Delineating the Popular in Game Studies: A Survey of Hardcore Gamer Culture', *Popular Texts and Their Audiences Conference*, Liverpool: John Moores University, 24–28 November 2005.

Udon (2005) *Street Fighter: Eternal Challenge*, Chicago: Devil's Due Publishing.

Games

Bruce Lee (1984), Datasoft.

Bushido (1983), Ebenel Enterprises.

Chuck Norris Superkicks (1983), Xonox.

Devil May Cry series (2001–), Capcom.

Fantasy Zone series (1986–91), Pony Canyon Inc.

International Karate (1985), System 3 Software Ltd.

Karate Champ (1984), Data East.

Karateka (1984), Broderbund.

Kung-Fu Master (1985), Irem Software Engineering Inc.

Raiden (1991), Seibu Kaihatsu Inc.

Resident Evil series (1996–), Capcom.

Sonic the Hedgehog (1991), Sega.

Splatterhouse series (1991–93), Namco.

Street Fighter (1987–), Capcom.

Streets of Rage series (1991–93).

The Sims (2000), Maxis.

The Way of the Exploding Fist (1985), Beam Software.

Yie Ar Kung-Fu (1984), Konami.

1942 (1985), Capcom.

Notes

1   Capcom is an acronym for Japan Capsule Computers; the company is today one of Japan's premier developers, founded in 1979. Their output has been characterized by a strong emphasis on gameplay and the retention of an 'arcade aesthetic'. Though not explicitly dealing with film adaptation, series like Resident Evil (Capcom 1996–present) and *Devil May Cry* (Capcom 2001–present) have been characterized by a prominent cinematic quality, with similar echoes

of the same Asian action cinema that underpins the aesthetic conventions of the *Street Fighter* series.

2 The allocation of names for the North American and European release differed from the original Japanese release. The boxer Balrog was originally named M. Bison, widely recognized to be a play on the name of celebrity boxer Mike Tyson. For reasons unknown (though most probably because of potential action from Tyson) Capcom changed boxer M. Bison to Balrog. Balrog was the original name of Vega the Matador, and Vega the original name of M. Bison. What is interesting here is the mobility of names, and the way in which the meaningfulness of the characters extends largely from their range of moves, win poses and victory remarks. These boss characters became playable in the subsequent release *Street Fighter II: Championship Edition* (1993).

3 A 'combo' is a sequence of hits in which the attacking player's timing ensures that a combination of hits make contact without space for the other player to block. Now a central part of *Street Fighter* gameplay across the series and various spin-off videogames, the capacity to combo was initially considered an erroneous element of the game design, though its integration into gameplay by players provoked Capcom to recognize it officially, with a 'combo counter' element in the user interface of the 1993 release *Super Street Fighter II*.

4 One important distinction between the Japanese and Western popular reception of Street Fighter is in its voice acting. As a consequence of the mass appeal of Japanese animation or *anime* voice actors have attained a degree of celebrity status, and are often quizzed as to the lifestyles and motivations of the characters they represent. For instance Katashi Ishizuka and Toshiyuki Morikawa have voiced Ryu throughout the series.

13

The trouble with *Civilization*

Diane Carr

What follows is an exploration of meaning, information and pleasure in *Sid Meier's Civilization III*. Various theorists, including Poblocki (2002) and Douglas (2002) have argued that games within the *Civilization* series[1] perpetrate a reductive folk-history that positions Western-style technologically orientated progress as 'the only logical development' for humanity (Poblocki 2002: 168). Such critiques are warranted, but they share a tendency to focus on the game's rules and pseudo-historical guise, at the expense of its more playful, less quantifiable aspects. The intention here is not to redeem *Civilization* or save it from its critics. The point is, rather, to examine aspects of the criticism that has calcified around the series to date, and question some of the conclusions that have been drawn.

Given the complexity and volume of information in this game, and the fact that games are played and re-played, it would be quixotic to pursue a single, definitive account of the meaning of *Civ III*. One analysis might focus on the game's rules, conditions and goals in order to show that it embeds a pro-Western stance. Alternatively, an interpretation could draw on evidence relating to the playing of the game by different users. Or the meaning of the game could be discussed in terms of its relationship to earlier fantasies of imperial conquest and Western self-reinvention in the space of the 'other'. These approaches might be classified as focusing on, in turn, rules, play and culture. These categories are borrowed from Katie Salen and Eric Zimmerman's *Rules of Play* (2004). According to this useful book, rules involve the 'intrinsic mathematical structures of games' (2004: 102). For the sake of this discussion, this would be broadened to include the multiple modes and address of the game-as-text. Their second schema or conceptual framework is 'play' – the experience through which the potentials of the game-text are actualized, the 'player's interaction with the game and with other players' (102). Salen and Zimmerman's third schema is that of culture, the contexts of play in a wider sense. This frame involves looking past 'the internal, intrinsic qualities of games toward the qualities brought to the game from external contexts' (104). Salen and Zimmerman stress that these categories are inter-related and that the borders between them are permeable.

So a credible investigation into the meaning of *Civ III* could be staged at the level of rules, or play, or culture. Any of these strategies could result in a valid, if partial, analysis. The point at which such an exercise in interpretation might fracture is where the discussion shifts or slips between a consideration of the rules, or of play, or of cultural context, with insufficient care and caution. Furthermore, if a pattern is clearly discernable in two of the schema, the resemblance is suggestive of a relationship, but it does not automatically follow that any such link is straightforward – nor does it follow that it will result in a particular outcome within the remaining schema. To be more specific: to identify patterns within a game's rules is one thing. To point out parallel or analogous patterns within wider culture is fair, and to see this as evidence of a relationship, reasonable. To establish the reasonable possibility of a relationship, however, is not the same as determining its nature. To assume that tropes discernable in either the rules, or the wider cultural context – or both – will necessarily result in a particular repercussion (of whatever kind) at the level of play is problematic.

Civ III is a turn-based strategy game. The player establishes a settlement that with luck, skill, diplomacy, mercantile savvy, technical attainment and military guile will expand to thrive for six thousand years – or for as long as acquisitive, game-generated, neighbouring nations can be bribed, befriended or outgunned. The player begins each game by selecting from an array of non-contemporary leaders (Catherine the Great, Hiawatha, Cleopatra, etc.), and options relating to the tailoring of a game-world: climate, geology, number and aggression of other inhabitants. Each selection involves ramifications. Choosing a small planet, for instance, will result in a short, intense game. There are six difficulty levels, and the opportunity to exclude various victory conditions. Each of the leaders is attached to a particular tribe (Russia, Iroquois, Egyptian, etc.) that begins with different 'starting advances' and that will go on to develop a special military unit (Cossack, mounted warrior or war chariot, for instance).

When gameplay begins only a small area in the first settlement's vicinity is exposed on screen. Exploration reveals more of the terrain, including the location of various resources and luxuries. As well as exploring the game-world, the player needs to move through a range of screens where information of strategic importance is accessed and manipulated. There are six screens that relate to government and development. Each has a lightly characterized advisor who can be consulted on trade, domestic or military issues, or international relations. The science advisor is linked to the game's 'technology tree' – a flowchart of scientific research projects. The level of taxes set, raised and invested by the player decides the rate of technological advancement. By accumulating technology, the civilization is able to produce more advanced military units, and build a greater variety of facilities, from libraries to aqueducts, each of which involves quantified advantages (such as increased research or population) as well as costs. Players, if they care to, may investigate the relative advantages of each unit in the game's manual, or by 'right clicking' on the relevant icon in a city's 'construction box', or by checking the on-screen Civilopedia. New technologies also allow the player to undertake the construction of 'Great Wonders'. These involve a major investment of time and resources, but will generate considerable gameplay advantages. They are singular, in that if one civilization possesses the Great Wall (a defensive advantage) or the Great Library (a technological advantage) it precludes the competition from building it.

As play proceeds the game offers a wider variety of components and units. The player is likely to continue to seek to establish (or invade) additional cities, while managing and trading resources and directing city improvements. Players can actualize the game's potentials in a variety of ways. There are various trajectories to victory. Some goals could be described as diegetic because they are consistent with the represented world in that they involve diplomatic, cultural or military superiority over the AI competition.[2] Other goals would include the accumulation of points for the sake of a high score.

As this suggests, in *Civ III* the player attends and responds to an array of prompts, which are cased in varying degrees of guise: from teeth-gnashing rebel citizens, disgruntled advisers and patronizing allies, to blunt instructions such as 'press the space bar'. The player's components (worker, swordsman, tank) are mobile, and the player also moves: between menus and between the various demands and invitations of the game. The player's cities are viewed from an isometric, top-down perspective, yet it does not follow that the player's proximity is fixed. Distance, in this instance, is not determined solely by the visual because proximity relates to detail, and involves the stratification of information. The player's civilization is made up of different cities, each of which can be peeled like an onion to reveal more and yet more variables relating to management, resources and production. A player might be oblivious to some of these details, choose to ignore them by implementing default options, or delegate particular responsibilities to the 'city governor'. Thus the extent to which a player grapples with detail and complexity remains a matter of taste and proficiency. A player might also move between different attentive states, in that he or she could adopt a relatively distanced, calculating stance one minute, only to become engrossed pondering the movements of tiny, animated war elephants the next. The game is highly re-playable, so players are also mobile in the sense that over time their competency will increase. As an outcome, one layer of the game will become familiar, automatic, in which case the player might choose to re-incorporate novelty and challenge by playing at a higher difficulty level. While in theory it is possible to split the ludic aspects of the game (those parts of the game – including rules, goals, chance, components and winning or losing outcomes – that make it a game) from its representational aspects (the portrayal of the game world and its inhabitants), the emergence of the game, through play, involves a weaving together of these facets.

Civ under siege

In 'Becoming-state: The Bio-cultural Imperialism of *Sid Meier's Civilization*', Poblocki points out that the game wears a veneer of equity, in that the player may select his or her leader from a range of backgrounds (including Iroquois, Chinese, Hittite, Russian and Mayan), any of whom might achieve world domination if they clamber up the technology tree first. Yet this, Poblocki writes, only means that they have 'equal opportunity to become the United States of America' (2002: 168). Poblocki suspects that the cultural and historical bias embedded in the game's rules and goals mean that 'we can write anything we want as long as it is the master narrative of globalization' (175). Elsewhere other authors have expressed similar concerns in relation to the invisible assumptions that underpin real-world governmental policy simulations (Starr 1994). Such concerns are justified, yet in all likelihood policy makers, sociologists and civil servants looking to scientific simulations for evidence and players enjoying games (with 'made-up' rules and fictional geography where they play the role of a leader who lives for 6000 years) will differ in what they are looking for, and how they are likely to interpret and apply what they find. Salen and Zimmerman (2004) make a related point when they contrast an online game with an online medical database. The use of the database involves goals that are extrinsic, whereas playing the game is 'an end in itself' (2004: 332), its goals are intrinsic – the 'game is not a tool being used to fill an external, utilitarian need' (332)[3].

Poblocki discusses *Civilization* as a history simulation. The problem, he writes, is that 'basing computer simulation on nineteenth-century models of natural history is not adequate to explore contingencies of human history, but instead in a quasi-scientific fashion in fact reinforces the well established narratives of cultural imperialism' (2002:174). The reinforcement Poblocki mentions is an effect on the player, who, through his or her identification with the power offered by the role of leader, internalizes the rules of the game, because 'a critical distance to a process one is part of is difficult to assume' (175). In this process the player gulps down the logics of American imperialism, which, Poblocki speculates, could influence how the player-subject then orientates him or herself 'towards the current ideological rhetorics and policies of the United States' (174).

Positioning *Civilization* as a simulation or as a game might seem moot – given that it is a game that incorporates a simulation, but in the context of this discussion the distinction is important. Simulation games (such as *The Sims* or *SimCity 2000*) have made life difficult for theorists attempting to define games, precisely because they do not rely on goals and winning or losing outcomes (Juul 2003: 33; Salen and Zimmerman 2004: 82). Strategy games like those in the *Civilization* series, on the other hand, present the player with clear goals (and sub-goals), each of which relates to and recalls the game's rules, conditionality and constraints. A simulation game involves the pleasures of playful experimentation with the simplified model of a system, more or less for its own sake. If analysing rules (or the effects of rules on players), then the presence or absence of overt goals and winning or losing outcomes is of import – because they play a part in determining the player's relationship to a game's rules (and thus to any power or ideology embedded in those rules). Subsequently, in this instance, the conflating of the genres is problematic.

This is not to say that questions of simulation are irrelevant to *Civ III*. The point is that simulation-orientated play and more goal-orientated play are simultaneously on offer, and each invites a particular style of participation. These two modes of play recall the distinction made by Caillois between *paidea* and *ludus* (cited by Eskelinen 2001; Frasca 1999, 2003). The difference between paidea and ludus is 'similar to the distinction between play and game' (Eskelinen 2001), while for Gonzalo Frasca (2003) the 'difference between paidea and ludus is that the latter incorporates rules that define a winner and a loser, while the former does not'. When the user is playfully experimenting with the system, running around for the sake of exploration, or pursuing alternative, self-initiated goals (getting their roads to form a pattern, for example) they could be said to be leaning towards the paidic potentials of the game. When players focus more specifically on competition, goal attainment and strategic progression, they are drawing more intently on the game's ludic facets. If asserting, as Poblocki has done, that the player's relationship to the patterns embedded in the rules has ramifications (on the meaning of the game, and on the effect of any such meaning on the player) then it is expedient, yet ultimately misrepresentative, to overlook the diversity of the game's offers and the scope for the player to exercise her or his prerogative.

David Myers has taken issue with readings of *Civ*, including Poblocki's, that interpret the game's meaning according to external frameworks. For his forthcoming article, 'Bombs, Barbarians and Backstories: Meaning-making within *Sid Meier's Civilization*', Myers has scoured the online discussions between expert *Civ* players. There he found evidence that for these experienced users there is little or no link between the various in-game variables (be it barbarians, nuclear weapons, character ethnicity or despotism) and the real-world instances of these phenomena. He writes that the 'most frequently discussed aspects of the game within dedicated player forums (e.g., Apolyton.net) are the relationships among in-game signifieds – without reference to or really any concern about their significance (or signification) outside the game context' (Myers, 2005).

For these experts, argues Myers, the game's components and units only matter in terms of their ludic attributes: the function they have within the game's economy. Such players operate with the representational equivalent of X-ray specs, cutting through the cosmetic wrapping of the game (such as the depicted landscape, or characterization). Objects and actions – their value, status and meaning – are read solely in terms of their role and strategic value within the closed world of the game. The meaning of a Celtic swordsman, for example, does not hinge on his bold, bare-chested sprinting and sword brandishing, or his floppy mop of ginger hair, or his race and gender. The swordsman's meaning would relate to its capability as a defensive or an attack unit, the number of squares per turn that it can travel and the amount of resources involved in its construction and maintenance.

It is certainly true that players discussing *Civ III* might use language that is only intelligible to those familiar with the game, as this quote from a player suggests:

> This is an interesting scenario. I'm playing on Emperor level. I'm so behind that my only hope is to stay at war – so all the people have turned into entertainers and everyone is starving to death. It's switched to anarchy by itself so I'm going to go communist for a while then go back to democracy – which is ok, because I'm religious. (Player P, comment to the author during play)

At one level this player's remarks support Myers' argument. The comment about being religious, for instance, is not an affirmation of the player's faith, but a reference to the element of his civilization's identity that will determine the number of turns involved in a change of government.[4] Yet having observed this player at length I know that a proportion of his game-play does not involve the manipulation of components based purely on their meaning as determined by their ludic value. On the contrary, his gaming involves 'on-the-fly' interpretations that knit in-game and extra-gamic information together in a manner that is idiosyncratic, piecemeal and inconsistent (or playful, in other words). Some information is learnt during the course of play, other information might be deliberately sought out (in the manual, for instance). Obviously a player can only interpret a component in terms of its ludic attributes if they are known – if curiosity or strategic necessity has previously motivated the player to research (and remember) the relevant information. Given this, and the sheer volume of variables in the game, it is only to be expected that the comparative advantages posed by the attributes of certain nationalities (seafaring versus agricultural, for example), or the benefits provided by a particular 'Great Wonder' might remain uninvestigated. In such cases, the assessment of a variable might be informed by personal, extra-gamic connotations or associations – the upshot is that a player might remain disinterested by a particular Great Wonder or combat unit simply because it is felt to be a bit 'boring' or 'useless'.

These comments from players give some indication of just how differently individuals might approach the challenges posed by *Civ III*. The second player (Player L) has been playing the game over a longer period, yet the first (Player W) attains notably higher scores. The first player peers straight past the representational aspects of the game to efficiently milk the system for points, while the second takes pleasure in less quantified goals:

> *Player W*: Scored over 6000 the other day in CIV III. Now trying deity level. ouch.
>
> *Player P*: Bloody hell! – how did you manage that?
>
> *Player W*: I gradually conquered all of the [neighbouring civilizations] and then, in the end, I left one tiny village in the desert and surrounded it. This leaves time to research all the technologies and maybe even add some future tech, build temples and cathedrals everywhere to make all happy, turn all mines into irrigation to maximise growth, build mass transit everywhere to reduce pollution, and so on. (Player W and P, email correspondence 21 April 2004)

> I enjoy running around opening up the dark areas in search of huts and opponents, so I can quickly get an advantage over my opponents in terms of knowledge so that I can build the wonders of the world first. I don't care about reaching space age ... I'm not too fussed about getting on the scoreboard. In terms of strategy, I don't think I have much of one, apart from opening up areas, getting the huts and building more cities. Initially, I chose [a leader] randomly, wasn't too fussed. [Now] I play the Aztec characters, because they have a jaguar unit ... you don't have to use too much resources to make them ... the pictures of the 'leaders' are not that pretty to look at anyway and you can't change their features (Player L, interview 9 March 2005)

Such diversity suggests that Myers' evidence reflects the context from which it was extracted. The material that he collected from online *Civ* discussion forums is produced by a particular community of committed players, or fans, who are motivated to participate within a collaborative secondary realization of the game (in that their solo gaming becomes a shared experience, after the fact), and this results in a certain homogeneity of interpretation. As Henry Jenkins has shown, fandom involves a particular 'mode of reception' as well as 'a particular set of critical and interpretive practices' (1992: 277–278). Still, Myers' argument derails simplistic conclusions concerning the links between objects inside and outside the 'magic circle' of the game[5] (Johan Huizinga, cited in Salen and Zimmerman 2003:15). He also points out that the expert's perceptions of the game's components and configurations may differ from that of the newer user:

> it is only during initial and novice play – which is most compatible with a linear reading of the game as text – that Civilization game signs and symbols (i.e. game *signifiers*) might be reasonably associated with those pre-existing – often normative – values corresponding to the use (or misuse) of real-world factories, fossil fuels, and nuclear energies (i.e., real-world *signifieds*). (Myers 2005, original emphasis)

Myers draws on the online communications of experienced *Civ* players to argue that the values accorded to in-game objects or phenomena bear little or no direct relationship to their real-world counterparts and, for this reason, Sybille Lammes' paper 'On the Border: Pleasure of Exploration and Colonial Mastery in *Civilization III: Play the World*' makes for an interesting comparison. Like Poblocki, Lammes (2003) is concerned with the ideology of the *Civ* series, particularly its construction of categories such as culture or barbarism, and the question of whether playing with these dynamics involves the subversion or merely the reaffirmation of colonialist tropes.

As noted, the first stage in playing a game of *Civ III* involves wading through a set of options relating to the size of planet that the player would prefer: the land masses (continents, islands or archipelagos), the geology and climate, the presence or absence of indigenous inhabitants (of varying degrees of ferocity), the amount, identity and aggression levels of the other civilizations on the planet, and the identity of the player's own civilization. Lammes works her way through these opening menus while drawing attention to her inexperience – 'I cannot fathom the consequences of these qualities yet and have to concentrate on choosing from all the options on screen' (2003: 124). Unlike Lammes, a veteran user would be in a position to contextualize the various options faced during this initial 'set up' phase. Lammes documents her decision to play a particular mode of the game ('Capture the Princess') – without describing what this entails, beyond the probable inclusion of a princess: 'I am curious about the function of the princess amidst all these rules and choose for that option' (2003: 124). While she later describes the appearance of the princess component, Lammes still omits a description of its ludic function: 'I can now see the princess again … I try to move her as well. This does not prompt her to shift however. It only activates her to give off a giggling sound.' (125)

As a new player Lammes is attentive to the representational aspects of the game – the cutscenes, the princess's giggles. The rules of the game, however, remain largely a mystery. Lammes' inexperience with *Civ III* is not in itself a problem. What is absent, perhaps, is a clear acknowledgement that the analyst's novice status situates and shapes her interpretation. I concur with Myers that a user's level of experience informs the likelihood of his or her drawing on internal or external referents while making sense of *Civilization*. However, I would stress that the point is not that either the novice or the expert is more 'right' about the meaning of *Civ*. The crucial issue is that the user's level of experience (which will alter as a consequence of play) will constitute the interpretive frame for that user. Furthermore, this shows that the meaning of *Civilization* – whatever it might be – is neither universal, nor static.

Western entertainment, art and literature are rife with instances of chauvinistic marginalization and biased simplifications of history. It is possible to locate such dynamics in the rules of *Civilization*, as Lammes, Poblocki and others, including Douglas, have done. Yet it is one thing to show that *Civ* accommodates these patterns as rules, and another to conclude that it follows that *Civ* propagates these patterns as ideology or effect (as in 'an effect of play on the player'). If a novice and an expert 'read' the princess and the barbarian in an entirely disparate way, then the meanings of the game are clearly not constant. Objects, actions and outcomes within *Civ* will mean one thing to beginners and another to experts: meaning shifts, depending on the user, and users alter as well.

In *Civilization*, writes Poblocki, 'power is almost invisible because, at least at the level of rhetoric, it belongs to us' (2002:175). Poblocki is concerned that because of interactivity the politics embedded in the game are more likely to impress themselves on the player – that the player's collaboration with the text's values (expressed as rules) leads to the internalization of these values by the user. Douglas is also concerned about the capacity of games to instill or 'rehearse' ideology (2002: 14). He writes that while 'some might find the game's recognition of historical contingency progressive and liberating, I would argue that its ultimate effect is to reinforce the pattern of interaction between the colonizing power and the aboriginal' (15). Again, in this instance, the revealed meaning of the game is posed as an effect on the player; where the player-subject's values are at stake. Douglas suggests that 'games may work on their operators to configure our expectations of the real, our sense of history, national identity, race and gender, or economic justice, not just in terms of representation, but in the way that rules teach universal laws and routine behaviour' (16). By opposing nature to culture, and civilized to indigenous, writes Douglas, *Civ* reiterates the myth of *terra nullius* – the fantasy that until the arrival of Europeans, the 'new world' was legally vacant.

As with Poblocki's, much of Douglas's argument looks in to the rules of the game, and out to wider culture (philosophies of history, postcolonial theory), but when it comes to considerations of meaning there is a move from these schema, to that of play. It is as if the internalization, reinforcement and reconfiguration linked in their analysis with meaning, is something that happens *to* the player through exposure (like a form of radioactivity). In moving from a critique of the game's rules and the prejudicial bias that they house, to the continuity of such myths within Western popular culture, and then to statements about the effect of the game on its users, these discussions stray across Salen and Zimmerman's three schema: evidence tends to be collected from two schemas (rules, culture), yet conclusions are drawn in a third (play). The trouble with such critique is that play is the schema of the experiential, and it involves the actualization, interpretation and configuration of the game in real-time by users. As soon as play enters the equation, the assertion that barbarians, for instance, necessarily mean anything specific begins to disintegrate – not least because a player loading a new game can simply choose to omit barbarians from the scenario. Players look to the game, experience the game and interpret the game, in a multitude of ways.

The relationship between rule and play is complex, and its innumerable and varied ingredients will impact on the (eventual) production of meaning by individual players. Constituents of this relationship would include the multiplicity of offers featured by the game-as-text and the scope of the player's manoeuvrability in relation to these. Also to be considered would be the player's continual motion through the game-world, around the various menus, and towards greater competence and familiarity. Sliding further along the continuum between rule and play would involve, eventually, confronting the subjectivity of an individual user. This would seem to be the most likely site for the production of meaning, and it is also the point at which the contexts of play (environmental and social) would become an issue, and the influence of the broadest schema – that of culture – would inevitably become a factor. I would argue that this means that a discussion of the meaning of *Civilization* cannot, on the one hand, position meaning as an effect of play, while at the same time fail to note that play is expressive, and that the realization of the game's myriad offers during play involves selectivity on the part of the user. The player's own (complex and culturally situated) subjectivity is a variable within the system through which the meaning of a game is produced.

From literature to comics, from horror movies to militaristic FPS games, it is not difficult to find examples of Western texts that feature cultural or political bias. Yet it is one thing to identify such patterns within the structure of a text, and another to conclude that this is what that text *means* to its audience. That would entail making assumptions about who is watching (or reading, or playing). As active reader theorists, cultural philosophers and media studies pundits have long argued, describing the structure or the production of a text is different from describing its reception and interpretation. In addition to which, it has not been demonstrated that games are more likely to impress a particular perspective on their users due to interactivity or agency. The opposite could just as convincingly be argued: that because of play, interactivity and agency, the 'reading position' of the player is more multiple and contesting, more critical and assertive, than that offered to viewers, gazers or readers. The second proposition is more theoretically feasible, but that does not make it any easier to prove.

My emphasis on the provisional and shifting nature of meaning in *Civ III* is informed by my own gaming preferences. I have played *Civ* games regularly for a couple of years, but I am not a high scorer. When I want to rule the planet I play on an easy setting. When my goal is mere survival, I play at a much higher difficulty level. At times I focus on the manipulation of components according to their ludic value, yet at other times I take the flattery or unfriendly actions of the game's AI characters personally. I will often start a new game only to abandon the new world if it is missing iron, or if it is too dry, too swampy, or too light on luxuries such as silks, gems or incense. I associate fresh water and green land with wealth, and I think ocean travel is boring. I like the detailing in the tiny animated figures. I think Medieval Infantry units are useless, whatever their official attack rating is – although I know they only appear feeble because I keep sending them into combat with insufficient defensive support. Discovering each world feels like unwrapping a present or rifling through a toy box, and if I don't get what I want, I can toss the world away and generate another. I never play online, or contribute to *Civ* fan sites. Generally we (my partner and myself) play out the same scenario in parallel, taking turns on the computer, and comparing the two worlds that emerge. In the immediate context of play (our house) the game itself is regularly accused of cheating. 'Travelling in time' (reloading at an earlier save point to thwart the AI neighbours) is our preferred way to 'cheat back'. While I have played to completion and won, I frequently lose, and I am much more likely to abandon a game, or repeat a single scenario several times, than play it through to a particular conclusion. My point is that *Civ III* is a game, and games are played. This cannot be ignored when meaning, values or assumptions in computer games are under investigation.

Conclusion

Some of the dissatisfaction expressed by critics of *Civilization* seems founded in disappointment. The rhetorical subtext of their analysis is that play should be edifying. *Civilization* is not edifying – and so it must be corrupting. It is self-evident that *Civ III* involves a dog-eat-dog vision of history, and that this aspect of the game is reflected in its rules. It is true, also, that the game reflects its particular cultural, commercial and historical roots. However, if meaning is associated with reception and interpretation, then a significant portion of the meaning of *Civ III* is generated by or emerges through play.

This discussion is not intended, in any way, to be a reiteration of arguments on the limits of textual analysis. On the contrary, the analysis discussed in this chapter demonstrates the need for textual analysis. We need a better understanding of the multiple connotative fields and codes that are a part of a game's rules, representational agenda and inter-textual reach. Textual analysis, however, needs to embrace (rather than shun) the complexity and multiplicity of offers, invitations and demands accommodated and communicated by games.

The meaning of a game does not reside in 'one place', but once an analyst has decided, for the sake of a particular discussion, to investigate meaning within the schema of rules, or in play, or in terms of wider culture, that should in turn suggest the theory and the methods that are applicable, and the outcomes that can be realistically or usefully reached. Situating the research question in one schema, the proof and discussion in a second, and the conclusion in a third, without the complexities of each being considered, is not especially helpful.

The historical trajectory modelled by *Civ III* is certainly reductive – but criticizing a simulation for being reductive is nonsensical.[6] Cultural codes and assumptions may well be embedded in the selective inclusions and omissions that constitute a simulation (or a model, or a representation), but these need to be considered alongside game design processes and marketing, and not in isolation. By describing meaning as an effect (an ill-effect, or side-effect) of play some critics, despite their having a progressive agenda, risk inadvertently painting themselves into a reactionary corner. Like many popular texts before it, the *Civilization* games feature Western chauvinism, as Poblocki, Lammes and Douglas have argued. What is more difficult is proving that this continuity reveals anything other than that these fantasies are persistent (which is not a trivial point). The game, at least at the level of its rules, proposes that history is linear; that nations are culturally homogenous, that technical progression coupled with democracy leads to happy and productive civilian populations, and that the value of land resides in its yield and usability. The question is whether the meaning of *Civilization III* is limited to this; whether this fully accounts for the meanings of a game that captivates its players through the variability of its emergent play, and the sheer volume of information that is on offer.

Works cited

Caillois, Roger (1979) *Man, Play, Games*, trans Meyer Barash, New York: Schocken Books.

Douglas, Christopher (2002) '"You Have Unleashed a Horde of Barbarians!": Fighting Indians, Playing Games, Forming Disciplines', *Post Modern Culture*, 13.1, September 2002.

Eskelinen, Markku (2001) 'The Gaming Situation', in *Game Studies*, 1:1, www.gamestudies.org, accessed May 2005.

Frasca, Gonzalo (2003) 'Simulation versus Narrative: Introduction to Ludology', in Mark J.P. Wolf and Bernard Perron (eds) *Video Game Theory Reader*, New York: Routledge, www.ludology.org, accessed May 2005.

——(1999) 'Ludology Meets Narratology: Similitude and Differences Between

(Video)games and Narrative', Finnish version originally published in *Parnasso* #3, Helsinki, www.ludology.org, accessed May 2005.

Jenkins, Henry (1992) *Textual Poachers*, New York: Routledge.

Jenkins, H. and K. Squire (2003) 'Understanding Civilization (III)', *Computer Games Magazine*, September 2003, www.educationarcade.org, accessed May 2005.

Juul, Jesper(2003) 'The Game, the Player, the World: Looking for a Heart of Gameness', Keynote lecture, *DIGRA Level Up Conference*, Utrecht, November 2003, Conference Proceedings eds Marinka Copier and Joost Raessens,Utrecht: Universiteit Utrect/DIGRA, 30–47.

——(2002) 'The Open and the Closed: Games of Emergence and Games of Progression', in *Computer Games and Digital Cultures Conference Proceedings* ed. Frans Mäyrä, Tampere, Finland, 323–329, www.jesperjuul.dk/text/openandthe closed.html, accessed May 2005.

Lammes, Sybille (2003) 'On the Border: Pleasures of Exploration and Colonial Mastery in *Civilization III Play the World*', Paper presented at *DIGRA Level Up Conference*, Utrecht, November 2003, Conference Proceedings eds Marinka Copier and Joost Raessens,Utrecht: Universiteit Utrect/DIGRA, 120–129.

Myers, David (2005) 'Bombs, Barbarians, And Backstories: Meaning-Making Within Sid Meier's *Civilization*', in Matteo Bittanti (ed.) *Ludologica: Videogames D'autore: Civilization and its Discontents. Virtual History. Real Fantasies*, Milan, Italy: Edizioni Unicopli, www.loyno.edu/~dmyers/F99%20classes/ Myers_BombsBarbarians_DRAFT.rtf.

Poblocki, Kacper (2002) 'Becoming-State: The Bio-Cultural Imperialism of Sid Meier's *Civilization*', *Focaal European Journal of Anthropology*, 39, 163–177, www.focaal.box.nl/previous/Forum%20focaal39.pdf, accessed May 2005.

Salen, K. and E. Zimmerman (2004) *Rules of Play: Game Design Fundamentals* Cambridge, MA: MIT Press.

——(2003) 'This is not a Game: Play in Cultural Environments', Keynote lecture, *DIGRA Level Up Conference*, Utrecht, November 2003, Conference Proceedings (eds) Marinka Copier and Joost Raessens, Utrecht: Universiteit Utrect/DIGRA, 14–29.

Starr, Paul (1994) 'Seductions of Sim; Policy as a Simulation Game', *The American Prospect*, 5:17, 21 March 1994, Online at www.prospect.org/print/V5/17/ starr-p.html, accessed May 2005.

Acknowledgements

This research was undertaken with the support of the Eduserv Foundation.

Games

Sid Meier's Civilization (1991), MicroProse Software Inc/MicroProse Software Inc.
Sid Meier's Civilization III (2001), Firaxis Games/Infogrames.
SimCity 2000 (1996), Maxis.
The Sims (2000), Maxis/Electronic Arts.

Notes

1   The main subject of this paper is *Sid Meier's Civilization III*, or *Civ III* (released in 2001, developed by Firaxis Games, published by Infogrames) and its various expansion packs. Here, when it is expedient, and where distinctions between the games are not an issue, the title *Civilization* or *Civ* is used to refer to the game series as a whole, from *Sid Meier's Civilization* (released in 1991, developed and published by MicroProse Software Inc) onwards. Of course in the contexts of a different discussion, distinguishing between the various games may be necessary. The game can be multi-played, but here it is considered in its offline solo-player incarnation.

2   AI, or Artificial Intelligence, in this instance simply means that the other civilizations in the game are aspects of its programming, and not the avatars of other human players.

3   Kurt Squire has used the game as an education tool. In order to use the game in the history classroom with any success it was necessary first to create particular 'episodes' or mods, and then to ensure that gaming sessions were bracketed by teaching that enabled students to critically frame the proceedings (Jenkins and Squire 2003).

4   In a later conversation on *Civ III*, religion and anarchy it transpired that Player P thought that the game was proposing that a religious population adjusted faster to changes in government because 'faith grants the population strength or resilience', whereas Player D (the author) had always thought the game was saying that a religious population is more biddable or docile.

5   Whatever the resemblances or overlaps between being inside or outside of a game, there are still things that will set the game apart. Consent, for instance, is so fundamental to our playing a game, that without consent, it would not be play, or a game. However 'realistic' it looked, the presence of consent means that we know it is a game, and thus the meaning (of gestures, acts, signs and objects) will be irrevocably 'different'.

6   That would be like disparaging a map for not being life-size.

14

Killing time: time past, time present and time future in *Prince of Persia: The Sands of Time*

Barry Atkins

> In my quest for redemption, not even my death can stop me.
> (Promotional copy on the box of *Prince of Persia: The Sands of Time*,
> Ubisoft, 2003)

It is a familiar experience of play to be found, with only minor variations, in any one of many 3D platform adventure games, from *Super Mario 64* (1996) to any of the iterations of *Tomb Raider*. The player is presented with a screen populated with a complex arrangement of architectural features in which a representation of her or his avatar stands. In this particular case the player sees a distressed environment of fractured and broken masonry inside a ruined palace. Fallen blocks of stone are scattered on the floor of a chamber. Intricately decorated pillars stretch towards a ceiling high above, some broken seemingly at random along their length. A balcony appears initially inaccessible, but the way in which it is bathed in a shaft of soft light from a barred window grille makes it an object of curiosity. The game controls allow not only for a sophistication of movement, but for a sophistication of looking, with a panning of the in-game camera possible independently from the movement of the avatar, and the game's artists have given the player something aesthetically pleasing to look at. More importantly, however, the game's level designers have also provided the player with something interesting to engage with as activity rather than spectacle. For experienced players of such games the landscape itself is understood as a series of potential pathways and routes, with heights and distances suggesting the way forward, and the very textures and lighting of the landscape drawing the player onwards and upwards with subtlety. It is no accident, the player knows, that the blocks resemble an untidy staircase, or that the thin pillars that support the vaulted ceiling are placed just the right distance apart for the avatar to leap from one to another across the room, gaining height from broken pillar to broken pillar to eventually allow access on to the enticing balcony space. It is one of the most basic challenges of such games that the player be able to read the space before her or him and imagine progress across what Henry Jenkins (2005) has called its 'narrative architecture', and one of the most basic pleasures of such games rests in the player's ability to decode the landscape according to the key provided by the available movements of the avatar.

From here on in, however, things get a little physical for both the avatar and for the player manipulating the control interface. The climb up the blocks and the leap to the first pillar is straightforward enough, but traversal of the sequence of broken pillars is increasingly difficult, and the consequences of failure become greater as the player climbs. Videogames demand not only that the player sees, but that the player acts, and there is something interesting in the way 3D game space suggests a possibility of almost infinite action (it resembles the world of lived experience, and we might therefore expect it to behave like the world of experience) and yet relies on the player reducing that space, consciously or not, to a sequential puzzle to be solved in a series of button and trigger presses alongside the manipulation of the analogue sticks. Even in the most complex of games there is a fairly low range of available actions. The console controller may look fiendishly complicated to the non-gamer, with its multiple button array, direction pad, shoulder triggers, and analogue sticks, but the actual possibilities open to the player point more to the limit of possibility than to its potential. Some game genres, such as those adversarial fighting games commonly referred to as 'beat-'em ups', feature extremely complex button-pressing sequences (combinations, or combos), and PC and console games that approach the simulation of machine control (PC flight simulators and some robot piloting games such as *Steel Battalion* (2002), for example) might have significantly more complex keyboard or dedicated peripheral input. The 3D platformer, however, remains largely consistent in offering little more than run, jump and climb options for movement that communicate variety mostly by having different expression and consequences dependent on context. Specific games offer specific variations, and *Prince of Persia: The Sands of Time* (2003: hereafter referred to as *Sands of Time*), for example, adds wall-running to the mix (the ability to combine a forward run with a gravity-defying ability to adhere to vertical surfaces for a limited time) but the player of one 3D platform game is likely to be able to transfer the understanding of movement through game space fairly easily from one game to another even when potentially more innovative controls are attempted, such as in the 2004 game *Galleon*. *Galleon* combined the process of looking with movement, with the direction of the camera determining the direction of the walk or dash forward in a manner that surprised an audience that had thought that the basic control scheme for platform games had become more or less fixed. But the game space remained an essentially navigational puzzle that could be unlocked through manipulation of the game controls where a state of jeopardy for the avatar is introduced by the knowledge that the player may make either a cognitive or physical mistake, and send Rhama plummeting to his death, and the player to the reload screen. The basic logic of such games, including the logic that failure to understand game space or exercise careful control over the avatar will often lead to her or his in-game death and expulsion from the 3D game space, remains constant.

This chapter explores the significance of this potential for avatar death for any understanding of games in terms of the pleasures available to the player. It considers the player as someone who plays with the possibility of avatar death at any given moment, and who navigates not only a complex spatial architecture of ruined spaces, but a complex relationship between life and death and a past, present and future of ruined bodies as he or she moves intermittently through game space. That many games in particular genres revolve around the simulation of acts of killing is obvious, and in part fuels the continued negative reception of violent games in some quarters. That games also revolve around the imagination and visual reporting of acts of dying, and specifically the dying of a representative of the self, is subject to less scrutiny. What is explored below is the question of whether the pleasures made available by repeated moments of avatar annihilation might not be sufficiently accounted for by considering that death as the negative consequence of poor or ineffective play. Death, here, is treated as anything but a departure from play, and instead as a continued presence within the game that has been strategically accommodated by games designers and developers in ways that can be illuminated through the lens of the close analysis of the specific example of *The Sands of Time*. The single player adventure game or platformer is not like some sporting contest in which one's success is made all the sweeter by the failure of the defeated other: the other against whom our success is measured is our other self, who we either see or imagine as already having failed each potentially lethal task.

For the moment we will assume, however, that the player in our initial example achieves the perfect balance of judgement of which direction in which to jump within the compensation for error allowed by the game. The avatar might even make the leap from pillar to pillar to balcony with some fluidity and grace depending not only on the skill of the player in manipulating the control interface, but on the skill of the level designers and animators in producing a pleasing aesthetic experience. Having negotiated this space the player can be satisfied with their performance. There is something both cerebrally and physically satisfying about traversing game space, of the player having mapped the potential route in her or his mind and then having converted such mapping into successful movement. At the same time, however, the successful traversal of such a space presents the game's designers with something of a problem. The players of games demand both a novelty of experience and a consistency of experience. A consistency of behaviour in terms of the control of the avatar within the game space is certainly demanded of a game within the platform genre or the 3D adventure genre where so much of the focus is on movement through potentially lethal space.[1] Arbitrary changes in what is possible would depart from a basic contractual arrangement made between game and player, where the possibilities for action inherent in the control scheme are the toolset the player then uses to overcome the obstacles the game's designers put in her or his way. This then leads to a dilemma in terms of design: the player demands both more of the same (in terms of control methodology and outcome at least) alongside a demand for a perpetually novel experience. There are only so many variations on climb/jump/climb/jump, and so many architectural variations one can include without an infinite budget for the modelling and texturing of art assets, before the player becomes aware that he or she has been here before, or done this before, and the game risks falling into the tedium of repetition where the nature of the challenge to the player shifts noticeably from 'How do I do this?' to 'How did I do this last time?'.

One obvious way in which variation is introduced is through the inclusion of combat with non-player characters (NPCs), who might be more mobile than the scenery, but might similarly be understood as providing a puzzle in miniature for the player to solve or unlock. In the *Tomb Raider* games, which equip Lara Croft with her twin handguns with infinite ammunition and a variety of alternative weapons that automatically lock onto potential targets, the puzzle each NPC presents might be quite limited in form, with possible options being limited to the order of target selection, choice of weapon, and the pressing of the fire button, but puzzle they remain. In games such as *Sands of Time*, with its range of clearly differentiated opponents with markedly varied attack and defence routines that must be overcome by particular and specific combat strategies, there is an additional level of sophistication, but again, unless the developers are going to spend a huge amount of resources on the creation of different assets, each demanding not only unique models and animations but behaviours, then the player will quickly tire of the repetition. Indeed, anyone following the popular reception of *Sands of Time* on various internet discussion forums and fan sites would have been aware that even a game that was greeted with extensive critical acclaim was occasionally criticised for the lack of variation in its handling of combat.

A far more interesting method of producing a range of challenge within a game, at least in the context of this essay, is related, but not restricted, to one function served by the introduction of the opponent NPCs that populate the game space. Like the dizzying heights ascended by the avatar, the NPCs act to introduce the sense of jeopardy, of the possibility of imminent and catastrophic failure that will be forcefully communicated to the player through the death of the avatar. But the NPCs also introduce a sense of urgency to the game, often removing the possibility of peaceful and extended contemplation of the game space and acting to make the player act on her or his navigational decisions rapidly and even instinctively. Time becomes a significant factor as the player acts to dispatch wave after wave of opponents, who in the case of *Sands of Time* respawn on death to make such sections of the game sometimes lengthy tests of the player's sustained skill with the control scheme. With the introduction of the aggressive NPC the game recalls the arcade roots of contemporary videogames far more forcefully than when concentrating on the visual presentation of graphics at the cutting edge of the available technology, insisting on swift reaction and a rapid response from players that is simply not demanded in the more contemplative architectural sections of such games. Time, in such circumstances, threatens to run out of the control of the player, and the resulting experience is far more frenetic, and far more obviously a question of survival of the game's challenges on a moment-by-moment basis. I will return to a consideration of games as essentially performative – and as a question of 'live' performance where attention is focused, always, on the present moment of play – later in the chapter, but it is important to note here that aggressive NPCs are used not just to raise the stakes in the player's constant battle for control over an environment that always threatens the in-game death of the avatar, but to deny the player control over time.

For reasons of economy alone many games seek to place time pressures on the player without always simply throwing NPCs at her or him in ever increasing numbers, and actually move to apply the pressure of what Mark Wolf (2001: 88–91) refers to as the 'ticking clock' through a variety of means, including the release of poisonous gases, submersion underwater, door releases driven by clockwork, or walkways that only remain substantial enough to move across for a limited time, to name but a few. Timed challenges have certainly been a feature of 3D platform games at least since *Super Mario 64*, and remain a staple feature of the genre with visual and audio markers of clocks running down being a recurring and familiar presence. Even the occasional single player first person shooter videogame which can, as in the original *Half-Life* (1998), borrow somewhat incongruously even the basic jumping mechanic from the platform genre, has drawn on the change of pace and the introduction of pressure by the timed challenge, most successfully perhaps in instances such as the final dash to escape against the countdown to a massive explosion that concludes *Halo* (2003). The rationing of time, and the imperative to act 'in time', as well as in space, is an established weapon in the designers' armoury of challenges, often providing an adrenaline-fuelled reminder of the material body of the player.

To return to a second specific example of how the player acts in the encounter with game space, we can imagine our player faced with another area within the same ruined palace as before, but having moved on to a stage where the static immobility of the earlier room of broken pillars is replaced with a dynamic and shifting landscape which will actually respond to the movement of the avatar. In this case a broken walkway protrudes over an abyss, and the player can just about map out a route that will involve a brief wall-run and a leap away from the wall and across the abyss to grasp a small section of ledge below a corridor entrance lit by a flickering torch. So far so routine. As the player moves the avatar forward, however, the floor beneath her or him begins to drop away into the depths below, and the player must move the avatar forward at speed without pause once committed to action. As an additional demand on the player the jump must be carefully timed, or the avatar will fall into the gulf.

This is the location of a crucial tension in single player games. The pattern to be decoded is not just spatial, but is also temporal, and the successful player must be able to manipulate the controls within the constraints of time as well as of space. In a 3D platform game it is not just the action performed, but a question of timing, that determines the distinction between success and failure. The moment of the leap therefore has to be finely judged, and calls on the player's hand–eye coordination and the dexterity with which he or she manipulates the controller, as well as on an understanding of when is just the right moment to act. It is obvious here, as it was in the room of pillars, that any mistimed jump will bring the avatar crashing to the floor now far below. A slight error in the timing of the jump, or failure to move with speed off the collapsing walkway, and the avatar falls. Impact is accompanied by a sickening crunch and a short cry abruptly cut off. A death animation plays. The health bar slides immediately to nothing. The avatar is dead. The player has failed to negotiate this particular puzzle sequence, and that fact has been forcefully communicated back to her or him. We are still firmly in the realm of videogame convention. The death of the avatar is routine, as is the absolute break in play represented by the expulsion to the save management screen.

Where *Sands of Time* attempts something new, however, is that there is no automatic expulsion from the game-space at this point, and by pressing and holding down a single trigger the player can simply attempt the challenge again. That the player who has failed this challenge is allowed to try again comes as no great surprise: this is the basic function of the save/reload sequence that is present in most such games. But *Sands of Time* accommodates something close to the save/reload *inside* the game-space, and *within* the game's internal logic. Fatal decisions and actions are reversible, quite literally, with the player able to 'rewind' play (and watch that rewind in process, adding several layers of functionality familiar from the video cassette to the in-game camera) to a point at which the challenge can be attempted again. The developers had used the opening cutscenes to establish not only the narrative back-story that provides the basic context for the game's hero, his quest, and the rationale for the game's aesthetic look and feel, but also to establish a conceit for this in-game manipulation of time. The Prince who stands as the player's avatar has acquired a magical weapon, the Dagger of Time, that acts as a container for the also magical Sands of Time, a renewable and expendable resource that may be gathered (like Mario's coins) from the landscape, or from the corpses of slain NPCs, which does little more than place *Sands of Time*, in plot terms at least, in the universe of hokum fantasy with its enchanted weapons and overuse of portentous proper nouns that would be familiar from any number of other videogames.

The real departure made by Ubisoft, however, is located in the function the Dagger of Time serves when activated (in the PlayStation 2 version at least) by depressing the upper left shoulder trigger. By spending the accumulated Sands of Time stored in the Sand Tanks of the Dagger the player is able to either move into slow motion, or to reverse time. As the player's ability to manipulate in-game temporality is summarized as a selling point on the game's outer case: 'Wield the almighty Sands of Time: rewind the past, freeze the present, behold the future and slow down time itself, but use the power wisely.'

In doing so, *Sands of Time* recognizes the way in which such games are played, and accommodates that recognition within its own logic. Players will cause the avatar to die. If they don't, then the designers have offered an insufficiency of challenge. The rewind facility offered by the Dagger of Time does not remove the consequences of in-game death any more than does the quicksave facility offered by many games. The exclusion of the consequences of the failure that this represents from the game-space proper in most games, however, indicates that it stands outside normal gameplay (and constitutes an index of failure) rather being integral to the game. And such an assumption would be straightforward enough if our understanding of games is essentially linear, and one of a progressive movement in time and space towards a finite ending where the interruptions of avatar death are inconvenient moments that must be quickly erased from the consciousness of the player lest they detract from the experience of mastery and triumph that drives us on. What I shall seek to show in the remaining sections of this chapter, however, is that this is not the dominant experience of play, even if it is the dominant mode of *post-hoc* narrativization of the play experience, and has subsequently come to obscure the extent to which we need to refine our understanding of what it is we are describing when we describe play experience. If nothing else, we need to fully understand the pleasures, as well as the frustrations, offered by the multiple and frequent deaths of our avatars.

At the time of its first appearance *Sands of Time* had as much claim to be at the cutting edge of what was then achieved in contemporary commercial videogames as any other mainstream release. Developed in the mid-point of the life cycle of the then current generation of consoles (although initially a PlayStation 2 exclusive, it was subsequently released on Gamecube, Xbox and PC platforms) it managed to exploit the capabilities of the available technology with something more than mere competence. Its game engine, the driving code of the game that handles the image on the screen and all the variables of player input and the game's artificial intelligence, was comparatively free of bugs, sustained an acceptable frame-rate, and had allowed a detailed and often aesthetically stunning landscape to be rendered. Despite the inclusion of the manipulation of time, it made no great radical departure with regard to genre, building on its declared relationship to the original *Prince of Persia* (1989) 2D platform game to handle the move into three dimensions with rather more success than the much less well received *Prince of Persia 3D* (1999) that had seemed to have once put the final nail in the coffin of the *Prince of Persia* franchise. Released not long after the critically and popularly mauled *Tomb Raider: The Angel of Darkness* (2003), *Sands of Time* actually benefited from direct comparisons made within its genre classification. Its manipulation of time was certainly seen as a marketable asset, and when a sequel was produced, *Prince of Persia: The Warrior Within*

(2004), it retained the princely power over time, even if the delicacy and subtlety of the original's visual aesthetics, with their muted washes of colour and billowing silks was eradicated in favour of far more conventional videogame stylings. In drawing attention to issues of temporality in games, however, it highlighted its own structure as a videogame even as it might appear to have attempted to conceal the artificiality of this key aspect of the practice of videogame play through providing an internal justification for temporal manipulation through the Dagger of Time. *Max Payne* (2001) had featured a variant of 'bullet time' that had, in its nod to *The Matrix*, both declared its cinematic ambition and provided some in-game utility, and *Blinx: The Time Sweeper* (2002) had also offered player control over time. Whereas *Sands of Time* actually laid bare some of the most crude mechanics of how time is handled in contemporary videogames in a particularly forceful way.

That time was at issue, and subject to contestation and challenge over ownership, just as much as space is obvious. The plot tells the player so. The mechanics of the game tell the player so. The puzzles reinforce the point. The proleptic visions triggered at the save checkpoints, the cinematic flash-forwards that aid in the mapping of game-space, remind anyone in danger of forgetting. This explicit concentration on time might even be thought to reflect a contest for ownership and control of the player's time that is a feature of the videogame industry as a whole. Sure, what the developers and publishers want is the consumer's money, but what they have to compete for in order to get the pounds, euros, dollars or yen is their time. *Sands of Time* takes as its subject matter something that is at the heart of concerns about videogames, whether from those who decry the form and have concerns about so much time 'wasted' in the pursuit of such activity or those who celebrate it and often appear to place value on the amount of time a specific game will demand. The current trend towards the production of games that boast upwards of 30 or even 40 hours of gameplay is related to a straightforward attempt to express economic value where the current publishing model insists that the expense of contemporary development be recouped through high unit prices, which then imposes a need for perceived value for money in terms of time they take to play.[2] The central question that would seem to be of critical interest, then, is not so much why videogames put such substantial time demands on their players, as how games attempt to sustain that interest despite the limits of interactive possibility (detailed above). It certainly appears that those critics of games who do not play, but have seen what appears to be the monotonous repetition of manipulation of the control interface, are unable to understand the motivation for such extensive periods of play.

Things were much more simple in the days before the dominant practice of play moved from the arcade and into the living room. Then the economics of games, for the player, were always positioned on the knife-edge of failure and potential mastery, where 'Game Over' was immediately followed with 'Insert coin to continue'. In terms of a transaction it was clear that it was in the interests of the maker of the game to expell the player as often as possible from the game-space, but only if they had offered enough information to the player so that they believed that next time they would overcome the challenge and be able to sustain their period of play. It is difficult to imagine an arcade shoot-'em-up that would have previewed the attack patterns of the next wave of enemy ships just to lure the player into going on. Such knowledge had to be paid for, at least once the first few levels had been overcome. Merely to stay in the game was a potentially public and significant signifier of mastery and skill.

Through the introduction of the Dagger of Time *Sands of Time* brings into the foreground a basic and fundamental characteristic of single player narrative videogames as they are played moment by moment, which can sometimes be obscured by their overarching structures of progression and the inclusion of a far more sophisticated narrative framework than their arcade forebears. It is a rare game in any genre that does not offer a progressive structure in the accumulation of points, its ramping up of difficulty, its levelling up of characters, its sequential acquisition of skills, abilities or weapons, and (particularly) in its movement through space level by level and stage by stage until a final encounter is reached and a final challenge is overcome. In narrative games, those games I have referred to elsewhere as 'game-fictions' (Atkins 2003), this basic progressive structure is even more marked. This structure, that appears to match our expectations of the orderly linear progression we imagine in time passing, however, rarely matches the actual experience of play. The player plays, obviously enough, driven on at least in part by these overarching imperatives to progress reinforced by the game's structure and narrative emplotment, but in the full knowledge that this will not be a straightforward journey.

We might no longer have to feed the machine with loose change, but the experience of play will be, even for the most adept player, broken and intermittent. And players expect this of their games. There is an interesting dialogue present in the manual for the first person shooter *Doom 3* (2004), for example. What might be thought of as the authoritative and impersonal voice of the game's manual presents one version of the presence of the save/reload facility in the game in a standard typeface:

> You can save your game at any time. Your game is also autosaved when entering a new level. To save or load a game, press Esc to pause the game and reveal the in-game menu. You can also avoid the menus by using DOOM3 hotkeys. To quicksave, press F5. To quickload your last saved game, press F9.

A second voice immediately follows, presented as a hand-written note to the reader, and representing what might be thought as of the voice of a gamer offering advice to a fellow gamer, rather than the impersonal voice of authority:

> Save and Save often … Unless your health is really low.

Despite the fact that such an injunction inevitably risks developers being accused of being lazy in terms of their design and using save/reload to avoid having to balance the gameplay themselves, id were doing no more than communicating a basic understanding of how their game, and many other games operate – it is more sensible to err on the side of difficulty in terms of challenge than to ease that difficulty, because players are accustomed to, and even expect, the death of the avatar. Even games that have eschewed the quicksave and rely solely on checkpoint saves, such as Crytek's *Far Cry* (2004), have eventually bowed to public pressure and introduced saving outside of specific checkpoints in later patches to the game. All that Ubisoft have done is provide this process with its rationalization through plot conceit.

That the avatar dies in our games is not a particular torment or bar to pleasure.[3] Indeed, we are often offered the spectacle of our own demise as if it were a gift or a reward, as anyone who has seen the death animations of Lara Croft or the Master Chief would attest. If there is any form of identification in these games, and everything that is claimed (negatively and positively, commercially and academically, and possibly informed by common sense) would imply that there is, then there is something potentially surprising here. We die, or at least the avatar dies, again and again. It would certainly be simplistic to assume that there is an absolute identification of the player with the avatar, however. When the Prince 'speaks' to add his voice-over commentary when the game is paused ('Shall I go on?') or when we exhaust the rewind ability of the Dagger of Time and are expelled to the reload screen despite our second chances, (when he rather critically offers the comment 'Wait … that is not how it happened') he is not so much representative of the player who plays, with all the flaws and failings of the all-too human player who will fail and will make mistakes, but of some posited ideal Prince. This is foreshadowed in the cutscenes offered in the form of visions triggered when the player enters the save checkpoints before each major challenge – a Prince who never fails, who never falls to his death, and who stands outside the game. In fact the distinction between this Prince and the player is even pointed up in some of the dialogue, as when he asks 'Do *you* wish *me* to leave before finishing *my* story?' (my emphasis).[4] This Prince, according to the internal logic of the game, and the plot of redemption for the mistake in releasing the Sands of Time in the first place, has already completed all the actions the player is attempting to perform.

This is also a matter of tense. When we describe our practices of play we, like the Prince, use the past tense. While we play, however, our focus is on a future of multiple and uncertain possibilities, and our attention is firmly fixed on that future. Players of games value the sense of revelation and disclosure offered in narrative games in particular, as is indicated by the demand for warnings of spoilers in published reviews and commentary on games. The yet-to-be-played (or completed) game unfolds for the player in this sense as a cumulative series of revelations and – often quite literal – giving up of its secrets. On the local level of the individual play experience, however, an iterative re-encounter with what has already been seen is an essential component in allowing the player to construct that future. In a game without the time manipulation of *Sands of Time* the player might have to assemble the same basic pathfinding data to be found in the proleptic visions only through multiple deaths, but such a multiple reviewing and re-experience of game-space is often necessary. What is obvious is that we should consider videogame play as a matter of live performance in the moment of play, rather than a matter of straightforward reception or de-coding where meaning is only revealed when the text is decoded in full. In prioritizing the action of the player in the ever changing now of the present moment we must recognise that games played in real-time demand a constant renewal of attention on the screen that is not produced by the guarantee of novelty. What encourages the player to play is a different kind of pleasure that is non-linear, and rejoices in its struggle to wrestle the unstable future into the completed past. The connections between fragments of play experience may have narrative implications, and delivery of plot or story is certainly important to many players, but a distinction must be made between the local event of play in the moment, and the larger context for play provided by the game's narrative.

This is the danger present in over-emphasizing narrative accounts of games that has been pointed to before by many videogame scholars.[5] It is notable, for example, that two existing academic accounts of the experience of play that focus on narrative are as silent on the subject of avatar death as are the online walkthroughs whose very purpose is to erase the need for the avatar to die. Drew Davidson (2005) and Jason Rhody (2005) both position avatar death through this silence as an aberrant departure from the normal state of play, or even as not play at all.[6] To Davidson, occasions of repeated avatar death threaten to make him turn his back on the game altogether. But it might be that it is the very intermittence and fracture of the videogame text that mobilizes at least some of its pleasures. To draw upon the work of Roland Barthes, it is at least possible that this is the ultimate text of plural *jouissance*, of the movement from *petit mort* to *petit mort*, from little death to little death, with an ecstatic loss of control revisited in multiple climactic moments that generates the pleasure of the text.

Narrative games are notoriously linear, wedded to their advance to closure, and yet our death, the protagonist's death, is not the moment of philosophical finitude that has so fascinated critical theorists over the last decade or so. Nor is it a signifier of a failure of play or reading (or even, necessarily, of skill) that alienates the player from potential pleasure. Death – my death, our death, the avatar's death – and resurrection, the move from apparent absolute control through an absolute loss of control, only to regain control, to begin again, to begin our negotiation with the text again, to attempt to overcome our rejection from the text, by the text, is a core pleasure of a certain kind of videogame. If we are to talk of textual mastery then this is not philosophy's 'mastery of death' that has been a subject of debate and critique since Plato's *The Death of Socrates*. When Socrates downs the hemlock it is a moment of absolute ending and absolute finitude. He cannot reload and choose not to drink the dodgy potion like some *Baldur's Gate* hero, or be saved from death by *Sands of Time*'s rewind. Plato, one supposes, would certainly have been disappointed had he done so. The death of Socrates is the greatest of deaths, the grandest of deaths – the death of the avatar is the smallest of deaths, truly a *petit mort*, not the philosophical mastery of death, but the corporeal, physical and sensual lack of mastery of the climactic ending and beginning.

Which is not to ignore the frustration felt when the player is expelled from the game by in-game death through no fault of their own. To give the in-game death the meaning of pleasure the game has to listen to us, to pay us attention, to recognize that it is being courted by the player. The moment of death must always be personal to the player, always be theirs. If the game ignores us, then there is little pleasure to be had. The experience of the game's past must always point to a future of possibility. Game death must always be imminent, always be possible, always be round the next corner, but it should never be arbitrary. The lurking presence of in-game death adds a dark frisson to the pleasure of play (it might even be reminiscent of Freud's 'harbinger of death' that Diane Carr (2003) has described in relation to the protagonist of *Silent Hill*) and that imminent presence of death might even offer its own spectacular pleasure as we view the impossible event of our own demise, but if it is random then it offers little sustainable or iterative pleasure. And yet any unproblematically linear understanding of games collapses in the face of our in-game death. Each fragment of the text completed, each obstacle overcome, is a pleasure in and of itself, of course. There is even a cumulative pleasure of textual unfolding and delayed disclosure and unlocking – but this is not the text solely of penetration, domination or possession of the full secrets of the vanquished text. Each textual fragment is stolen like an illicit pleasure, wrestled with mouse or keyboard or twin analogue sticks from the reluctant text. To take pleasure in the moments of my life-in-game it must be punctuated by a death from which the avatar has emerged and a death to which he or she will return.

The textual fragment pleases because it is a fragment, a stolen moment. The player seeks not simple revelation – the text laid bare in all its anatomical detail – or mastery of the text, but incomplete glimpses of the perfect textual body that give pleasure only in their partiality. To borrow Barthes' theorization (and eroticization) of literary textual pleasure;

> Is not the most erotic portion of a body *where the garment gapes?* … it is intermittence, as psychoanalysis has so rightly stated, which is erotic: the intermittence of skin flashing between two articles of clothing (trousers and sweater), between two edges (the open-necked shirt, the glove and the sleeve); it is this flash itself which seduces, or rather: the staging of an appearance-as-disappearance. (Barthes 1975: 51)

We seek not only immersion in our games, but court rejection – to assume full immersion in the text, and to tell seamless tales of lives in-game, misrepresents the experience of play. It is the intermittence of the text, its broken/fragmentary/discontinuous nature, that is the site of pleasure, even (in Barthes' terms) of bliss in each instance of *petit mort*. As Barthes commented on the reading of language:

> The pleasure of the sentence is to a high degree cultural. The artefact created by rhetors, grammarians, linguists, teachers, writers, parents – this artefact is mimicked in a more or less ludic manner; we are playing with an exceptional object, whose paradox has been articulated by linguistics: immutably structured and yet infinitely renewable: something like chess. (51)

As readers of texts, even linguistic texts, we have always been engaged in play. We take our pleasure in the absolute singularity of the rules set and infinite renewability of the encounter with those rules in the moment. The moments of bliss in the videogame text are generated through reference to an imagined perfect text, the platonic absolute or ideal which is always absent from actual play – not the intermittent fragmentary text we have on screen, but a text that exists in potential only in our imagination. Were the over-arching meta-text of the imagination ever to be realized as so many narrative accounts of play seem to imply (with no dissonance, no disruption, no in-game death, no understanding of the ludic living-in-the-game/dying-in-the-game distinction) then the pleasures of the videogame text would be very different. The player takes their pleasures from a text in which they play with dying, and not solely with a text where they play with killing. *Sands of Time* declares itself to be story, and to be a playing out not only of event, but of an act of telling, but what it brings to our attention most forcefully is not the way in which narration after event can erase recognition of the stuttering and intermittent progress through the text but the degree to which videogame play offers a very different temporal experience than our other media.

Works cited

Aarseth, Espen (1997) 'Aporia and Epiphany in *Doom* and *The Speaking Clock*', in Marie-Laure Ryan (ed.) *Cyberspace Textuality: Computer Technology and Literary Theory*, Bloomington, IA: Indiana University Press.

Atkins, Barry (2003) *More Than a Game: The Computer Game as Fictional Form*, Manchester: Manchester University Press.

Barthes, Roland (1975) *The Pleasure of the Text*, London: Hill and Wang.

Carr, Diane (2003) 'Play Dead: Genre and Affect in *Silent Hill* and *Planescape Torment*', in *Game Studies*, 3:1, www.gamestudies.org/0301/carr/, accessed November 2005.

Davidson, Drew (2005) 'Plotting the Story and Interactivity of the *Prince of Persia: The Sands of Time*', in *Media in Transition*, 4, Cambridge, MA: MIT Press, http://web.mit.edu/comm-forum/mit4/, accessed November 2005.

Eskelinen, Markku (2004) 'Towards Computer Game Studies', in Noah Wardrip-Fruin and Pat Harrigan (eds) *First Person: New Media as Story, Performance and Game*, Cambridge, MA: MIT Press, 36–44.

Jenkins, Henry (2005) *Game Design as Narrative Architecture*, www.electronicbook review.com/thread/firstperson/lazzi-fair, accessed November 2005.

Juul, Jesper (2004) 'Introduction to Game Time', in Noah Wardrip-Fruin and Pat Harrigan (eds) *First Person: New Media as Story, Performance, and Game*,

Cambridge, MA: MIT Press, 131–142.

Newman, James (2004) *Videogames*, London: Routledge.

Rhody, Jason (2005) 'Game Fiction: Playing the Interface in *Prince of Persia: The Sands of Time* and *Asheron's Call*', DiGRA/Simon Fraser University, www.gamesconference.org/digra2005/papers/265d6765298a689956d 2420f440e.doc accessed November 2005.

Wolf, Mark (2001) *The Medium of the Video Game*, Austin, TX: University of Texas Press.

Games

Blinx: The Time Sweeper (2002), Microsoft, Artoon.

Doom 3 (2004), Activision, id.

Far Cry (2004), Ubisoft, Crytek.

Galleon (2004), SCI, Confounding Factor.

Half-Life (1998), Sierra, Valve.

Halo (2003), Microsoft, Bungie.

Lara Croft Tomb Raider: The Angel of Darkness (2003), Eidos, Core.

Max Payne (2001), Gathering, 3D Realms/Remedy.

Prince of Persia (1989), Brøderbund.

Prince of Persia: The Sands of Time (2003), Ubisoft.

Prince of Persia: The Warrior Within (2004), Ubisoft.

Prince of Persia 3D (1999), Learning Company, Mattel.

Steel Battalion (2002), Capcom.

Super Mario 64 (1996), Nintendo.

Notes

1   James Newman (2004: 71–90) offers an astute commentary on time in games, and also touches on related issues specific to the platform game genre, such as the presence of mini-games to provide another form of variety.

2   Concrete statistics of actual completion rates for games (even if we ignore the difficulty in defining a meaning for game completion) remain difficult to come by, but anecdotal evidence would suggest that games developers are caught in something of a contradiction in that players are perceived as demanding value for money measured rather crudely as potential play length, while rarely remaining engaged to the point of seeing the end game. Somewhat perversely, this would suggest that something is wrong, on one side or another, about what represents 'value' in terms of games.

3   Something that is different, of course, in the area of permanent death or 'permadeath' in online games where investment in the development of a unique character, often measured (again) in terms of time investment, raises fierce

emotions in many players.

4   The final plot revelation, that makes it clear that this is a dialogue between the Prince and Farah, does not erase the in-game experience of separation from identification with the avatar that this provokes, even if it does rather neatly tie the voice-overs into the game's story.

5   In his essay 'Towards Computer Game Studies' Markku Eskelinen rightly focuses on the function of time in computer games. What he terms the dominant temporality of the intersection between 'user time' and 'event time' certainly describes the action of play, which recognizes the twin activities of manipulation of the game interface in 'user time' (whether it is the engagement with the controller, the joystick, the keyboard or the mouse) and the feedback of the consequences of that manipulation in 'event time' (on screen, through the vibration of the controller and through changes in audio content). As a means of describing the activity of play this works well, and achieves Eskelinen's stated desire to show the specificity of games when compared to traditional forms of print and cinematic narrative. Eskelinen draws on significant work by Espen Aarseth (1997) in his examination of time in games, and further examination of in-game time can also be found in the work of Jesper Juul (2004).

6   Davidson's account of his individual experience of play is to be applauded, and in its self-reflexive analysis of his own pleasures in traversing the game stands as a useful and often insightful addendum to the usual kinds of walkthrough whose focus is more instructive than analytic.

Index

Aarseth, Espen 40, 125–6, 151
Adventure 176
Althusser, Louis 63, 115
American Mcgee's Alice 115
Atkins, Barry 38
Auster, Paul 30

Bakhtin, Mikhail 133–4
Balpe, Jean-pierre 10
Barthes, Roland 15, 212, 250
Battalion Commander 86
Battlezone 165
Benjamin, Walter 106
Brothers in Arms 60
Buffy The Vampire Slayer 115
Butler, Judith 120

Caillois, Roger 26, 62, 226
Calvino, Italo 40
Carr, Diane 250
Civilization 83
Civilization 3 213, 222–6
Conflict: Desert Storm 78
Conflict: Desert Storm 2 78
Conflict: Global Terror 80
Conflict: Vietnam 66–82
Combat Leader 86
Conway's Game of Life 192, 201

Crawford, Chris 12, 17
Crogan, Patrick 61
Crumey, Andrew 37
Csikszentmihalyi, Mihaly 192

Daikatana 146
Darley, Andrew 14
Davidson, Drew 249
Dekerckhove, Derrick 31
Disney, Walt 159
Doom 12, 139–43, 176
Doom II 145
Doom III 139–57
Douglas, Christopher 213
Douglas, Nick 134
Dune II 87–8
Dungeons & Dragons 71

Elder Scrolls III: Morrowind, The 12
Everquest 12, 101, 109, 115
Exhibition 184
Eye of The Beholder 88

Façade 21–4
Far Cry 247
Final Fight 218
Fiske, John 211
Frasca, Gonzalo 152, 226

Full Spectrum Warrior 52–65

Galatea 183
Galleon 239
Global Conquest 87
Go 12
Grand Theft Auto III 187
Grand Theft Auto: San Andreas 191
Grand Theft Auto: Vice City 46
Grossman, Erving 193

Half-Life 242
Halo 242
Haraway, Donna 120, 129
Herz, J.C. 147
Hodge, Robert 53
Hughes, Linda 200
Huizinga, Johan 53
Hunt, Leon 208

Jakobson, Mikeal 109
Jenkins, Henry 14–17, 77, 229, 238
Johnson, Steven 39
Juul, Jesper 26, 40

Kennedy, Helen 70
King, Geoff and Krzywinska, Tanya 142,
    146, 206–7, 213
Kline, Jeff 70
Koster, Ralph 192
Kracouer, Siegfried 207
Kushner, David 144

Lacan, Jaques 115
Lammes, Sybil 229
Laurel, Brenda 124–5
Lem, Stanislaw 42
Lister, Martin 42, 126

Mactavish, Andrew 143
Mannovich, Lev 152
Martin, George R.R. 107

Max Payne 12, 245
Maxwell, Richard 29
Modem wars 87
Montani, Pietro 44
Morris, Dave 124
Morrissey, Judd 12
Motte, W.F. 26
Myers, David 227
Myst 16, 176
Mystery House 148, 183

Ndalianis, Angela 149, 215
Neidich, Warren 10

Pitfall 185
Pobliki, Kacper 225
Poole, Steven 17, 43, 219
Primal 115
Prince of Persia 244
Prince of Persia 3D 244
Prince of Persia: The Sands of Time 237–
    53

Quake 12, 120–38, 146, 165
Quake II 146
Quake III: Arena 123–4
Queneau, Raymond 11

Road to Hill 30 60
Rouse, Richard 141

Salen, Katie and Zimmerman, Eric 40,
    181, 222
Savoir Faire 175–90
Scramble 191
Second Life 158–74
Simcity 29–51, 166
Simcity 3000 41
Simcity 4 38, 41, 46
Simcity: Rush Hour 46
Sims, The 12, 17–19, 24, 31, 46, 166,
    206

Sims 2, The 18–19, 191
Sims Online, The 25
Spacewar 148
Space Invaders 141
Stafford, Barbara Maria 33
Stankovic, John 86
Stern, Eddo 102
Stewart, Susan 34
Street Fighter 209–10
Street Fighter 2 204–21
Suits, Bernard 17
Super Mario 64 242
Super Street Fighter 2 Turbo 213

Taylor, T.L. 109, 121
Tetris 12
Tomas, David 70
Tomb Raider 240
Trial, The Trail, The 165
Tripp, David 53

Turkle, Sherry 113

Ultima Online 109, 159
Unreal 165
Unreal Tournament 130

Varicella 175

Warcraft 83, 88–9
Warcraft 2: Orcs and Humans 89–91
Warcraft 3: Reign of Chaos 83–100, 105
Wardrip-Fruin, Noah 11
War Zone 2100 73
Winnicott, D.W. 80
Wittgenstein, Ludwig 22
Wolf, Mark J.P. 141, 241
Wolfenstein 3D 149
World of Warcraft 85, 101–19, 200
Wright, Will 41, 45